WHOLE-LOAN CMOs

WHOLE-LOAN CMOs

Editors:

FRANK J. FABOZZI

CHUCK RAMSEY

FRANK R. RAMIREZ

with the
assistance of
David T. Yuen

Published by Frank J. Fabozzi Associates

Designer and Managing Editor: Stephen Arbour
Consulting Editor: Patricia Peat
Cover Design Consultant: Chuck Ramsey
Distribution Manager: Scott Chambers Riether

ISBN 1-883249-04-X

Printed in the United States of America
1 2 3 4 5 6 7 8 9 0

TABLE OF CONTENTS

PREFACE

The dominant types of collateralized mortgage obligations outstanding are those backed by Fannie Mae and Freddie Mac, popularly referred to as *agency CMOs*. Today, an equally important sector of the CMO market is developing: the market for *whole-loan* or *non-agency CMOs*. These CMOs are issued by private entities and, unlike agency CMOs, they expose investors to credit risk. While investors in agency CMOs have focused totally on prepayment risk, investors in whole-loan CMOs must concentrate on both prepayment risk and credit risk.

Because the whole-loan CMO market is relatively new, opportunities for enhanced returns abound. Current and potential investors in the whole-loan CMO market must have the skills to identify and then capitalize on the opportunities available. The purpose of this book is to provide investors with the tools to effectively participate in this market.

Whole-Loan CMOs is divided into five sections. Section I introduces the reader to the whole-loan CMO market, while Section II describes the unique investment characteristics of these products. A detailed explanation of how to assess the credit quality of whole-loan CMO structures is presented in Section III where, in addition, the state-of-the art databases available to analyze whole-loan CMOs are discussed. In Section IV, the prepayment characteristics of whole-loans CMOs are documented. Finally, Section V sets forth the characteristics of one sector of the whole-loan market, the market for commercial MBS.

To be effective, a book of this nature should offer a broad perspective. The experiences of a wide range of experts are more informative than those of a single expert, particularly because of the diversity of opinion on some issues. We have chosen some of the best known practitioners actively involved in the evolution of this market to contribute to this book.

We wish to thank the contributors and their organizations for participating in this project. David T. Yuen contributed significantly to this project. The production team for this book greatly facilitated its completion. The team includes Patricia Peat, who edited the manuscript, and Scott Chambers Riether, who provided copyediting and proofreading assistance. Stephen Arbour designed, typeset, and coordinated the production of this book.

Frank J. Fabozzi
Chuck Ramsey
Frank R. Ramirez

ABOUT THE EDITORS

Frank J. Fabozzi is an Adjunct Professor of Finance at Yale University's School of Management and the editor of the *Journal of Portfolio Management.* From 1986 to 1992, he was a full-time professor of finance at MIT's Sloan School of Management. He is on the board of directors of the BlackRock complex of closed-end funds and the board of directors of the family of open-end funds sponsored by The Guardian Life. Dr. Fabozzi is a Chartered Financial Analyst and Certified Public Accountant who has authored and edited many books on investment management.

Chuck Ramsey is a principal of Alex. Brown & Sons and a partner and chief executive officer of Mortgage Risk Assessment Co. He was previously a general partner and senior managing director of Bear Stearns where he was responsible for mortgage-backed securities sales. Mr. Ramsey is known as the architect of specified pool analysis and is responsible for the development of computer systems designed to more accurately value these securities.

Frank R. Ramirez is a principal of Alex. Brown & Sons. Mr. Ramirez earned a J.D. from the University of California at Berkeley and an MBA and BA from Stanford University. His prior positions were as a managing director of Bear Stearns and as a staff attorney for the Securities and Exchange Commission. Mr. Ramirez specializes in the use of derivative mortgage-backed securities to enhance total returns and match liabilities.

LIST OF CONTRIBUTORS

Clifford Scott Asness — Goldman Sachs Asset Management
Sean Becketti — CS First Boston Corporation
Douglas L. Bendt — Mortgage Risk Assessment Corporation
Kimbell R. Duncan — Nomura International PLC
John N. Dunlevy — Hyperion Capital Management
Richard Ellson — CS First Boston Corporation
Frank J. Fabozzi — Journal of Portfolio Management and Yale University
Evan Firestone — CS First Boston Corporation
Thomas Gillis — Standard & Poor's
David Jacob — Nomura Securities International
Andrew B. Jones — Duff & Phelps Credit Rating Company
Richard M. Lerner — CS First Boston Corporation
Mary Sue Lundy — Fitch Investors Service, Inc.
Jojy Vaniss Mathew — MIS, Inc.
Chuck Ramsey — Alex. Brown & Sons, Inc. and Mortgage Risk Assessment Corporation
Peter Rubinstein — Donaldson, Lufkin, & Jenrette
Cathy Smiley — Alex. Brown & Sons, Inc.
David Sykes — Alex. Brown & Sons, Inc.
Edward L. Toy — Teachers Insurance and Annuity Association
Karen Auld Wagner — CS First Boston Corporation
Mark Warner — BlackRock Financial Management
Eva A. Zeff — Oppenheimer Management Corporation

LIST OF ADVERTISERS

Chase Manhattan Mortgage Corporation
Coopers & Lybrand
Duff & Phelps
EJV Partners
Ernst & Young
GAT
Hyperion Capital Management, Inc.
Information Management Network
Interactive Data
Intex Solutions, Inc.
KPMG Peat-Marwick
MIS Inc.
Mortgage Risk Assessment Corporation
Nomura
Residential Funding Corporation
Standard & Poor's
The Trepp Group

Section I

INTRODUCTION TO THE WHOLE-LOAN CMO MARKET

CHAPTER 1

The Whole-Loan Mortgage Market: Background and Overview

David Sykes, Ph.D.
Principal
Alex. Brown & Sons, Inc.

Cathy Smiley
Senior Analyst
Alex. Brown & Sons, Inc.

INTRODUCTION

The mortgage securities market comprises two major sectors: the agency sector and the non-agency whole-loan sector. Securities from both sectors are collateralized by pools of mortgages that are secured by residential real estate.

In the agency sector, mortgage securities are issued by any one of three agencies: the Government National Mortgage Association (GNMA), the Federal National Mortgage Association (FNMA), and the Federal Home Loan Mortgage Corporation (FHLMC). To qualify for agency securitization or purchase programs, loans must conform to agency underwriting guidelines and size amounts (at this writing, $151,725 for GNMA and $203,150 for FNMA and FHLMC).

Non-agency securities are generally issued by private mortgage companies such as Chase Mortgage Finance, Countrywide Mortgage Conduit, and Capstead Mortgage Corporation. One important exception is the Resolution Trust Corporation (RTC). From 1991 until the spring of 1993, the RTC's issuance volume and standards of information dissemination did much to foster the growth and development of the whole-loan market.

The mortgages that collateralize whole-loan securities usually do not conform to agency criteria. The primary category of non-conforming loans is the "jumbo" loans, that is, loans that exceed agency size limits. Highly populated metropolitan areas with high-cost housing such as New York, San Francisco, Los Angeles, and San Diego produce most of the jumbo loans. Consequently, a pool of jumbo loans is usually more regionally concentrated than a conforming pool. For example, it is not uncommon for a jumbo pool to have a California concentration in excess of 50% as compared to a typical conforming pool's concentration of around 25%.

A second category of non-conforming loans is defined by loans made to borrowers who fail to meet the agency underwriting standards. This category is known as the *B/C credit market*. These loans can arise out of a variety of circumstances. A borrower may have a poor or inadequate credit history, volatile income flows, and/or inadequate documentation. Borrowers in the B/C category are usually required to provide more equity than other borrowers to buffer against delinquency and/or defaults.

Investors in both agency and whole-loan securities generally face prepayment risk. Credit risk on agency issues is essentially eliminated by virtue of agency guarantees, but investors in whole-loan paper may still be subject to credit risk. Should the underlying collateral experience defaults and subsequent foreclosures, payment delays and/or ultimate losses may be passed through to investors.

The whole-loan market has developed a variety of structuring techniques to protect investors against default risk, event risk, and delays in payment of principal and interest. These techniques include insurance, letters of credit (LOC), and subordinated securities within a structure that enable the senior securities to obtain triple-A or double-A ratings from the rating agencies.

HISTORICAL HIGHLIGHTS

In the early to mid 1980s the whole-loan sector was largely overshadowed by the soaring growth in the agency market. Thrifts were the dominant players in the whole-loan sector, where they engaged primarily in the traditional business of originating 30-year fixed-rate mortgages funded by short-term financing. As long-term rates dropped and the yield curve flattened, this process of financing long-term paper with short-term financing led to the demise of many thrift institutions. Faced with an ever-shrinking spread over funding costs, thrifts predominantly shifted their focus from fixed-rate products to adjustable-rate mortgages.

Mortgage banks and conduits emerged as the dominant force behind fixed-rate mortgage originations. The rapid growth of this industry was fostered by advances in computer and communications technologies that made possible the collection and dissemination of credit information, geographic underwriting data, local and national market rates, and other pertinent information.

Unlike thrifts, mortgage conduits do not hold in portfolio the product they originate. Instead, they typically securitize and sell their originations as either whole-loan passthroughs or multi-class Real Estate Mortgage Investment Conduits (REMICs). Consequently, the funding requirements of the mortgage conduits are limited to a relatively short warehousing period and, therefore, their interest rate exposure is limited to short-term rate risk.

The RTC has played a vital role in the evolution and development of the whole-loan market. Created by an act of Congress in 1989, the RTC is a corporation wholly owned by the United States Government with the legal authority to issue full faith and credit obligations of the Government, equivalent to the pledge of GNMA.

The primary function of the RTC has been to manage and liquidate the assets of savings institutions seized by regulatory authorities to minimize losses to the government's Savings Association Insurance Fund. In this capacity, the RTC was an active issuer of whole-loan securities only from 1991 to the spring of 1993. During this time, however, the RTC did more to transform the whole-loan market into a major sector of the mortgage market than any other issuer, issuing a record $9.6 billion in single-family whole-loan securities in 1991, followed by $15.1 billion in 1992 (Exhibit 1).

Exhibit 1: Top Private MBS Issuers

1993 Rank	Issuer	Volume ($Billions)			Market Share (%)		
		1993	1992	1991	1993	1992	1991
1	Prudential Home MSCI	27.2	16.9	5.6	27.6	18.9	11.3
2	Residential Funding Corp.	13.0	11.9	7.4	13.2	13.3	15.0
3	GE Capital Mortgage	8.0	2.9	1.0	8.2	3.2	2.0
4	Ryland/Saxon Mortgage	7.5	6.5	3.1	7.6	7.3	6.2
5	Countrywide/CWMBS	6.2	0.0	0.0	6.3	0.0	0.0
6	Chase Mortgage Finance	4.8	5.9	2.6	4.9	6.2	2.6
7	Citicorp/Citibank Housing	4.3	5.8	4.4	4.3	6.4	8.9
8	Capstead/CMC	3.4	4.4	1.8	3.5	8.8	3.7
9	Bear Stearns Mortgage	2.9	1.2	0.5	2.9	1.3	1.0
10	Securitized Asset Sales-Pru	2.5	0.0	0.0	2.5	0.0	0.0
	Resolution Trust Corp.	3.2	15.1	9.6	3.1	16.9	19.4

Source: *Inside Mortgage Securities*; *Bloomberg.

This enormous volume caught the attention of mortgage market participants. Moreover, new types of bond and credit structures were introduced to a market that had been largely dominated by plain vanilla sequential-pay structures enhanced by a variety of credit supports. Credit supports included insured deals, letters of credit (LOC), surety bonds, corporate guarantees, and reserve funds. The RTC's subordinate structures appealed to the many investors who had expressed increasing discomfort with third-party guarantees. Senior/subordinate credit structures comprised 85% of 1993 issues compared with 30% in 1987 (Exhibit 2).

Prior to 1991, private issuers were generally resistant to providing detailed information on the collateral backing whole-loan issues, primarily because of the foreboding amount of information processing involved. The advent of the RTC greatly softened their resistance. Never before in the history of the whole-loan market had a large issuer worked via the traditional Wall Street dealer syndicate process to actively market, trade, and issue whole-loan securities. Through this process there was a coordinated distribution of information, laying the groundwork for much higher dissemination standards. However, standardization was limited because many of the RTC transactions involved unusual or unique collateral. Nevertheless, the efforts of the RTC in providing collateral information effectively prodded the private issuers to provide data regarding their underwriting standards and collateral performance in order to develop and maintain liquid markets in their own securities. The advanced level of information dissemination and standards found in the whole-loan market today would not likely have occurred were it not for the RTC.

Exhibit 2: Private-Label Issuance by Credit Enhancement Type (Percent of Total Issuance)

Credit Enhancement Type	1993	1992	1991	1990	1989	1988	1987
Internal Credit Enhancement Methods:							
Subordination	82.81	48.48	70.03	49.47	62.43	78.68	29.73
Reserve Fund	1.19	16.90	0.00	0.00	0.00	0.00	0.00
Super-Senior	1.86	2.92	10.58	0.00	0.00	0.00	0.00
External Credit Enhancement Methods:							
Pool Insurance	10.72	28.10	10.28	23.24	10.11	3.97	0.00
Surety Bonds	1.64	1.56	0.24	4.5	2.18	4.04	17.57
Letter of Credit	0.00	1.08	4.93	15.38	13.27	0.00	0.00
Corporate Guaranty	0.00	0.00	0.30	2.62	12.01	13.31	52.70
Multiple Support	0.80	0.96	3.64	4.79	0.00	0.00	0.00
Other	0.98	0.00	0.00	0.00	0.00	0.00	0.00
Total Issuance (Dollars in Billions)	98.51	89.48	49.70	24.43	14.24	15.85	11.10

Source: *Inside Mortgage Securities*

In general, the RTC's participation in the whole-loan market was an important milestone in the history of the market. *They* forced rating agencies and investors to deal with new issues and products. The government's guarantee of the representations and warranties was a major benefit to the RTC issuance and to the whole-loan market.

GROWTH

1989 through 1994 has been a remarkable period of growth for the whole-loan market. Total issuance from 1977 through 1984 amounted to only $3.8 billion. As shown in Exhibit 3, the pace of issuance began to accelerate significantly after 1986, with issuance for 1993 alone totaling $98.5 billion.

As a percentage of total mortgage security issuance, the whole-loan sector has come from a 6.6% market share in 1989 to a 14.9% share in 1993. Similarly, in terms of total mortgage securities outstanding (see Exhibit 4), whole-loan securities currently account for about 10.8% of the mortgage market, up from only 4% in 1987.

As shown in Exhibit 5, the percent of all nonconforming mortgage originations being securitized has also grown substantially. In 1990, only about 27% of these mortgages went into private-label mortgage-backed securities (MBSs). By 1993, the portion of non-conforming originations being securitized grew to about 46%.

Exhibit 3: Whole-loan Issuance ($Millions)

Year	REMICs	ARMs	Total Whole-loan Issuance	%Total Mortgage Market
1982	NA	NA	253	NA
1983	NA	NA	1,585	NA
1984	NA	NA	236	NA
1985	NA	NA	1,956	1.8%
1986	NA	NA	6,993	2.6%
1987	9,044	2,057	11,100	4.5%
1988	3,303	12,118	15,420	9.3%
1989	7,812	6,426	14,238	6.6%
1990	16,812	7,619	24,431	9.4%
1991	30,599	18,750	49,349	14.9%
1992	63,448	26,018	89,466	16.5%
1993	77,759	20,734	98,493	14.9%

Source: *Inside Mortgage Securities*

Exhibit 4: Securities Outstanding Whole-loan Versus Agency ($Millions)

Year	Agency	% Total	Whole Loan	% Total	Total
1987	668,427	96%	27,800	4%	696,227
1988	745,183	96%	34,865	4%	780,048
1989	870,789	95%	43,325	5%	914,114
1990	1,017,470	95%	53,335	5%	1,070,805
1991	1,156,388	93%	84,000	7%	1,240,388
1992	1,272,009	91%	132,000	9%	1,404,009
1993	1,348,620	89%	164,000	11%	1,512,620

Source: *Inside Mortgage Securities*

Exhibit 5: Securitization Rates Whole-loan Versus Agency ($Millions)

	Agency		Whole Loans	
Year	Originations	Securitized	Originations	Securitized
1990	367,820	63.9%	90,620	27.0%
1991	449,660	59.6%	112,410	35.4%
1992	714,940	63.6%	178,730	41.6%
1993	845,100	67.2%	211,280	46.1%

Source: *Inside Mortgage Securities*

Exhibit 6: Conforming Loan Limits FNMA and FHLMC

Year	Loan Limit
1985	$115,300
1986	133,250
1987	153,100
1988	168,700
1989	187,600
1990	187,450
1991	191,250
1992	202,300
1993	203,150

The growth in the whole-loan sector is especially impressive because it has occurred at a time when the agency sector has also been growing rapidly. Growth in both sectors has been fueled by the massive refinancings that occurred throughout 1992 and 1993. Total originations jumped from $458.44 billion in 1990 to $1.1 trillion in 1993. However, the agencies have also been eating away small slices of the non-conforming jumbo market as they have raised their loan limits over time. For example, the FNMA/FHLMC limit has grown annually from $115,300 in 1985 to its current 1993 level of $203,150 (Exhibit 6).

INVESTORS

The rapid growth in the whole-loan market is a testimony to the investor appetite for whole-loan product. Virtually all the major institutional categories are involved. In recent years, pension funds and insurance companies have each carried roughly between 25% to 30% of all institutional holdings, while banks, thrifts, and mortgage funds each hold between 12% to 15%, and foreign investors carrying the balance of about 5%.

Attractive Spreads

For many investors, the appeal of whole-loans arose out of a growing aversion to the "event" risk associated with corporate high-yield bonds. Rather than being concentrated on any single economic entity, the credit risk of whole-loans is generally diversified across a pool of many individual borrowers. Thus many high-yield investors have been attracted to the whole-loan market.

This is especially true for buyers of subordinated pieces, which can trade anywhere from 200 bps over Treasuries for triple-B credits to as wide as 1,000 bps for unrated pieces. The spread range reflects the range of credit quality available.

The triple-A rated senior tranches typically trade 30-40 bps cheaper than comparable agency securities. While the subordinate tranche spread advantage is dominated by credit considerations, the spread advantage on the triple-A bonds can be roughly decomposed as follows: 10-15 bps for liquidity, 5 bps for credit risk, 5 bps for risk-based capital weighting, and 10-20 bps for greater prepayment volatility.

In addition to the diversification of event risk, the multi-class whole-loan security structures provide investors with a richer menu of options than is typically associated with high-yield corporate debt. The available bond types include most of the tranche types found in the agency market such as sequential-pay bonds, planned amortization classes (PAC), targeted amortization classes (TAC), floaters, inverse floaters, principal-only classes (PO), interest-only classes (IO), PAC IOs, PAC inverse IOs.

Federally Regulated Investors

The substantial appetite for whole-loan product has been particularly impressive given the increasingly inhibiting regulatory environment faced by depository institutions. Regulatory capital requirements favor securitized agency loans over whole-loan securities.

For example, federally regulated banks must assign a senior tranche from a whole-loan issue a 50% risk weight under the risk-based capital guidelines, while comparable agency securities have a risk weighting of only 20%. Any whole-loan security below the senior tranche falls in the 100% risk weight category, regardless of the rating.

Under the Secondary Mortgage Market Enhancement Act of 1984 (SMMEA), thrift institutions can place certain qualifying whole-loan securities in the 20% risk weight category. An SMMEA-qualifying security must have at least a double-A rating and be collateralized by first lien residential mortgages.

Depository institutions were confronted with adjusting to both the Federal Financial Institutions Examination Council (FFIEC) policy statement of 1991 and the Financial Standards Accounting Board (FASB) Financial Accounting Standard (FAS) 115 in 1993. The FFIEC policy statement requires depository institutions to subject CMO securities to a high-risk test: the base case projected average life cannot exceed ten years; for a 300 bps parallel shift in the yield curve, the price of the security cannot change by more than 17%, and the average life cannot extend by more than four years or shorten by more than six years.

ARMs and LIBOR indexed floaters are subject only to the price volatility test as long as the coupon is less than the lifetime cap. Securities that do not pass the high-risk test can be purchased only as actively managed, mark-to-market, hedging vehicles.

Under FAS 115, very restrictive conditions must be met for a security to qualify for historical amortized cost accounting. Essentially, the institution must demonstrate that it has both the "intent and ability" to hold a given investment to maturity. Once a security is classified as held-to-maturity, the institution may not sell it without running the risk of having part or possibly all of its held-to-maturity securities reclassified into one of two mark-to-market categories. Securities held as available-for-sale are marked-to-market with gains/losses reported as a special component of shareholders' equity; securities categorized in a trading account are marked-to-market with gains/losses reported in the income statement.

These rules and regulations, designed to strengthen the industry, have a distinct impact on the nature of the investment process. In general, institutions are expected to liquidate products that do not conform to current or anticipated guidelines. Given the uncertainty associated with this environment, the rapid growth of the whole-loan sector is indeed impressive.

ISSUERS

The stability in the issuance of whole-loan securities has also been impressive. Both small and large originators rely on whole-loan conduits for the distribution of their product. This has led to a relatively limited number of strong conduits that have survived a variety of mergers and failures over the years. Private-label issuance has been consistently dominated by names like Pru Home, Residential Funding Corporation, and GE Capital Mortgage Services. As can be seen from Exhibit 1, these three issuers accounted for nearly 50% of total private-label MBS production in 1993.

THE SECURITIZATION PROCESS

The process of securitizing residential whole-loan product may involve existing or newly originated pools of mortgages. While existing pools can be securitized, the market is dominated by newly originated mortgages. The process for securitizing newly originated pools is outlined in Exhibit 6. In general, the primary players include: (1) an origination network of mortgage bankers ("the correspondents"); (2) a master correspondent; (3) a special-purpose, bankruptcy-remote entity; (4) a trustee; and, of course, (5) investors.

Exhibit 7: The Securitization Process

```
        ┌──────────────────────────┐
        │   Origination Network:   │
        │      Mortgage Banks      │
        └──────────────────────────┘

           Loans        ↓

        ┌──────────────────────────┐
        │  Master Correspondent/   │
        │        Servicer          │
        └──────────────────────────┘

                  ↓

                                    ┌──────────────────────┐
      Pools of Loans    ←           │  Issuer/Bankruptcy-  │
                                    │    Remote Entity     │
                                    └──────────────────────┘

                  ↓

        ┌──────────────────────────┐
        │      Trustee/Bond        │
        │     Administration       │
        └──────────────────────────┘

         Bond Payments   ↓

        ┌──────────────────────────┐
        │        Investors         │
        └──────────────────────────┘
```

The master correspondent monitors both the investor and lender sides of the market, compiling a daily pricing sheet that informs the participating mortgage bankers of the levels at which raw loans will be purchased. As the mortgage banks sell into the master correspondent's warehouse, the individual loans are accumulated into pools that are then assigned and endorsed to the trustee on behalf of the issuer's special-purpose, bankruptcy-remote entity. The special-purpose entity is a wholly-owned subsidiary of the issuer, essentially a legal vehicle that shields the integrity of the whole-loan issue from any future economic demise of the parent company and/or the servicer.

The master correspondent will often act as the on-going servicer of the loans once they are securitized. Finally, when the issuer is a large conduit operation such as Residential Funding Corporation, the master correspondent role is often performed in-house. When investment banks issue whole-loan deals, the master correspondent role is typically performed by an outside party.

The trustee acts on behalf of the investors. Its primary responsibilities include monitoring the integrity of the overall process and the monthly bond administration. This includes generally overseeing the servicing activity, receiving monthly cash payments from the servicer, forwarding the cash flows, as paying agent, to the investors, and maintaining any reserve accounts called for by the bond structure. In some instances, the trustee may subcontract with a separate party to carry out all or part of the bond adminis- trative process. In any case, the administrative details are transparent to the investor, just as they are with agency deals.

THE STRUCTURING PROCESS

Rating agencies determine the level of credit support required by a structure depending upon the collateral type, the issuer, and the desired rating. The loss coverage required mirrors the historical performance of mortgage pools. Initially, the principal balance is reduced almost exclusively by pre- payments. As good loans prepay, however, the proportion of bad loans in the pool increases. Thus, although the pool balance has declined, the credit risk has not.

   This view of early prepayments and their negative effect on credit risk is called "adverse selection." To counteract the effects of adverse selection, rating agencies require that the initial loss coverage be maintained until the pools are sufficiently seasoned that their performance character can be ascertained. Experience has shown that fixed-rate pools are adequately sea- soned after 5 years, ARMs after 10 years, and negatively amortizing ARMs after 15 years.

   To avoid a rapid drop in loss coverage, rating agencies generally require three levels of loss coverage: a fixed period of time where the loss coverage remains constant (usually 4%-5% for 15-year fixed-rate collateral, 6%-8% for 30-year fixed-rate collateral, and 10%-12% for ARM collateral), a 4 year period where the loss coverage steps down provided the pools have proven to season well, and a seasoned period where the loss coverage required becomes a fixed percentage of the outstanding pool balance.

   Although delinquency coverage, also known as liquidity coverage, may be provided by the same credit enhancement technique covering losses, it is kept separate from loss coverage and must remain constant. Rating agencies require that any third party providing delinquency cover- age be assessed no lower than one rating level below the desired rating on the security.

   Although the rating agencies vary in the methods in which they assign ratings, all agencies review the risk characteristics of the pool and the security's structure.

Collateral Issues

Agencies review the aggregate features of the pool in addition to each loan comprising the pool. On the micro level, the contractual features and the prop- erties securing each loan are examined. On the macro level, the overall pool characteristics, such as the number of loans in the pool and the geographic concentration of those loans, provide the final elements for assigning a risk weighting to the collateral.

Loan-to-value ratio: The loan-to-value (LTV) ratio is the ratio of the loan balance to the minimum of the purchase price and the appraised value of the property. As the borrower's ownership interest in the property is inversely related to the LTV ratio, and defaults normally occur because of low equity in the property, the origination LTV ratio is a key factor in assessing the probability of default. A high origination LTV ratio reflects poorly on a mortgagor's credit quality. Rating agency studies indicate that mortgages with 90% LTV ratios are 1.5 times more likely to default than mortgages with 80% or lower LTV ratios, and loans with 95% LTV ratios are 3.0 times more likely to default.

Mortgage type: Fixed-rate loans default less frequently than loans with variable payments. Rating agencies assign higher risk weightings for buydown loans, graduated payment mortgages (GPM), growing equity mortgages (GEM), tiered-payment mortgages (TPM), and adjustable-rate mortgages (ARM) because these mortgages usually experience an increase in payments that may cause "payment shock." The risk of payment shock causing defaults and ultimate foreclosure is particularly high for borrowers who would not have qualified for the mortgage at the full payment rate. Characteristics of ARM loans that affect the risk weighting include the adjustment frequency, interest rate caps, the existence of teaser rates, the volatility of the underlying index, and the possibility of negative amortization.

Mortgage term and coupon: A loan's amortization schedule is a function of the loan balance, term, and coupon. Lower terms and/or higher coupons cause a faster buildup in equity, thereby decreasing the LTV ratio. Typically, rating agencies will assign lower risk weightings to a mortgage whose original term is less than 30 years. A higher risk weighting will be assigned to a mortgage whose coupon at origination was higher than the then-current prevailing rate, as that may indicate a mortgagor's poor credit history.

Documentation standards: Full documentation standards for conforming loans require the lender to conduct verification of income (VOI), verification of employment (VOE), verification of down payment (VOD), assessment of credit reports, and property appraisals. The VOD and the property appraisal are especially important as they add validity to the LTV ratio. However, nonconforming loans may not be fully documented. Rating agencies account for the deviation in documentation standards when assigning risk weightings.

Mortgage purpose: Purposes for a mortgage range from financing a primary residence or refinancing a mortgage, to financing a vacation home or investment property. Rating agencies assign a higher risk weighting to loans that finance properties other than primary residences, as the probability of a borrower defaulting on a second property is much higher than on a primary residence. Investment properties are particularly risky because poor investment decisions may affect the borrower's ability to cover mortgage payments. Straight refinancings do not reduce the equity in the property and hence cause no additional risks. However, takeout refinancings increase the LTV ratio and, therefore, are assigned higher risk weightings.

Seasoning of loan: Research performed by Standard and Poor's (S&P) indicates 95% of losses generally occur by the seventh year of a pool's life. As a loan ages, appreciation in property values and principal paydown cause the LTV ratio of a loan to decrease, reducing the risk associated with the loan. However, as with the adverse selection theory, the recent record low mortgage rates and the consequent refinancings could cause the risk associated with a pool to increase as the remaining loans comprising the pools may have been unable to take advantage of the opportunity to refinance due to poor credit.

Secured property type: The default risk is lower for loans secured by owner-occupied, detached, single-family properties than those secured by multi-family dwellings, planned unit developments (PUD), condominiums, and townhomes. Although housing prices usually decline during a recession, single-family detached homes experience less price volatility as renters and other homeowners are able to purchase homes. Consequently, townhomes, PUDs, condominiums, and multi-family dwellings experience an even sharper price decline. As the value of the property declines, the LTV ratio increases, and also the risk of default. In the event of default, single-family detached homes are more liquid because the initiation of foreclosure proceedings is less difficult.

Geographic diversification: Economic diversification and regional special hazards must be considered when analyzing the default risk of a loan. Rating agencies assign higher risk weightings to pools with a concentration greater than 5% per zip code, and only 1% per zip code in a special hazard prone area. Loans originated in a specialized economic environment are more susceptible to declines in a local industry, such as that seen in the Texas economy's dependence on the energy industry, and therefore receive a higher risk weighting. Investors have become particularly concerned that in the event of an earthquake, pools composed of a high concentration of California loans may experience losses in excess of the required special hazard coverage. In response to this fear, S&P conducted a study in late 1993 of the credit performance of loans secured by properties exposed to earthquakes. Reportedly, S&P found that homeowners rarely sustained damage in excess of the equity in the property, causing minimal defaults due to earthquakes. Consequently, S&P lowered the amount of special hazard insurance required from 1% to 0.5%. Additional special hazard insurance may be required for properties located near faults or frequent seismic activity, or for poorly constructed homes.

Structural Issues

Once the quality of the collateral has been established, the rating agencies verify that the collateral cash flow adequately supports the structure of the deal. A scrutiny of the infrastructure of the deal provides the final element in assessing the credit enhancement required for a security.

Trustee/servicer credit quality: Many of the servicer's functions are critical in terms of the underlying credit risk to which investors are exposed. In addition to collecting the monthly payments and passing the cash flows to the trustee, the servicer handles delinquency issues, initiates foreclosure procedures, and liquidates properties when necessary. To help maintain the timely payment of principal and interest, the servicer typically covers losses due to delinquency and foreclosure, receiving reimbursement as loans emerge from delinquencies or properties are foreclosed and liquidated. Due to the critical role of the servicer, some issues provide for a back-up servicer or additional credit enhancement such as LOCs, corporate guarantees, or bond insurance. Rating agencies allow the servicer to be rated one level lower than the security, but only if additional credit enhancement is provided. Generally, the trustee, however, must be at least AA for any issue.

Interest shortfall: Investors expect to receive interest based on a full 30 day period. However, prepayments that occur between monthly payments can cause a shortage of interest available to bondholders. Some whole-loan issues provide for the servicer to pay compensating interest to cover the shortfall up to a specified percentage of the monthly servicing fee. In the event that the interest shortfall is not fully compensated, the loss is shared on a pro-rata basis by all classes composing the MBS passthrough or multi-class REMIC. In structures that do not pay compensating interest, losses can be significant in a high prepayment environment.

Credit Enhancement Techniques

As we have seen, credit risks associated with mortgages include short-term delinquencies and unrecoverable losses caused by special hazards, bankruptcy, origination fraud, and foreclosures. Agency guarantees of the timely payment of principal and interest eliminate credit risk from agency mortgage securities. (Note that FHLMC PCs guarantee only the timely payment of interest and ultimate payment of principal.) To protect investors from the credit risks associated with whole-loan mortgages, non-agency security structures include a variety of credit enhancement techniques. The techniques can be categorized according to whether they are internal or external to a security's structure. External credit enhancement techniques are provided by either the issuer or a third party; internal credit enhancement techniques are built into the structure.

External Credit Enhancements

Regardless of the credit enhancement used to cover losses and delinquencies, most lenders require mortgagors to provide primary mortgage insurance (PMI) and standard hazard insurance. PMI protects the lender from high LTV ratios and is usually written to cover 20% - 25% of the original loan balance. Normally when the LTV ratio falls below 80%, PMI insurance is no longer required. The mortgagor may also be required to purchase special hazard insurance if the property is located in an area where natural disasters are likely. Because pool level insurance policies require the PMI policy to take a first loss position, if the provider of PMI has a lower rating than the desired rating on the security, additional credit enhancement is required. External credit loss coverage usually comes in the form of pool insurance, letters of credit (LOC), bond insurance, or corporate guarantees.

Pool insurance: Pool insurance normally covers losses due to defaults and foreclosures. The amount of pool insurance purchased is dictated by the desired rating on the security. Some pool insurance policies are designed to step down in size as the pools season and, accordingly, less loss coverage is required by rating agencies. Additional credit enhancement techniques must be used to cover bankruptcy, origination fraud, and special hazards.

In the event of bankruptcy, a bankruptcy bond provides coverage against a court order that modifies the mortgage debt by decreasing the interest rate or reducing the unpaid principal balance. Such a reduction in mortgage debt is known as a *cramdown*.

Individuals can file for bankruptcy under Chapter 13 and Chapter 7 of the Internal Revenue Code. Chapter 13 bankruptcy filings allow individuals to retain their assets while restructuring or forgiving debts. Under Chapter 7 bankruptcy filings, personal assets are liquidated to pay debts; cramdowns are not allowed. In the 1993 case of *Nobleman vs. American Savings*, the U.S. Supreme Court disallowed cramdowns under Chapter 13 filings as well.

While cramdowns are allowed under Chapter 11 bankruptcy filings, Chapter 11 is primarily used by businesses. Thus, given the relatively unlikely event of bankruptcy, most rating agencies would normally require as little as $100,000 to $150,000 of loss coverage on a $250 million pool of high-quality mortgages.

Because pool insurers will not cover losses stemming from fraud during the loan application process, rating agencies require fraud insurance coverage of 1% - 3% of the original pool balance. Fraud coverage is allowed to decrease over the first six years as rating agencies assume the risk of losses due to fraud declines as the pool seasons.

Letters of credit: The issuer of a whole-loan security or a third party can provide a letter of credit in the amount required by the rating agencies to enhance the entire deal or in a lesser amount designed to complement other forms of credit enhancement. Additional insurance is required to cover losses caused by bankruptcy, origination fraud, and special hazards as LOCs rarely cover losses due to these risks. To protect the investor from event risks, some LOCs are designed to convert to cash if the issuer is downgraded. The servicer normally covers short-term delinquencies, but LOCs can be written in a manner requiring the provider of the LOC to cover short-term delinquencies.

Bond insurance: Bond insurance normally covers all types of losses. Capital Markets Assurance Corporation (CAPMAC), Financial Guarantee Insurance Corporation (FGIC), and Financial Security Assurance (FSA) issue bond insurance that covers all losses. General Electric Mortgage Insurance Company (GEMICO) provides bond insurance that covers only credit-related losses. Typically, bond insurance does not take the first-loss position in the credit support structure and thus rarely provides standalone credit support. Bond insurance is frequently used to provide additional credit support to upgrade a double-A-rated security to a triple-A rating.

Corporate guarantees: Corporate guarantees cover all losses and can be used as standalone credit support or with other forms of credit enhancement to provide the loss coverage required to obtain a particular rating.

Under the "weak-link" test used by the rating agencies to evaluate the creditworthiness of a security, if a primary credit supplier's rating is reduced, the security is subject to re-evaluation, and the rating of the security may decline as well. For example, when Citibank was downgraded in the early 1990s, many of the securities enhanced by Citibank corporate guarantees were downgraded also. The popularity of external credit enhancement techniques has declined due to the rising costs of third-party credit enhancement and a dwindling pool of highly rated third party credit suppliers. The percent of private-label issuance externally enhanced declined from 70% in 1987 to only 14% in 1993. See Exhibit 2.

Internal Credit Enhancement

Internal credit enhancement techniques allocate a portion of the collateral cash flow to supply the support needed to obtain a desired rating for the security. This self-insurance aspect of internal credit enhancement structures eliminates the event risks associated with external credit enhancement methods. The most popular form of internal credit enhancement available is the senior-subordinated structure. Other internal structures include reserve funds and spread accounts, both of which are normally used in addition to a subordinate class.

Senior-subordinated structures: In this structure, one or more subordinate classes are created to protect the senior classes from the risks associated with whole-loan mortgages. The original senior-subordinated structures were composed of two classes. The A class, or senior class, is insured against credit loss by the B (subordinate) class, which assumes a first-loss position. If a loss is experienced, funds that would normally be directed to the subordinate class are redirected to the senior class. Should payments due to the A class exceed the total cash flow available one month, resulting in a payment shortfall, and no funds are available from an additional credit enhancement policy or short-term delinquency coverage account, the A class accrues the payment shortfall. In subsequent months, payments due to the B class would be diverted to pay off the shortfall. The A class is protected from losses until the B class is exhausted.

Prepayment risks cause an uncertainty as to the amount of coupon interest due. Hence rating agencies require the total amount of loss coverage in the form of principal. Thus the subordinate class size must be at least as large as the initial required coverage amount. For example, a $100 million 30 year fixed-rate pool that requires an initial 8% loss coverage would need a subordinate class of size $800,000 to provide sufficient loss coverage to receive a Triple-A rating on the senior class.

With the original A/B structure, the subordinate class was usually held by the issuer. Interest in subordinate classes has increased as investors have gained expertise with mortgage-backed securities. One variation to the A/B structure is the three-class senior-subordinated structure, which breaks the B class into a speculative-grade rated bond and an unrated bond; the two subordinate bonds share the losses sequentially.

In 1991 the A/B structure evolved further into a mezzanine structure composed of four types of classes: super-senior, semi-senior, super-subordinate and subordinate classes (Exhibit 2). Each class can be further structured into a variety of bonds, such as PAC-companion structures or floater-inverse floater structures, suiting the needs of a diverse investor population. The two most popular forms of senior/subordinated structures are the reserve fund structure and the shifting interest structure.

Reserve fund structure: Generic senior-subordinated structures use reserve funds to meet loss coverage requirements. Recall that on a fixed-rate pool, the first level of loss coverage must be maintained at a constant level for the first five years. If the subordinate class receives any principal during this period, the amount of loss coverage falls below the required level of coverage. Thus during the first level of loss coverage, the subordinate class's share of principal is directed to the reserve fund. Since scheduled principal payments are initially low, to increase the size of the reserve fund more rapidly, both principal and interest due to the subordinate class are diverted to the reserve fund until a targeted amount is reached, normally 1% of the original pool balance. The amount of principal diverted from the subordinate class declines as the pool seasons and the required amount of loss coverage declines. The reserve fund combined with the expected future cash flows of the subordinate class represent the loss coverage.

Although a third party could provide delinquency coverage, normally the issuer contributes the required amount of delinquency coverage to the reserve fund. Once the reserve fund reaches the required amount, subordinate principal is diverted to reimburse the issuer. The structure becomes fully self-insured once the issuer has been reimbursed.

Rating agencies require that the reserve fund can be invested only in short-term high-quality securities. Thus the owner of the subordinate class experiences a decline in yield without a corresponding decline in risk. This disadvantage led to the development of the shifting interest structure.

Shifting interest structure: Instead of diverting subordinate cash flows to a reserve fund, the shifting interest structure diverts subordinate cash flows to the senior class. The adverse selection theory can be used to argue that only the percentage of prepayments due to the subordinated class needs to be diverted to the senior class. As prepayments are used to reduce the balance of the senior class, a shift in ownership interest occurs; hence the name shifting interest structure.

Similar to the reserve fund structure, as the pool seasons, the required amount of loss coverage declines. For the first five years, 100% of the prepayments due to the subordinate class are diverted to the senior class. For the next four years, the percentage of prepayments diverted from the subordinate class decreases relative to the percentage decrease in overall loss coverage required. Finally, no further diversions are made and the two classes pay pro rata. The subordinate class balance remains proportionally constant to the outstanding pool balance, satisfying the third level of loss coverage.

Because the senior class receives portions of the prepayments due to the subordinate class, the senior class has a higher effective prepayment rate than the collateral, while the subordinate class has a lower effective prepayment rate. This causes the subordinate class to have the average life stability of a PAC or super PAC.

Although reserve funds are occasionally used, delinquency coverage is usually external to the shifting interest structure.

Spread accounts: Excess interest, the interest that is not directed to any class, can be siphoned into a spread account. This account can then be used as additional credit support. Spread accounts must work in conjunction with another form of credit enhancement since rating agencies require the loss coverage to be supported by principal. Spread accounts are most often used to help support a senior/subordinated structure with ARM collateral.

PREPAYMENTS

FNMA and FHLMC securitization programs require loans to meet guidelines that limit servicing fees, loan size, weighted average maturity dispersion, and underwriting criteria. The homogeneous nature of the collateral and an abundance of historical data have facilitated the creation of sophisticated prepayment models. Whole loan prepayment rates are more difficult to model, however, because the collateral is less homogeneous than conforming loans. In general, historical data on prepayments, defaults, and foreclosures are relatively sparse. Fortunately, many of the larger whole-loan issuers such as the RTC, Prudential, RFC, Ryland, Chase, and Citibank have begun making more timely prepayment information available to investors and dealers.

When attempting to forecast whole-loan prepayment rates, investors must consider the traditional factors influencing prepayments (loan rate, age, and seasonal effects) as well as the geographic concentration, term, LTV ratios, origination standards, and the loan sizes and types composing the pool. Typically, greater variance in loan types tends to increase prepayment rates of whole-loan securities over that of similar coupon agency securities.

As with conforming loans, whole-loan prepayment rates tend to increase when interest rates decline, and as the loans season. During 1993, non-conforming loans responded much faster than conforming loans to interest rate changes, surprising the market with their efficiency. Some whole-loan securities in the refinance-sensitive coupons (8.5% to 10%) experienced prepayment rates as much as 50% to 100% faster than similar conforming loans.

Since non-agency securities are frequently backed by a large number of jumbo loans, the collateral often has a relatively high regional concentration. Hence, the prepayment performance of a whole-loan security is often tied to a particular region's economic condition. Jumbo loan borrowers are relatively quick to react to declining interest rates because of the substantial impact a lower mortgage rate can have on the borrower's monthly payment. As property values increase, the more affluent jumbo borrowers may trade-up to better homes. Likewise, as property values decline, jumbo borrowers are less likely to move. As the jumbo loans composing a pool prepay, the credit risk of the pool may increase through adverse selection. However, the increase in credit enhancement resulting in a shifting interest structure should alleviate this risk.

SUMMARY AND OUTLOOK

From 1988 to 1993, the non-agency, whole-loan market has grown over six-fold, from $15.4 billion securities issued in 1988 to $98.5 billion issued in 1993. The market will continue to mature and gain more investor acceptance as continued progress is made in organizing and disseminating deal- and issuer-specific pool level data on prepayments, defaults, and delinquencies. These wheels have been set in motion by the RTC, and many of the private issuers. Specialty firms such as Mortgage Risk Assessment Corporation have also been established to specialize in collecting, processing, and analyzing whole-loan collateral data at the individual loan level. With this foundation for the crucial information infrastructure beginning to take shape, investor opportunities in whole-loan securities in the 1990s compare with those in the agency securities in the early 1980s.

Section II

CHAPTER 2

Structural Nuances in Non-Agency Mortgage-Backed Securities

Peter Rubinstein, Ph.D.
Senior Vice President
Donaldson, Lufkin, & Jenrette

This chapter was written while the author was employed as Chief Mortgage Economist at Moody's Investors Service.

Non-agency residential mortgage-backed securities are incredibly complex. The usual risk present in all fixed income securities — the fluctuation of interest rates — is both amplified and distorted in whole loan passthroughs by features that hamper liquidity: credit risk, prepayment risk, a lack of data, and structural complexity. This chapter focuses on some of the least understood structural aspects of these securities — nuances that may appear small, but in fact significantly impact yield.

By nuance, we do not mean the way CMO tranches prioritize cash flows, or differences in credit structuring techniques. These are major issues that we assume the reader is familiar with. Instead, this chapter examines more subtle structural issues that are sometimes referred to in the prospectus, but often are fully disclosed only in the pooling and servicing agreement. These include: advances of delinquent principal and interest, claims adjustments for liquidated loans, compensating interest for prepayments, ratio stripping, and interest subordination (including potential payment delays to subordinated classes). While we discuss specific structures of certain issuers, these structures change over time, so all references to specific issuers and their policies describe some, but not necessarily all, of their transactions.

ADVANCES

Advances are funds servicers loan to the trust to allow the trustee to make timely payments of interest and principal to investors. Servicers advance only to cover homeowner delinquencies, not shortfalls for other reasons. For example, reduced interest collections due to mid-month prepayments, the Relief Act, or "cramdowns," are not reasons for advancing because these are not events of default; homeowners are allowed in these circumstances to make reduced payments.[1] Nor do servicers advance principal to cover defaults in the final repayment of balloon loans.

In most non-agency MBSs, advancing is performed by the master servicer from its own funds. In some transactions, reserve funds may be used to support advancing, and occasionally subservicers have the primary obligation to advance. No interest is paid the servicer for advanced funds; instead, the servicer usually keeps all late penalties collected from delinquent borrowers as additional compensation. Virtually all transactions require a back-up servicer to provide advancing in case the primary servicer fails to advance; this function is usually performed by the trustee. Advanced funds are recouped by the servicer when either the homeowner pays delinquent interest

---

[1] The federal Soldiers' and Sailors' Civil Relief Act of 1940 allows certain military personnel to pay reduced interest rates on home mortgages during times of war. A cramdown is a reduction in either the mortgage interest rate or the mortgage principal amount imposed by a bankruptcy court.

and principal or when the property is foreclosed and sold. In either case, advances are repaid before cash is distributed to security owners.

Forms of Advancing

The obligation to advance in the private-label market is limited and varies substantially by issuer. The best and most common form of advancing offered in the non-agency market is called *mandatory* advancing.[2] Mandatory advancing calls for the servicer to advance both interest and principal on delinquent loans. Failure to advance is an event of default unless the servicer determines that there is no reasonable chance of recouping advanced funds from the ultimate disposition of the property.

A few issuers, such as Countrywide Funding Corporation and Countrywide Mortgage Conduit (recently renamed Independent National Mortgage Corporation), offer a slightly weaker form of mandatory advancing. In deals sold under the "CWMBS, Inc." description, they advance interest but not principal for loans that have progressed to REO (i.e., loans that have completed the foreclosure process).[3]

Other issuers, such as Chemical Mortgage Securities, Inc., and PNC Mortgage Securities Corp., offer a slightly stronger form of mandatory advancing. They will advance even when advanced funds are not deemed recoverable from the specific loan that has gone bad so long as credit support is available to absorb any loss.

The next best form of advancing, found in a fair number of transactions, is called *optional* or *voluntary* advancing. In these transactions, the servicer intends to advance but is not legally required to do so. In other words, failure to advance is not an event of default.

Generally, optional advancing works as well as mandatory advancing as long as the pool is performing well, but in some transactions optional advancing has stopped because of extremely high delinquencies. For example, in many ComFed transactions advancing has stopped.

A variation on optional advancing offered by Citicorp Mortgage Securities, has optional advancing by the master servicer but mandatory backup advancing by the trustee. Operationally, this arrangement is as good as normal mandatory advancing as long as the back-up servicer is highly rated and acapable of servicing.

Although less common now, many older transactions offer even weaker forms of advancing. In transactions with *limited* advancing, the ser-

---

[2] Servicers of pools with first-lien mortgages virtually always advance both scheduled interest and principal. Servicers of securities backed by second-lien mortgages (such as home equity transactions) traditionally do not advance principal.

[3] In this sense, CFC and CMC resemble Freddie Mac, which guarantees the ultimate return of principal rather than the timely payment of principal on most of its earlier transactions.

vicer must advance, but only up to some specified limit. The most common types of limits are: (1) a preset, fixed dollar amount; (2) a floating dollar amount, typically tied to the amount in the reserve fund; or (3) a maximum number of missed payments per loan.

In transactions with *partial* advancing, funds are advanced only to the extent needed to make up for missed payments to the senior classes. The weakest and most unusual form of advancing, of course, is no advancing at all. We are unaware of any publicly offered transactions that completely lack advancinga multi-class structure with many "skinny" mezzanine classes, a lack of advancing makes payment delays to the mezzanine classes far more likely.

THE IMPACT OF ADVANCING

The primary purpose of advancing is to smooth a pool's cash flow stream. At the same time, advancing also shifts cash flows forward in time. With no advancing, a pool generates smaller monthly payments whenever homeowners fail to pay, followed by larger cash flows when homeowners cure or the property is liquidated. The advancing of missed payments provides larger pools cash flows earlier in the deal, followed by smaller cash flows when the servicer reimburses itself, which, *ceteris paribus*, is a benefit because of the time value of money.

Ultimately, however, the impact of advancing on investors depends upon how the transaction is tranched. For transactions with internal credit support, the benefit of advancing is far more important to subordinated classes. Senior classes in modern senior-subordinated REMIC structures receive interest and principal first, so a lack of advancing will cause a payment delay to the senior class only if delinquency shortfalls exceed the total amount due the subordinate class.[4] Such events are rare in a two-class structure, although in a multi-class structure with many "skinny" mezzanine classes, a lack of advancing makes payment delays to the mezzanine classes far more likely.

Advancing is an important benefit for transactions enhanced with only a pool policy. Without advancing, highly rated classes will surely experience at least some small payment delays, and could suffer significant payment delays. Note that the risk is twofold: (1) the investor will lose interest on delayed payments, a reinvestment risk, and (2) the maturity of the security is extended by payment delays, a duration risk.

---

[4] Older grantor trust passthroughs first pay senior interest, then subordinate interest, followed by senior principal and then subordinate principal. In these structures interest and principal payments from homeowners retain their original character — principal cannot be used to pay interest and vice versa — so operationally the senior class is always paid first.

Exhibit 1: Advancing Policy

Issuers Typically Offering Mandatory Advancing

Prudential Home Mortgage Securities, Inc.

Residential Funding Corporation

SBMS, Inc. (Salomon Brothers Mortgage Securities, Inc.)

Housing Securities Inc.

Ryland (mandatory for subservicers, limited for Ryland as backup servicer)

Countrywide Funding Corp. (interest only on REOs)

Countrywide Mortgage Conduit, Inc. (interest only on REOs)

Merrill Lynch Prime First

Chase Mortgage Finance Corp.

PNC (will advance on non-recoverables if subordination is still intact)

Paine Webber

Sears

Chemical (will advance on non-recoverables if subordination is still intact)

Issuers That Have Transactions With Optional Advancing

ComFed (advancing has stopped on many transactions)

Citicorp Mortgage Securities Inc. (mandatory back-up advancing)

Republic Federal S&L Assn.

Glendale Federal S&L Assn.

California Federal S&L

Issuers That Have Transactions With Limited Advancing

Home Owners Federal S&L Assn.

Sandia

Columbia S&L Assn.

Issuers That Have Transactions With Partial Advancing

Imperial Savings Assn.

Advancing has different effects in the case of CMO/REMIC cash flow tranching. Since a primary objective of these structures is to control maturity by sequentially allocating all pool principal to one tranche at a time, serious delinquencies coupled with no advancing could cause extension risk, particularly to the class receiving principal at the time of the delay. While the level of risk depends partly on the specific cash flow prioritization scheme used in the structure, a major portion of the risk also depends on how poorly the collateral is performing (i.e., the level of delinquencies) and on how quickly the collateral can be liquidated.

In Georgia, for example, the foreclosure process is fast, typically three to six months, so delays will be minimal even if delinquencies are severe. In New Jersey and Massachusetts, on the other hand, the foreclosure process is slow, often taking two years. Because the impact of a delay in the receipt of principal can be funneled into just one tranche at a time, a lack of advancing could cause substantial extension risk to the currently amortizing tranche in a pool with high delinquencies (i.e., shortfalls beyond the amount that can be absorbed by subordinate classes) on collateral originated in slow foreclosure states.

Exhibit 2 provides an investor checklist for advancing.

Claims Adjustments

Between 10% to 20% of all non-agency mortgage-backed securities are enhanced with pool policies. Pool policies typically pay 100% of any loss due to borrower default, but only if the servicer "properly" manages the delinquency, which generally means that the servicer must manage the delinquency to minimize losses.[5] If the insurance company finds that the servicer has not properly managed the defaulted loan, it can reduce the amount of the claim paid.

Claims adjustments are common. For example, insurance companies have refused to pay for losses due to penalties imposed when the servicer failed to pay property taxes on time. Adjustments have also been made because of servicers' failure to notify the insurance company in a timely fashion of the default, in which case the adjustment is usually to deny coverage for interest during the period for which the notification was late. Other adjustments have been made because the servicer paid excessive legal fees or repair costs on liquidated REO property.

---

[5] Standard pool policies cover 100% of each loan's loss up to the overall policy limit, with the exclusion of losses due to fraud, special hazard, or bankruptcy. A variation, called a modified pool policy, covers no more than 25% of each individual loan's balance. Note that in some foreclosures the insurance company manages the disposition of the property, in which case the problems that could cause a claim adjustment are mitigated.

Exhibit 2: Investor Checklist for Advancing

<u>Key questions</u>

- Is there advancing?
    - Is the advancing mandatory, optional, limited, or partial?
    - What is the credit rating of the advancing party? Can it honor its commitment?

- Is there back-up advancing?
    - Is the backup advancing mandatory, optional, limited, or partial?
    - What is the credit rating of the advancing party? Can it honor its commitment?

Additional questions if advancing is optional, limited, partial, or non-existent

- What dollar volume of advancing is likely, given the collateral?
    - Are the loans from a fast or slow foreclosure state?
    - What level of delinquencies can be expected over the life of the pool? For example:
        - Does the pool have "A" quality credits or "B" & "C" quality credits?
        - Are the loans 30- or 15- year (15-year loans tend to have stronger borrowers)?
        - Are the loans fixed-rate or adjustable-rate? (ARMs tend to have weaker borrowers)?

- How will advancing interact with the credit and cash flow tranching?
    - How much cash is available from subordination to absorb a lack of advancing?
    - How sensitive is the tranche to extension risk if advancing fails?

For investors, the key concern with claims adjustments is that most transactions enhanced with pool policies have no other form of credit support, so any loss due to an uncovered claim flows directly through to senior bondholders. Such losses have been small to date because most issuers and servicers have been willing to absorb claims adjustments in order to maintain the goodwill of investors, but no formal mechanism exists in servicing documents for covering these losses. This is an issue worth watching because it could become a problem in the future. To mitigate the chance of losses from claims adjustments, investors should look for pools managed by reputable servicers.

Note that losses from claims adjustments are a distinct, separate issue from the loss in yield that investors can suffer when pool policy claims are settled in the middle of the month. This is similar to the "compensating interest" issue in that pool policies pay for lost interest only up to the date of settlement. The balance of the month's interest is generally covered only if and to the extent that the transaction offers compensating interest for pool policy settlements.

Compensating Interest

Compensating interest is the payment by the servicer to investors of a full month's interest on loans for which only a partial month's interest has been collected because of prepayment during the month. Some transactions also offer compensating interest to cover the loss of interest from mid-month liquidations and mid-month pool policy settlements.

The financial impact of compensating interest, which can be significant, is discussed in detail in Chapter 12. Here we discuss only the variations of compensating interest offered in the non-agency market. Exhibit 3 lists typical compensating interest provisions for some issuers.

The most important distinction among issuers is that compensating interest is simply not offered on many transactions in the non-agency market. For example, virtually all RFC transactions before 1994 do not pay compensating interest. Similarly, GE transactions issued in the beginning of 1994 and earlier as well as some of the early SBMS Inc. transactions do not pay compensating interest.

Of the issuers that do offer compensating interest, none fully reimburses investors in all circumstances. Most issuers limit compensating interest to be no more than the master servicing fee. In some instances, only part of the master servicer fee is made available for compensating interest. Since the size of the master servicing fee varies substantially, a part of a large fee may actually be more than all of a small fee.

Occasionally, subservicers must contribute all or part of their servicing fees to cover compensating interest, and some issuers allow their investment earnings on payments held for distribution (i.e., the float) to augment the amount available for compensating interest.

A second issue concerns what types of lost interest are covered. Whenever compensating interest is offered, prepayments in full are covered, but partial prepayments (i.e., curtailments) are often excluded. Payment of compensating interest on liquidations, mid-month pool policy settlements, and other loan terminations is uncommon.

A third aspect of compensating interest is how prepayment interest shortfalls (i.e., any partial month's interest that is not compensated for) are distributed among various cash flow tranches and credit classes. A common practice is to prorate any interest shortfall among various credit classes on the basis of the outstanding principal balance of each class, and then within each class, to distribute shortfalls to each cash flow tranche pro rata, according to the amount of accrued interest due.

Exhibit 3: Compensating Interest Policies of Select Issuers

Issuer	Limits
Prudential	Cover full prepayments up to 20 bps master servicing fee on fixed rate products, and 25 bps on ARMs. Partial prepayment shortfalls borne by subordinate tranche. Starting with 1994-26, full prepayments received before the 17th of the month are passed through in current month without interest. Full prepayment after the 16th of the month receive compensating interest but are passed through in the following month.
RFC	Virtually never offered before 1994-13.
GE	None on transactions before 1994-26.
Countrywide Funding Corp.	Prepayments before the 15th of the month passed through in current month without interest; full prepayments after the middle of the month are covered up to half the master servicing fee (half of 25 bps = 12.5 bps).
Countrywide Mortgage Conduit, Inc. (now called Independent National Mortgage Corporation)	Full and partial prepayments up to 12.5 bps of the master servicing fee.
Merrill Lynch Prime First	Full, partial, and liquidations covered up to master servicing fee (typically > 25 bps).
Citicorp Mortgage Securities Inc.	Full and partial prepayments up to servicing fee (typically 25 bps).
Sears	Full, partial, and pool policy settlements up to master servicing fee.
Paine Webber	Full and partial prepayments up to master servicing fee (typically +/- 29 bps).
Home Owners Federal S&L Association (older deals)	Full prepayments up to master servicing fee, but for senior class only.
Chase	Full prepayments, partial prepayments, and liquidations covered up to the master servicing fee.
Coast S&L (older deals)	None
Chemical	Full and partial prepayments up to the master servicing fee (fee varies)
Ryland	Full prepayments, partial prepayments, and liquidations covered up to the primary servicers' servicing fee (not master servicing fee)

Exhibit 4: Investor Checklist for Compensating Interest

• Is compensating interest offered?

• If compensating interest is offered, what types of loan terminations are covered:

> • full prepayments?
> • partial prepayments?
> • mid-month pool policy settlements?
> • other liquidations?

• What is the maximum amount available for compensating interest:
> • How large is the master servicing fee?
> • Are other funds available, such as float?
> • What percentage of the fee is made available?

• How are unsupported interest shortfalls allocated to investors?

• When are prepayments (or other terminations) passed through?

Some issuers, such as Countrywide Mortgage Conduit, Inc., treat their excess master servicing spread as a class (whether securitized or not) and allow it to absorb a pro-rata share of any prepayment interest shortfall. Other issuers, such as Prudential, allocate prepayment interest shortfalls from full prepayments across all classes, but allocate shortfalls due to partial prepayments to only the subordinate classes. This effectively gives the senior tranches full protection up to the master servicing fee so long as the subordinate classes are in existence.

A last dimension of compensating interest concerns the timing of payments. Most issuers pass full prepayments on to investors in the month following receipt. Partial prepayments are usually passed through in the same month of receipt if received before the determination date (i.e., the date on which payment to certificate holders is calculated).

Countrywide Funding Corporation, some of the newer PNC transactions, and new Prudential transactions have introduced a variation allowing the passthrough of full prepayments received before the middle of the month in the same month received, but without interest from the first day of that month to the day of prepayment. This essentially causes the same 25-day delay an investor would get with full compensating interest. Prepayments received after the middle of the month for these issuers receive normal compensating interest, but the prepayments are passed through in the following month.

Exhibit 4 provides a checklist for investors to evaluate compensating interest.

RATIO STRIPPING

Home mortgage rates vary substantially both over time and in different places, which makes it virtually impossible for issuers to assemble large, fixed-rate pools with homogeneous interest rates. Consequently, as individual loans prepay, the interest rate generated by the entire pool (i.e., the weighted average coupon or WAC of the pool) shifts, even if all the individual mortgages have fixed rates. To create large classes of securities with fixed interest rates, the pool cash flow must be modified.

A common method for creating a constant remittance rate is called *ratio stripping*. The procedure is quite simple. The issuer first picks the fixed remittance rate it wants to offer investors. Then, for all loans with mortgage rates above the chosen remittance rate, all interest above the remittance rate — called *stripped interest* — is assigned to someone else, typically either a separate tranche, a subservicer, or the master servicer. If the stripped interest is sold as a separate tranche, is often called a *WAC IO* (interest-only).

For loans with a mortgage rate below the remittance rate, on the other hand, the issuer "strips" off enough principal so that the interest on that loan in relation to the remaining principal equals the desired remittance rate. The right to receive the stripped principal is typically sold off as a separate tranche called a *WAC PO* (principal-only). The net result of this process is the creation of up to three classes; a large class that will always produce a fixed remittance rate, plus one or two strip classes. An example will illustrate this process.

Assume that a $30 million pool of new 30-year fixed-rate mortgages is composed of three groups of loans, each with a face value of $10,000,000. Assume the first group pays interest at 7%, the second at 8%, and the third at 9%; and assume that the current market rate is 8%. Suppose the issuer wants to offer as large a tranche as possible yielding 8%.

To accomplish this, 100 basis points of the interest stream from the 9% loans is stripped off and securitized as a separate WAC IO tranche, leaving a $10 million piece earning 8%. Similarly, $1.25 million face value of the principal from the 7% loans is securitized as a separate WAC PO tranche, leaving $8.75 million, which will effectively earn 8% because this remaining piece is entitled to 7% interest earned on the full $10 million $(7\% \times 10,000,000/8,750,000 = 8\%)$. By stripping off the excess interest and principal, the issuer creates a $28.75 million tranche that will always generate an 8% interest rate regardless of prepayments, assuming full compensating interest, mandatory advancing, and no losses due to default.

This synthetic 8% pool, however is not the same as, and will not perform like, a real 8% pool. Similarly, the WAC IO and WAC PO stripped securities created by ratio stripping are different from pure IOs and POs created by separating the entire interest and principal streams as, for example, in the

FNMA IO/PO program. The differences are caused by two factors: amortization and prepayments. Furthermore, the way prepayment rates are reported could mislead investors into overvaluing these securities.

Consider first the WAC IO. By definition, WAC IOs are created off relatively high-coupon collateral. High-coupon mortgages have two distinguishing characteristics: (1) they amortize more slowly than low-coupon mortgages, and (2) they prepay at a faster rate. The slower amortization means that WAC IOs will generate more cash flow each month (except for the first month) than pure IOs off any lower coupon pool as long as prepayments are comparable, because the balance on the underlying WAC IO pool is larger at any given time.

On the other hand, WAC IOs created out of relatively high-coupon collateral are likely to prepay faster than IOs based on current-coupon collateral. This means they will likely generate less cash flow, and should therefore be less valuable than "normal" IOs.

Usually the prepayment effect dominates. Unfortunately, however, prepayment rates are always reported for the entire pool. The pool contains a blend of low and high coupons, so the reported rate will understate the prepayment rate sustained on that portion of the pool underlying the WAC IO because the WAC IO is stripped off only the high-coupon mortgages. The risk is that investors could be misled into thinking that the collateral underlying the WAC IO is prepaying at a better (i.e., slower) rate than it really is.

At the same time, the WAC PO (like all POs) generates a fixed amount of aggregate cash flow over its life, regardless of amortization or prepayment rates. Only the timing of the cash flows is affected by these factors. By definition, WAC POs are created from relatively low-coupon mortgages. Lower-rate mortgages amortize faster than high-coupon mortgages. Since POs are similar to zero-coupon bonds purchased at a discount, the faster amortization makes the WAC PO more valuable than a "normal" PO stripped off an entire pool.

WAC POs created from relatively low-coupon collateral are, however, less likely to prepay than pure POs, which makes them less valuable. Usually, the prepayment effect will dominate. The amortization impact dominates only if rates rise sufficiently to choke off virtually all prepayments. As with the WAC IO, the reported pool prepayment rate will misstate (in this case, overstate) the prepayment rate experienced on the collateral subset underlying the WAC PO, so the investor could be misled into thinking the WAC PO is prepaying at a better (i.e., faster) rate than it really is.

Last, consider the large synthetic 8% tranche created by ratio stripping. Part of the tranche, $10 million, is composed of true 8% mortgages. These will amortize and prepay like any comparable group of 8% mortgages. Another $10 million (face value) of the collateral underlying the tranche will amortize and prepay like 9% mortgages, and the rest like 7%

mortgages. Under most interest rate scenarios, the pool in this example will prepay more rapidly at first than a homogenous 8% pool as the 9% mortgages refinance, and more slowly later on as the 7% mortgages are likely to remain intact.

INTEREST SUBORDINATION AND PAYMENT DELAYS

Interest subordination is the reallocation of all subordinate cash flow (principal and interest) as needed to reduce the principal balance of senior classes by more than their pro-rata share of the proceeds from a loan liquidation. In most transactions with interest subordination, the intent is to convert defaults into full prepayments, which are then allocated strictly to the senior class. Most senior/sub transactions issued from 1990 through 1993 are structured with some form of interest subordination, and many new deals still use this structure.

The cash flow taken from subordinate classes is technically not lost; it is borrowed. Operationally, however, the pool may never generate enough cash in the future to repay the first-loss subordinate tranche. On the other hand, mezzanine classes are more likely to be repaid after some delay. A simple example will best illustrate how interest subordination works.

Assume a new transaction has three credit tranches: a $90 million senior class, a $5 million mezzanine class, and a $5 million first-loss class. Assume for simplicity that the pool is composed of $100 million of identical, new, 30-year fixed-rate mortgages with net passthrough rates of 12% per year (1% per month). Assume that on the first payment date a loan with an original balance of $200,000 is liquidated, and assume that only $120,000 in cash is recovered from the disposition of the property net of all sales costs, generating an $80,000 loss to the pool.

Under most interest subordination programs, and assuming full advancing, the master servicer will attempt to pay the senior class $199,942.77 in principal: the original face value of the liquidated loan less $57.23 in principal already advanced. Most of the money ($120,000) is available from the liquidation proceeds. To make up the shortfall, the servicer will take interest and principal that would have been paid to the subordinated classes.

Each subordinate class would otherwise be entitled to 5% (their pro rata share) of 1% (the monthly interest rate) of $100 million (the principal balance), or $50,000 in interest, plus 5% of $28,612.60 (= $1,430.63) of scheduled principal repayments. Since this is more than enough to make up for the shortfall in liquidation proceeds, the senior class will receive a full, default-induced prepayment of $199,942.77, constructed as follows:

$120,000.00	liquidation sales proceeds
−2,057.23	advances that must be recouped by the servicer
+51,430.63	scheduled principal and interest due the first-loss class
+1,430.63	principal due the mezzanine class
+29,138.74	interest due to the mezzanine class
$199,942.77	reduction in senior balance

At the end of the month, the mezzanine class will still have a balance of $5 million, will receive the remaining $20,861.26 interest not taken for subordination, and will be owed $29,138.74 interest. The first-loss class will receive no cash flow and they will be owed $50,000 interest. In most transactions, the balance of the first-loss class will be adjusted such that the sum of all class balances equals the face amount of the pool. The senior class will receive a full interest payment of $900,000 and will have its balance reduced to:

$$\underset{\text{90,000,000.00}}{\overset{\text{Balance}}{\text{beg. of Month}}} - \underset{\text{199,942.77}}{\overset{\text{Liquidation}}{\text{Principal}}} - \underset{0.9(28,612.600)}{\overset{\text{Scheduled}}{\text{Principal}}} = 89,774,305.89$$

If the interest available from the subordinate classes had not been enough to cover the losses sustained, most transactions will take future months' subordinate interest until the senior class balance is reduced by the full liquidated loan amount.

Interest taken from the first-loss class is rarely capitalized, which means that the delayed interest does not earn interest. Treatment of delayed interest on mezzanine classes varies. In Chase Mortgage Finance Corporation transactions, interest taken from the mezzanine class is capitalized, effectively earning interest on interest. Other issues (Prudential transactions, for example) typically do not capitalize mezzanine interest taken.

Most transactions tie the amount of interest that can be taken from the subordinate classes to the shifting interest prepayment step-down schedule, so the amount of interest available for subordination diminishes over time. In fixed-rate transactions, the step-downs typically begin in year 5 and are fully implemented by year 10. In ARM transactions, step-downs typically begin in year 10 and are fully implemented by year 15.

For the senior class, interest subordination is clearly a benefit. To the extent that losses are first absorbed by subordinate interest, the subordinate principal balance is higher, in theory offering greater protection against future losses. For the subordinate class, of course, interest subordination is bad. It forces subordinate classes to wait for their money, and exposes them to credit risk for a longer period of time, and few transactions pay the subordinate classes interest on delayed interest.

Despite the problems interest subordination can cause for junior classes, this was not an issue in the markets until late 1992. Up to that date, many first-loss tranches were held by the original issuers, and those that were sold were almost never rated, so they were typically purchased by investors with sufficient credit expertise to evaluate the potential loss due to payment delays.

In November 1992, Prudential started to resecuritize large groups of first-loss tranches it had been holding. In summer 1993, a mezzanine tranche in one of these resecuritizations experienced a payment delay because a sufficient number of the underlying subordinate securities had experienced payment delays.

The delay caught some investors off guard. In the world of corporate and municipal bonds, a delay in the receipt of payment is an event of default; these issuers promise timely payments of interest and principal. In the world of agency (i.e., GNMA, FNMA, and FHLMC) mortgage-backed securities, a delay in the payment of *interest* is an event of default. With the exception of some FHLMC issues, a delay in the payment of principal is also an event of default, because the agencies also promise timely payments.

But in the world of non-agency mortgage-backed securities, payment delays (as opposed to a loss of principal or interest) are generally not an event of default because the transaction documents do not promise timely payment of interest and principal, but only the *ultimate* payment of interest and principal. The possibility of a delay is a fully disclosed feature of all interest subordination deals. Furthermore, as discussed earlier, virtually all other non-agency deals have some potential for delays because of advancing policies.

So interest subordination does pose some risk for junior tranches. For first-loss tranches, the impact can be substantial. For mezzanine classes, the expected timing, lower probability, short duration, and smaller size of any payment delays suggests that the impact on yield should be small.

Exhibit 5 lists issues typically structured with and without subordination.

CONCLUSION

In the non-agency mortgage-backed securities market, complexity is compounded by a lack of standardization. This chapter identifies some of the structural nuances that differentiate securities in the non-agency market, and explains their importance to the investor.

Exhibit 5: Issues Typically Structured
With and Without Subordination

Issues typically structured with interest subordination
>Prudential Home (prior to 1994-28)
>Chase Mortgage Finance Corp.

Issue typically structured without interest subordination
>Citibank, N.A.
>Countrywide
>GE Capital Mortgage Services, Inc.
>Household Bank, f.s.b. (under SASI shelf)
>Housing Securities, Inc.
>Household Bank (under SASI shelf)
>Paine Webber
>PNC Mortgage Securities Corp.
>RFC
>Sears Mortgage Securities Corp.

Not all structural issues are covered, and there are many non-structural issues that can have a significant impact on yield. The key lesson of this chapter is that the details of each transaction must be examined, because there is substantial variation across deals, and the differences can have a substantial impact on yield.

CHAPTER 3

Fundamental Differences Between Agency and Non-Agency Mortgage-Backed Securities

Clifford Scott Asness, Ph.D.

Vice President, Director of Quantitative Research
Goldman Sachs Asset Management

The author thanks Jonathan Beinner for his many helpful comments.

The most important differences between agency and non-agency mortgage-backed securities (MBS) are the extra yield available on the non-agencies and the chance of default on the non-agencies. This trade-off is easy to understand. An investor assumes the risk of default in order to get the benefit of extra yield.

If these were the only differences between agencies and non-agencies, choosing between them would be straightforward (not to say simple). The investor would weigh the estimate of the probability of default against the benefit of the extra yield.

Life is not that simple, however. There are many differences between agency and non-agency MBS that can affect our opinion about their relative value and risk. Examples are: (1) agency securities pay a full month of interest regardless of when a homeowner prepays, while non-agency securities may not; (2) the prepayment curve of non-agency MBS is often steeper and more extreme than their agency counterparts; (3) non-agencies often come with a "clean-up" call; and (4) a new issue purchase of a non-agency CMO can entail writing a delivery option that gives the security's seller the chance to over- or underdeliver.

These effects, which vary in their impact, have several things in common. First, each difference between agency and non-agency MBS has a negative effect on non-agency MBS value. Second, these differences hurt the value of non-agency MBS because they add to the negative convexity already present in most mortgage-backed securities.

None of these differences implies that an investor should avoid non-agency MBS. The substantial spreads available in non-agency products may well compensate or overcompensate an investor for the features we discuss. At the same time, it is important to understand the special characteristics of non-agency MBS. Besides affecting our judgment about value, the differences we describe can affect our estimates of duration and convexity.

This chapter explains and illustrates these differences between agency and non-agency MBS using a simple example. We explain the differences in detail, and we attempt to put in perspective the magnitude of each effect on the value of non-agency MBS.

AN EXAMPLE

We will examine a hypothetical non-agency CMO called NONAGENCY 94-1 E. The bond is a ten-year PAC bond issued off current-coupon non-agency collateral. It is rated AAA by several major rating agencies and is protected from prepayments between 100 and 400 PSA. Its coupon is set such that the bond is initially priced at par.

At issuance NONAGENCY 94-1 E is offered at a yield spread of 105 basis points (bps) over the on-the-run ten-year Treasury. This spread is 25 basis points more than for a seemingly comparable agency PAC.

Given the excellent credit history of most AAA non-agencies, it initially seems that a non-agency bond would be preferable to an agency PAC with a similar range of prepayment protection. There are, however, other differences between agency and non-agency MBS that can affect our judgment about value, and these affect NONAGENCY 94-1 E throughout its life.

DELIVERY OPTION

Commonly, when investors purchase a new-issue agency CMO, they receive and pay for at settlement the exact face amount agreed upon. With new-issue non-agency MBS, however, it is not uncommon for the issuer to have an option to over- or underdeliver.

For example, NONAGENCY 94-1 E is purchased on 1/1/94 for settlement 2/28/94. The agreed-upon face amount is $1 miilion, but the issuer has the option to over- or underdeliver by 5%. This option works against the purchaser. Say rates fall enough for the ten-year PAC to appreciate two points in between the trade date and the settlement date (a rate move of about 30 basis points). The issuer will then underdeliver by 5%. This costs the purchaser 5% of 2 points or about 3 32nds.

The delivery option is equivalent to the issuer owning a straddle written by the purchaser. Standard options mathematics can estimate this delivery option's value. For NONAGENCY 94-1 E, we estimate the value at about 2 32nds or approximately 1 bp in yield. While not very large, this effect is measurable and unambiguously negative. Furthermore, if unrecognized and unhedged, the effect could be significant.

PREPAYMENT CURVE

The normal trade-off when considering owning MBS instead of Treasuries entails receiving higher yield in exchange for taking on average life volatility. PAC bonds typically ameliorate this trade-off. They offer less of a yield advantage than many other MBS, but offer more average life stability. PACs, however, do not offer absolute protection, but protect against only a certain range of prepayments.

Generally, non-agency MBS exhibit different prepayment behavior from agency MBS. Non-agency prepayments respond faster to refinancing incentives. For MBS that have in-the-money prepayment options and are not very seasoned, non-agency MBS experience more extreme prepayments than agencies.

Exhibit 1: Average Life Variability for Non-Agency PAC and Corresponding Agency PAC

Interest Rate Movement (bps)	Average Life Agency PAC (years)	Average Life NONAGENCY 94-1 E (years)
– 200	7.7	4.4
– 100	10.8	8.8
+0	10.8	10.8
+100	10.8	10.8
+200	10.8	10.8

Exhibit 1 highlights these differences. For both NONAGENCY 94-1 E and a corresponding agency PAC, the exhibit shows what happens to each bond's average life using our model under different interest rate scenarios (parallel curve shifts).

Clearly, when rates fall the non-agency PAC shortens faster and more drastically than the agency PAC. This has a direct effect on the value of NONAGENCY 94-1 E.

The negative convexity of NONAGENCY 94-1 E is worse than that of the agency PAC because the non-agency will appreciate substantially less in a rally. This result is general. The "steeper" prepayment curve exhibited by non-agency MBS will usually make these securities less convex than their agency counterparts.[1]

The agency and non-agency PACs are not as comparable as we first thought. The non-agency PAC has more yield, but also has more negative convexity. Our models find that the option-adjusted spread (OAS) of the non-agency PAC is lowered by about 12 bps because of the steeper prepayment curve. Differing assumptions and models will assign different values to this effect, but an investor must explicitly consider this issue.

COMPENSATING INTEREST

When a homeowner prepays all or part of a mortgage, the timing of the payment does not always coincide with the normal mortgage payment date. When this happens, the homeowner pays interest only for the days the mortgage is outstanding. Thus the homeowner pays less than a full month's interest.

An investor in agency MBS does not have to be concerned. The

---

[1] Exceptions might include bonds priced far away from par. For example, a non-agency principal-only strip (PO) could be more convex than an agency PO.

agency investor is guaranteed to receive a full monthly interest payment regardless of when prepayment occurs.

Non-agency MBS are not always guaranteed to receive full monthly interest. Some non-agency securities do pay what is called *compensating interest*. This means that any interest shortfall due to intra-month prepayment comes out of the servicer's spread. Thus, the investor is protected up to the amount of the servicing. Some non-agencies, however, offer no protection. In this case the investor absorbs any loss of interest from intra-month prepays.

NONAGENCY 94-1 E has no compensating interest feature. Thus, investors are at risk of losing coupon due to intra-month prepayment. This effect will be greater (1) the more the days of interest lost, and (2) the higher the prepayment speed.

Exhibit 2 details the reduction in overall yield on this bond under different interest rate scenarios assuming all prepayments occur midway through the month (15 days' of interest lost on prepayments).

Unless rates fall and thus prepayments rise, the effect on the non-agency is minimal. When rates fall, though, the effect can be substantial. Furthermore, this is another source of negative convexity.

If rates do not change, or evolve according to forward rates, the effect of interest shortfalls is quite small. But if rates rally, the negative effect can be large. If rates rise, there is only a tiny gain. Considering only this feature, the investor is short volatility. Again, non-agencies have a source of negative convexity not present in agency MBS.

CLEAN-UP CALLS

For convenience, and to minimize expenses, it is common for non-agency CMOs to have rather substantial cleanup calls. For NONAGENCY 94-1 E, the cleanup call is at 10%. This means that when the mortgages collateralizing the CMO reach 10% of their starting balance, all the bonds may be called at par.

If we assume that the deal will always be called, i.e., the call is non-economic, then there is no major valuation problem. Some of the bonds are now simply shorter. If we assume that the deal is called randomly, then the bond's return has an additional source of noise, but no worse convexity.

If the call is exercised economically, however, the effect is more drastic. When rates fall, the value of the deal's collateral will be higher. An economic call would now be more likely to be exercised. The opposite occurs when rates rise.

Exhibit 2: Yield Loss Due to Compensating Interest*

Interest Rate Movement (bps)	Yield Loss Agency PAC (bps)	Yield Loss NONAGENCY 94-1 E (bps)
-200	0	13
-100	0	8
+0	0	1
+100	0	1
+200	0	0

* Assumes prepayments occur midway through the month.

If the bond being analyzed is similar to the underlying collateral, then the call usually has a negative effect.[2] The appreciation of the non-agency CMO in a rally will be reduced, while values would still fall in a trade-off. This effect is difficult to quantify, as it is not clear how economically these calls are actually exercised. But, for longer classes of CMOs in callable deals it is an important issue to consider.

As a side note, many discount bonds are mistakenly bought under the assumption that there is "upside" in the possibility of being called. If these bonds were called today it would obviously be beneficial as an immediate gain would be realized.

If the calls are economic, though, the bonds will usually be called only when the investor would benefit from them being left outstanding. That is, they will be called only when the market rallies and they would have been priced above par. Just because a bond is currently a discount does not mean an investor should give away a free call option.

CONCLUSION

When evaluating non-agency MBS, investors often focus on the trade-off between yield and credit risk. Similarly, when comparing non-agency MBS to more traditional fixed-income investments, they often talk of the credit history on the mortgages versus the credit history on similarly rated corporates.

Just as it is misleading to describe an agency IO or PO as low risk because it has agency credit, a non-agency MBS's credit exposure does not tell its whole story. This chapter has detailed several other important effects on value and risk that investors must consider. While the substantial extra spread available on non-agency MBS may still make them attractive, this conclusion should be reached only after explicitly considering the issues we raise.

---

[2] If a particular bond differs at all from the underlying collateral, there may be states of the world where it benefits from the collateral being called economically. Although specific classes may benefit, the value of the sum of each bond in the CMO structure is worth less in the presence of an economic call.

CHAPTER 4

Whole-Loan CMO Modeling Systems

Jojy Vaniss Mathew

Senior Structured Finance Consultant
MIS, Inc.

WHOLE-LOAN MODELING SYSTEMS: A PERSPECTIVE

The whole-loan CMO market today is a dynamic and sophisticated market driven by advancements in technology. Modeling systems are available to structure, reverse engineer, and analyze instruments in the whole-loan CMO market. These systems are an integral part of not only the whole-loan market, but also the aggregate structured finance market, which includes all types of collateral being securitized.

Any asset that generates cash flows can ultimately be securitized. Securitization activity is expanding today in the non-conforming loan market, multi-family and commercial markets, second mortgage markets and even B and C credit mortgage markets. The objective of this chapter is to explain what is required if a modeling system is to analyze even the least complex whole-loan deals.

Collateral loans in a whole-loan deal are pooled under a trust or special-purpose finance entity. The cash flows from the underlying collateral loans are pooled through to a bond structure, according to a set of predefined rules. These cash flows are allocated further to the tranches on the basis of additional rules of distribution. Depending on the type of collateral and bond structures, certain other structural enhancements are created to maximize the credit quality of the bond classes to the investor. Senior-subordinated structures, reserve accounts, letters of credit, and third-party insurance policies are used for credit enhancement purposes. Multi-family and commercial property collateral use credit enhancement even at the individual loan level.

Structured finance instruments have evolved into a wide array of bonds tailored to the needs of a diverse investor market. The varying maturities and offerings available facilitate the creation of portfolios that meet the specific investment criteria of investment managers. Tranches from CMO deals have become alternatives to investing in corporate bonds, depending on the investment guidelines of a portfolio manager.

As the market has evolved, so has the complexity and diversity of the bond classes offered to investors. The initial structures started out as sequential tranches. Modern structures range from PACs to TACs, Z (accrual) bonds to VADMs, floaters to inverse and super floaters, senior-subordinate tranches, and cross-collateralized tranches.

Hardware and software technology has fostered and sustained the development of this market. Each deal structure is unique in its own way. Whether you are on the sell side creating the deal structures, or on the buy side analyzing the tranches, the appropriate tools are needed to model whole-loan transactions. Structural and analytic methodologies have become more sophisticated as a result of modern computer technology. The simpler deals of the past could be modeled on spreadsheets. But today's complex deals require a highly specialized modeling system.

The purpose of this chapter is to evaluate the structures in the market today and to provide an insight into the components of a whole-loan modeling system that make these structures possible. The criteria for evaluating a modeling system are also discussed.

Insights into Deal Structures of Today

Portfolio managers buying a whole-loan tranche often face a scarcity of information on a particular investment. With the complexity of deal structures and the limited availability of updated collateral information, even the most popular commercial databases are often unable to provide cash flow data on whole-loan transactions. Thus, it often falls to the buyer of a whole-loan tranche to model and analyze the whole-loan holdings. Computer systems have evolved to fill this niche by providing the analyst with a specialized tool to model these sophisticated deals.

Reverse engineering is the process of modeling the different facets of a CMO deal. By recreating the deal (as structured by the underwriter or issuer), an analyst is able to analyze the tranches within a deal. The complex inter-relationships and architecture of a CMO deal require an evaluation of the entire deal, and not just a single tranche. The reverse engineering process and the deal structure created through this process give the user the flexibility to analyze the cash flow parameters of the transaction in more detail.

For example, in a simple A-B-C sequential deal, the structure requires the system to flow all principal to tranche A initially; when tranche A is paid off, tranche B is paid followed by C. The deal must be analyzed as a whole because the cash flow characteristics of B are dependent on the cash flow characteristics of A. The faster A pays, the sooner B receives cash flows. Thus, reverse engineering is the process of synthesizing and evaluating the rules of a deal structure in determining cash flow allocations.

Early CMO structures involved homogeneous collateral securitized into simple sequential bond structures. But as the market evolved, so did more complex and esoteric structures. The number of tranches went from few to many, and cash-flow allocation often involves more complex modeling parameters. The analysis of whole-loan structures requires increasingly sophisticated models with advanced computer technology requirements.

It is important to understand the collateral and bond structures of the market and how they impact the functionality of a modeling system. The underlying collateral of whole-loan CMOs is made up of residential mortgages, multi-family mortgages, commercial and office property mortgages, second mortgages, and B and C credit mortgages. See Exhibit 1 for a breakdown of the whole-loan CMO market by underlying collateral class.

Exhibit 1: Whole-Loan CMO Market

The most prevalent structure in the residential whole-loan market today is a senior-subordinate structure. In these structures, non-conforming collateral is pooled together to create a CMO structure. It is not uncommon for thousands of loans to be pooled together as collateral. Modeling requirements on the collateral side of these transactions involve definition and amortization of various types of mortgage assets, and definition and processing of prepayment assumptions and defaults.

On the bond side of a typical senior-subordinate residential whole-loan structure, senior tranches are usually accompanied by subordinate tranches. In the senior tranche structure of recent Prudential, GE, RFC, and other popular whole-loan transactions, the tranche structure is often similar to the tranche structures of modern agency CMOs. Bond classes often include Planned Amortization Classes (PACs), Targeted Amortization Classes (TACs), accretion tranches (Zs), accretion-directed (AD) tranches, and support (SEQ) tranches. The subordinate tranches often are concurrent/sequential tranches, which absorb loss allocations to provide credit support to the senior tranches.

The credit support that the subordinate tranches provide to the senior tranches distinguishes whole-loan structures from agency structures, and requires additional modeling from the structured finance system. Modeling the bonds involves combining the principal and interest collections from the underlying collateral, and distributing these cash flows to the bond structure and individual tranches. A system must be able to model the various tranche principal and interest types, perform a diverse array of analytics, and create reports.

Senior-subordinate structures that rely on multi-family/commercial/ office mortgage collateral have even more complex modeling requirements. Oftentimes, the collateral involves heterogeneous types of loans pooled together. For example, Phoenix Real Estate Securities Commercial/Multi-Family Mortgage Pass Through Certificates, Series 1993-1, include principal and interest types as diverse as interest-only mortgages, partially amortizing mortgages, and 15-year and 30-year fixed-rate mortgages. Mortgage coupon types in this deal include step-rate, fixed-rate, and rate-reset coupons.

In multi-family and commercial whole-loan transactions, special funds such as loan level reserves are set up to enhance the credit quality of the collateral. Thus, additional loan level variables, such as property-by-property reserves, net operating income (NOI) calculations, and yield maintenance payments, have to be addressed when modeling such deals.

Bond structures of these deals are typically senior-subordinate tranches, which are often sequential, and without PAC/TAC principal structures. The bond structure that is created is often more integrated with the collateral pools in allocating cash flows.

For example, cash flows from the adjustable-rate mortgages might flow only to the class A of the senior tranche set. Modeling often requires outlining logic that determines specific flows of funds from collateral to the bonds.

As banks and other institutions find spreads narrowing in the origination, servicing, and securitization of class A credit first mortgages, they are aggressively pursuing the market for second mortgages and class B and C credit first mortgages. As more types of collateral are developed and securitized, new deal structures are also created.

Collateral structures in senior-subordinated second mortgage securitizations and class B and C credit securitizations often use heterogeneous collateral. Various collateral types (loan types) are pooled together to create such deals. Modeling these securitizations involves modeling the various mortgage loans in the pool and flowing the cash flows to a senior-subordinated bond structure.

THE MODELING PROCESS

Whole-loan deal modeling can be thought of as a three-tier process as conceptualized in Exhibit 2. The first step in this process involves modeling the collateral and its characteristics. The second tier can be termed the "waterfall," defined as the process of taking the collateral cash flows and aggregating them into buckets of cash flows, as required by the deal structure. The final tier involves defining the tranches and directing cash flows from the waterfall to the tranches on the basis of a set of payment rules.

Exhibit 2: Whole-loan Deal Modeling Process

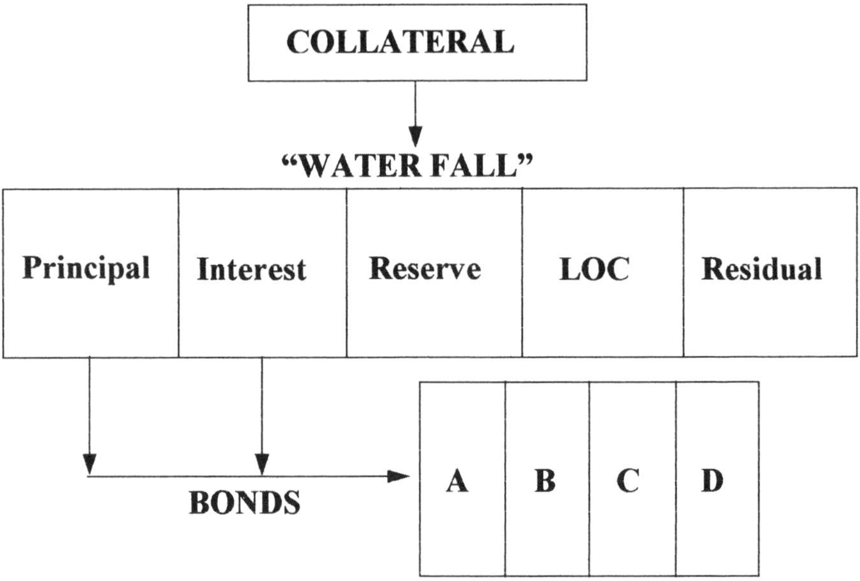

```
        ┌─────────────────────────────┐
        │        COLLATERAL           │
        └─────────────────────────────┘
                      │
                      ▼
              "WATER FALL"
┌───────────┬───────────┬───────────┬─────────┬───────────┐
│           │           │           │         │           │
│ Principal │ Interest  │  Reserve  │   LOC   │  Residual │
│           │           │           │         │           │
└───────────┴───────────┴───────────┴─────────┴───────────┘
      │           │
      │           │            ┌─────┬─────┬─────┬─────┐
      ▼           ▼            │     │     │     │     │
        BONDS      ──────────▶ │  A  │  B  │  C  │  D  │
                               │     │     │     │     │
                               └─────┴─────┴─────┴─────┘
```

Modeling the Collateral

The first step in collateral modeling is to define the collateral loan detail to be modeled. The process of stratifying collateral identifies the collateral to be modeled. This involves using a loan cracking system or similar technology to pool the collateral. A loan cracking system is a database system that takes servicer tapes, decodes the data, and populates fields in a database with the different loan characteristics. (See Exhibit 3.)

Some whole-loan issuers make collateral information available via their own electronic bulletin boards. Usually this data is provided in an ASCII format. For example, the Salomon mortgage tape format is a common ASCII layout for mortgage information. As the ASCII data on a servicer tape are decoded and read-in by computer software, they are typically posted to a database with predefined fields that identify and accept the data. Collateral with like characteristics can be grouped and filtered using database query methods.

Depending on the type of collateral in question, loan-specific parameters are identified. For example, all loans with weighted average coupons of 7.5 to 8.5 and with weighted average maturities of 356 to 360 months are identified and slated for securitization. The database of loans is queried for such measures, and assets meeting the specific criteria are identified. The final step in loan cracking is to process the queried data, and pass it on to a modeling system for analysis.

Exhibit 3: Loan Stratification Process

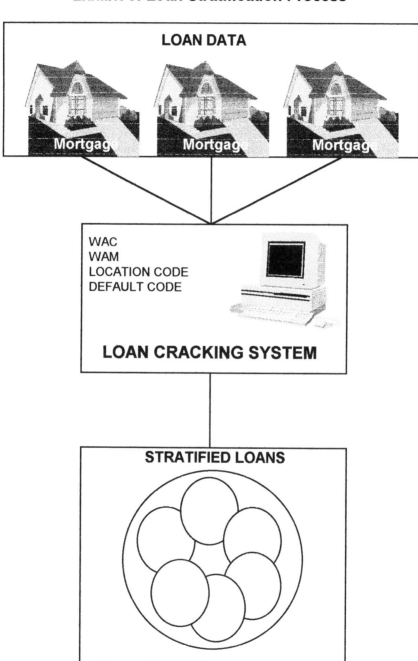

Exhibit 4: Defining Loan Data

Collateral Loan Data				
Loan Balance	Amortization Term	Remaining Term	Gross Rate	Service Fee
1000000.00	360	360	8.1	0.6
2000000.00	360	356	7.75	0.25
1000000.00	360	357	7.5	0.25
Loan X	Value X	Value X	Value X	Value X

To reverse engineer a deal, gathering the collateral information involves reading a prospectus and identifying the various pieces of collateral involved in that particular transaction, including identifying loan balances, amortization terms, remaining terms, coupons, collateral types, and servicer fees.

To create the collateral structure, the next step is to identify the stratified loan data or loan listings from the prospectus to a modeling system. Structured finance systems typically have the ability to import collateral data into the system. Import capability is an important criterion in selecting a system. The task of manually entering hundreds of loans is a time-consuming and inefficient process.

Once a system imports an ASCII file with the various loan-by-loan details, the next step is to identify the imported data to the system to perform collateral calculations. Structured finance systems accomplish this using variables. The most common method involves creating a delimited ASCII file listing data in rows, with each field identified by specific variable column headings, as illustrated in Exhibit 4.

The objective is to create collateral cash flows in the modeling system. This involves identifying a set of collateral parameters and having the system amortize the collateral and create cash flows. Amortization variables are defined on a loan-by-loan basis.

For example, in a spreadsheet @PMT function, identifying loan balance, term, and rate values enables the spreadsheet to calculate a payment value. Similarly, the system has to be able to read-in loan balance, term, and rate, and then calculate the payment and the associated amortization calculations.

Some systems also use screen-driven functionality; a user fills out a table of values such as loan balances, terms, and rates on which the system performs collateral calculations. This is especially useful when summary collateral information is used to perform collateral cash flow calculations.

In the modeling of collateral, the system should have the capability to apply prepayment and default methodology. The most common prepayment and default methodologies include the PSA, CPR, SMM, and ABS models. Some deals require systems to model defaults and prepayments on a loan-by-loan basis. Some RTC transactions require that prepayments on certain collateral loans be forecasted using the PSA methodology, while other loans are prepaid using the CPR methodology, all within the same deal structure. Analysts once used static assumptions, but more dynamic modeling now makes use of vector assumptions.

Another very important collateral function is the use of formula logic. The ability to write "if," "and," and other conditional logic statements is essential in the modeling of whole-loan collateral. For example, the coupon of a GPM mortgage requires writing a conditional "if" statement stating when the coupon changes take place. A logic statement that reads "if date is less than 970525, rate is 5.5%, but if date is greater than 970525, the rate is 7.5%" is an example of this type of formula logic functionality.

Tagging and directing collateral loans and associated cash flows to particular bond classes is a strategy used in some whole-loan deals. This involves identifying certain characteristics of the collateral on a loan-by-loan basis (e.g., geographic location based on ZIP codes), pooling loans that meet certain criteria, and creating collateral cash flows from these pools. Thus, a system has to have loan-by-loan capability to import information such as NOI, rent escalation rate, geographic location code, default code, and other descriptive codes.

Descriptive codes allow writing logic routines to tag and direct collateral cash flows. For example, in RTC 92-M4, collateral principal and interest are pooled on the basis of each loan's service fee before being flowed to specific tranches in the bond structure.

An advanced dimension of collateral modeling is creating calculated variables. These are essential in modeling commercial and multi-family deals with loan-by-loan reserve accounts. (See Exhibit 5.) These reserve accounts are established to guarantee the debt service payment on a loan. To evaluate such parameters, the system has to be able to create calculated variables based on formula logic.

An example is, "evaluate the loan-by-loan NOI versus the debt service requirement, and if the NOI is in excess of the debt service, calculate the excess and fund the loan-by-loan reserve to a cap. However, if the NOI is less than the debt service, there is a shortfall in making the payment, so draw from the reserve account and make the payment." Logic of this type is used in SASCO 1992-M4, a multi-family CMO transaction. To reverse engineer this deal, such calculated functionality needs to be incorporated into the collateral structure.

The process of collateral modeling in a system involves pooling the collateral, defining loan-by-loan variables, and performing calculations to generate collateral cash flows. The modeling system should be flexible and powerful in executing this functionality.

Exhibit 5: Modeling the Collateral

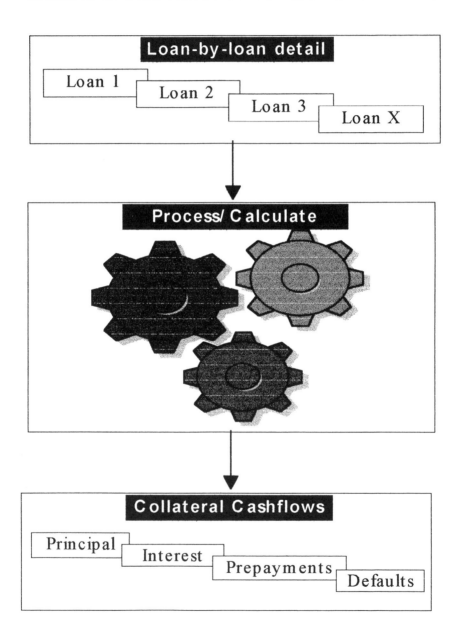

Modeling the Waterfall

The process of taking the collateral cash flows and aggregating them into buckets of cash flows or groups of cash flows as required by the deal structure, prior to distribution to the tranches can be conceived as a "waterfall." (See Exhibit 6.)

The waterfall is a staging process that creates funds to be distributed to tranches on the basis of a set of predefined rules. In a typical whole-loan structure, various layers of the deal have priority over others in terms of how cash flows are allocated from the available collateral cash flows. For example, in a simple senior-subordinate structure, the senior interest has the highest priority. Following payment of available funds as senior interest, the senior principal is next in line to receive cash flows. This is followed by subordinate interest, principal, and rights to any excess allocated to the residual.

The system at the aggregate collateral cash flow level has to be able to distinguish the senior and subordinate tranches, and allocate the incoming cash flows within the tiered structure. This requires a system to distinguish different types of collateral cash flows (e.g., scheduled principal versus prepaid principal) and accordingly allocate them to the waterfall (direct flows into the appropriate bucket) according to predefined rules for the pooling of collateral cash flows.

A structured finance system modeling whole-loan transactions has to be able to generate individually cash flows such as: scheduled gross interest, service fees, net interest, scheduled principal, prepaid principal, defaulted principal, servicer advances, yield maintenance payments, and other calculated collateral variables. Formula flexibility and predefined variables are needed to perform these functions. For example, if a system has a predefined variable that calculates yield maintenance premiums from the collateral, this variable could be used in logic formulas outlining yield maintenance premium distributions to the bond structure.

Formula flexibility and calculated variable functionality are critical in modeling whole-loan transactions. The ability to create logic formulas is often required in modeling the flow of funds within the waterfall.

A good example of this is shifting interest logic. In the most common form of shifting interest logic, the senior tranche is given the subordinate tranche's proportion of prepayments on the basis of a set of date rules. These date rules might dictate that "if the date is before May 25, 1997, pay 100%; between May 25, 1997 and May 25, 1998, pay 70%; and after May 25, 1998, pay 60%." In this instance, the system has to isolate prepayment flows in order to distribute them according to the logical condition.

Exhibit 6: The Waterfall Process

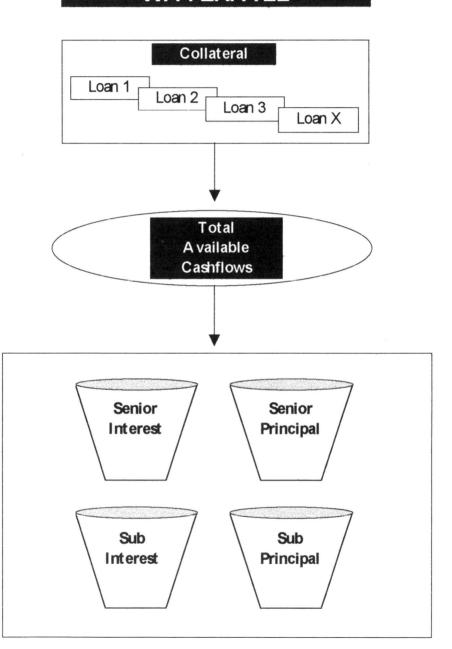

Formula and calculated variable functionality is also essential in modeling a ratio-stripped deal with principal and interest flows directed to a WAC PO or a WAC IO. To determine how much principal and interest to allocate to the WAC PO and WAC IO, the system must evaluate on a loan-by-loan basis whether the net mortgage coupon is above or below the deal average coupon, and strip (allocate) cash flows accordingly. In the waterfall structure, formula logic must be present to evaluate the underlying flows, in order to allocate specific cash flows to the WAC IO/PO on the basis of the strip ratios

At the waterfall level, the system has to be able to set up tiered accounts. This involves creating the necessary accounts and having the system capability to distinguish between senior and subordinated principal accounts. Additionally, the system has to be able to define and recognize rules for the priority of senior principal over subordinate accounts.

Scratch or miscellaneous variable functionality is also a requirement in certain whole-loan deals allowing the user to calculate variables such as outstanding percent of tranches in a specific tier. In these deals, the cash flow allocations are based on outstanding proportion of subordinate tranches to the senior tranches, as determined by the calculated variables.

Tiered principal accounts are also essential in modeling whole-loan deals. The system's ability to create separate senior and subordinate cash flow buckets allows determination of how tranche principal is allocated.

Senior tranches are entitled to their share of scheduled principal and prepayments. Additionally, the subordinate tranche set's share of prepayments is flowed as principal to the senior tranches in a shifting interest structure. Simultaneously, the subordinate tranche is entitled to its share of regular amortization and any remaining prepayments after the allocation of shifting interest to the senior classes.

In order to perform these tasks, the system must identify different tiers of principal accounts, and flow funds to these buckets. To allocate these funds, the system needs to integrate logic in the calculation routines. Certain deals require an interactive process of allocating collateral pieces to a specific bucket. Calculating flows from tagged collateral is a necessary system aspect of modeling RTC whole-loan transactions.

Loss allocation and distribution is a vital part of modeling a whole-loan deal structure. Loss allocation logic allows the user to channel losses of principal due to defaults, delinquencies, and foreclosures from the collateral to the bond structure. Loss allocation parameters determine when the balance of a subordinate tranche is written down due to principal losses from the collateral. Loss logic is also necessary in determining flow of funds from recoveries. Thus, creating loss allocation funds at the waterfall level is essential to modeling whole-loan structures.

The system must also model multiple levels of interest pools prior to distribution to the tranches. All interest due to the senior and the subordinate set of tranches must be identified and calculated separately. These pooled cash flows then have to be allocated to a particular tranche set. This means creating separate senior and subordinate interest accounts, where the senior has priority over the subordinate, and being able to set limits on how much can be allocated to each account.

In certain deals, the subordinate might receive only excess cash flows after the senior interest and other types of flows are paid. Other deals might pay certain tranches cash flows based on collateral spreads. This requires the system to process each piece of collateral to evaluate the spread flows and then direct the appropriate cash flows to the designated interest bucket (pool). This ability to create strip flows on a loan-by-loan basis is especially important in modeling WAC IO tranches.

Modeling multiple tiers of reserve funds is also an important requirement. In certain deals, multiple reserve accounts enhance the deal structure. With regard to cash flow allocations, these reserve accounts might be funded at various stages in the waterfall. The system must be able to set up an initial reserve, fund the reserve on an ongoing basis, set limits on cash flows directed to a reserve, and outflow funds from the reserve if shortfalls occur in the waterfall. Calculating earnings on reserve flows is also essential in accurately modeling deal parameters. Tiered letter of credit accounts are also a system requirement, with the functionality to fund and withdraw from these accounts, as well as forecast reinvestment earnings.

In many deals, funds must be flowed out as fees to trustees and guarantors. Additionally, funds from other deal-enhancing financial instruments (e.g., swaps, caps, floors) may also be flowed into the deal structure. Thus, inflow/outflow functionality is a modeling requirement for certain transactions. Usually, standard fees (such as trustee fees) are paid before any principal or interest is paid. Formula logic is often required in modeling these inflow/outflow funds and fee structures. An investor buying residuals must be able not only to model all the principal and interest structures, but also the fees involved in the deal, to forecast the cash flows on the residuals.

Residual funding capabilities and analytics for forecasting and pricing of residuals are also important in the modeling of whole-loan deals. The ability to calculate phantom income and OID amortization is also necessary in managing whole-loan transactions and calculating after-tax returns.

A system's built-in capabilities and formula logic provide optimum flexibility in modeling the waterfall of cash flows from the collateral. The modern whole-loan deal uses fund structures extensively, and the choice of an appropriate modeling system is a critical decision that merits careful study and evaluation.

Exhibit 7: The Flow of Funds

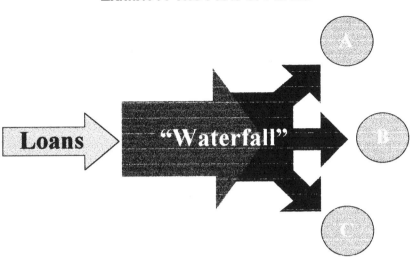

Modeling the Tranches

Once the cash flows are generated from the collateral and pooled under a waterfall, the final step is to make distributions to the tranches. (See Exhibit 7.) Modeling the tranches involves outlining the specific characteristics of each tranche type, principal and interest pay types, principal and interest payment rules, and linking each to the waterfall structure to determine the source of monies.

Modeling the waterfall is significantly impacted by the tranche structure. For example, if there are only two tranche sets in a senior-subordinate deal, only two sets of principal and interest buckets are required.

Early CMO structures had only one or two tranche types within a deal; now a single deal may contain as many as 20 different tranche types. A structured finance system should be capable of modeling every principal and interest tranche type in the market. Today's whole-loan deals offer tranche types ranging from a PAC principal tranche to a concurrently paying support tranche. The system must handle all principal tranche types, including collateral strips, PACs, TACs, ADs, and sequential (SEQ) support bonds. Flexible formula logic to model future tranche types or tranche structure is also a requirement because of the dynamics of the evolving marketplace.

To model planned amortization class (PAC) structures and other sinking fund structures, systems usually offer two alternatives. The first method accepts high and low PSA bands and then back-solves for the PAC schedules. The other imports PAC schedules and pays tranches accordingly.

In certain deals where PACs are segmented and divided into component classes (as in some Chase Home Mortgage deals), importing PAC schedules is the only way to model PAC tranches. This is because no specific structuring bands are available when creating certain component classes. This capability is also essential in modeling deals where the PACs are not optimized to a high/low PSA band.

Modeling accretion-directed tranches depends on the system's ability to create accretions from Z tranches and to pool them according to rules such as "accrete tranche Q until tranche P is paid off; pay accretion-directed tranches M and O with the accretion flows created." In this process, the system must be able to create accretion funds, know when to stop creating such funds, and distribute funds accordingly.

To model collateral strips such as WAC PO tranches, the process starts with the system's ability to evaluate collateral on a loan-by-loan basis, make logical decisions, and flow funds to a waterfall principal bucket containing all the strip cash flows. From this bucket, the cash flows can then be allocated to one or several strip tranches.

Definition of notional balances based on collateral, single tranches, and a blend of tranches is also a system requirement. The ability to refer to collateral and tranche balances, and use formula logic to interrelate them, allows for the modeling of these tranche types.

For example, assume tranche A is a normal tranche, and tranche B is an IO based on the notional balance of A. To model tranche B's cash flows, tranche A's principal balance is referenced as the notional balance. Tranche B's interest payments are calculated by multiplying tranche A's balance (notional balance of B) times the coupon rate of tranche B. Similar methods are used when modeling IOettes, making such functionality essential.

Defining various interest types is also a basic modeling requirement. When defining a standard fixed-coupon, floater coupon, graduated-coupon, inverse floater, or super floater coupon, forecasting tranche interest cash flows absolutely requires modeling flexibility. Before a floater or an inverse floater can be defined, the system has to incorporate various indexes such as LIBOR, COFI, and Treasury rates. Access to such indexes should be readily available within the system.

Often, vectors of indexes are used to forecast coupons. The system also has to define and use margins, floors, caps, and other variables associated with forecasting floating coupons. Some systems define coupon structures using an input table, while others use formula logic to define floating-coupon structures.

Z bonds created in deals require a system to accrete interest payments on the basis of various parameters. The ability to create accretion logic based on other tranches, date parameters, or period value parameters is a common modeling requirement in today's deals.

After the attributes of the individual tranches are established, the next step involves flowing cash flows from the waterfall to the tranches. In a senior-subordinate whole-loan deal structure, cash flows from the senior interest and principal buckets are flowed to the senior tranches, and from the subordinate interest and principal buckets to the subordinate classes. This is accomplished through a set of interest and principal rules (payment matrixes) that allocate cash flows to the tranches.

For example, in a senior-subordinate deal, assume there are three sequential tranches: A, B, and C. From the senior principal bucket (containing senior tranche's percent of scheduled principal and prepayment plus shifting interest prepayments from the subordinate classes), principal is allocated to A, B, and C. The rules might state "pay tranche A all available funds until zero; after A is paid off, pay tranche B all available funds to zero; followed by C to zero."

Modeling systems use table-driven functionality or rule routines to create the paydown matrixes. The ability to model multi-tiered accounts on the waterfall level and associated paydown matrixes on the tranche level is necessary in modeling whole-loan deals.

Approaches to Modeling

There are three approaches to modeling a deal:

1. The table-driven approach allows the user to enter data outlining the deal and tranche structures and create a bond structure.

2. The rule-based approach requires the user essentially to set up rule (formula) routines in creating a bond structure.

3. The final approach is table-driven functionality combined with rule-based language, and is often the most flexible and easy to use.

One of the most recent innovations in structured finance system functionality is called "term sheet reverse engineering." This allows an investor to model a deal structure on the basis of limited information available from a dealer term sheet. The process typically requires the user to input certain information from a term sheet, and have the system make additional assumptions and return a bond structure. This type of functionality is extremely useful in performing pre-acquisition analytics and gauging the risk-return profile of a CMO investment.

Exhibit 8: The System Process

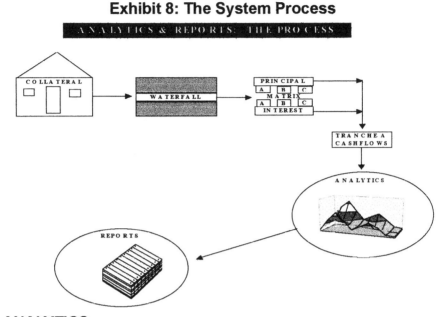

ANALYTICS

Analytics can be performed once a user has set up a deal structure encompassing collateral characteristics, waterfall structure, and tranche structure. Analytics functionality involves generating cash flows from the collateral, flowing these to a waterfall, and finally allocating cash flows to tranches based on a payment matrix. (See Exhibit 8.) Once cash flows are allocated to the tranches, various tranche-level analytics and reporting can be produced. This process also verifies the validity and accuracy of the deal structure by allowing the modeler to match the analytics against the calculations outlined in the prospectus.

The primary prerequisite for analytics is the ability to generate cash flows, as analytics are based on cash flow forecasts. To formulate tranche cash flows, several conditions have to exist within a system. The ability of a system to run collateral prepayment and default scenarios is essential.

The system must allow the user to run static and vector prepayment and default assumptions in forecasting collateral and bond cash flows. Standard prepayment methodologies, such as the PSA, CPR, SMM, and ABS, must be integral to the system to facilitate modeling. Default and credit sensitivity analysis are also an integral part of modern whole-loan analysis. Default/ delinquency analysis using PSA's standard default assumptions (SDA curve) has recently become widely used for whole-loan credit analysis. Additionally, some deals require generating analyses based on loan-by-loan assumptions.

Multi-scenario capability is also an integral part of analytical function- ality. Typically, once a deal is reverse-engineered, the next step is to verify that the model is accurate and matches the issuer's original structure. Pro- spectuses usually list multi-scenario bonds outstanding and price/yield tables for a deal at closing. Multi-scenario analytics let the user analyze multiple sce- narios and verify the bond structure under various assumptions.

Multi-scenario price-yield and yield-price calculations are a common analytic required in structured finance systems. The ability to enter a price (yield), shift the price (yield) up/down, and generate a table of values for yield (price) is essential to analyzing the feasibility of a tranche.

Tranche pricing is another valuable system capability. The simplest form allows a user to define a Treasury rate and spread, and calculate the price for the tranche. More advanced matrix pricing allows the user to define spreads by tranche types. These spreads are then used to price the tranches, by adding interpolated or current yield curve values based on calculated tranche average lives. The ability to incorporate pricing data from pricing ven- dors is also highly desirable, as many investors use third-party pricing ser- vices to evaluate their holdings.

Regulatory testing analytics are standard in modern CMO analysis. The FFIEC high-risk test, a banking regulatory test, requires the system to perform three different risk evaluation tests for a particular CMO. Often this test has to be performed using dealer median prepayment estimates, and thus the ability to import dealer median prepayment estimates has become important. The FLUX test is a newer cash flow volatility test adopted by the National Association of Insurance Commissioners (NAIC). This test forecasts cash flows under various interest rate scenarios to categorize a tranche as volatile or non-volatile. Another required regulatory test is the Regulation 126 test, which evaluates a tranche's performance characteristics under various interest rate scenarios.

The more advanced analytics available include interest rate models, user-defined prepayment models, option-adjusted spread (OAS) calculations, credit simulation, and credit-adjusted OAS. The interest rate models use sim- ulation methods such as binomial lattice, Monte Carlo, and Latin hyper-cube to generate future yield curve estimates.

Prepayment models assimilate historical and user-defined prepay- ment information to derive prepayment estimates based on inputs from the interest rate model. OAS uses cash flows generated from the interest rate and prepayment models to generate an OAS price, effective duration and convex- ity, and OAS dispersion values. Credit simulation and credit-adjusted OAS are the newest analytic tools available for whole-loan CMO analysis. Credit simu- lation generates random credit performance scenarios to determine default- adjusted cash flow scenarios and analytics based on such cash flows.

Reporting is also an essential part of a CMO system. Basic reports include tranche cash flow reports, price-yield and yield-price tables, and percent outstanding tables. Price-yield tables and percent outstanding reports are often used to verify the modeling accuracy of a reverse-engineered structure versus prospectus information. Custom reporting capabilities are also a plus in generating management reports and presentations.

Graphics functionality should also be considered when evaluating a system. Cash flow graphs including principal, interest, and total cash flows are often helpful in asset/liability matching functions. Additionally, average life, duration, and price-yield graphs offer insights into the cash flow and valuation characteristics of a tranche. OAS distribution graphs and three-dimensional surface graphs also add to the analytical prowess of a system.

It is also useful to export cash flows or analytics to other systems. Exporting to spreadsheet applications offers extended flexibility for analytics and reporting. Interfaces to other systems within your organization should also be evaluated, including trading systems, asset/liability management systems, and accounting systems.

EVALUATING SYSTEMS

Today's complex whole-loan deals often require modeling collateral at the individual loan level, incorporating a diverse array of variables. Bond structure modeling involves creating a waterfall structure, establishing tranche structures, and distributing cash flows to the tranches based on rules. Once a deal structure is established, analytics can be performed, and reports generated.

Advanced technology makes the modern securitized whole-loan market possible. Systems with specialized modeling functionality are required for proper evaluation of the structures underlying whole-loan transactions. The concepts outlined in this chapter are useful in evaluating structured finance systems and in responding to RFPs.

Appendix

An Evaluation Checklist
For Whole-Loan Modeling Systems

In evaluating structured finance systems, the following are a basic set of functional requirements:

Collateral
- —Collateral type independence
- —Predefined variables
- —Loan level functionality
- —Prepayment methodology
- —Default and delinquency methodology
- —Informational variables
- —Ability to tag and direct loans
- —Formula logic
- —Calculated variables
- —Links to bond functionality

Waterfall
- —Ability to segregate collateral flows
- —Ability to create levels of subordination
- —Fund types
- —Loss and recovery logic
- —Outflows/inflows
- —Formula logic

Tranche Structure
—Term sheet reverse engineering
—Defining tranche types
—Defining principal types
—Defining interest types
—Tranche coupon functionality
—Built-in logic routines
—Principal distribution matrix
—Interest distribution matrix
—Loss allocation matrix
—Arrears distribution matrix

Analytics
—Multi-scenario capability
—Prepayment scenarios
—Default scenarios
—Static speed/rate scenarios
—Vector speed/rate scenarios
—Cash flow forecasts
—Pricing
—Price/yield tables
—Regulatory tests, including FFIEC
—Interest rate forecasts
—OAS analysis and dispersion analysis
—Credit simulation and analysis
—Graphing functionality
—Data export functionality
—Interfaces to other systems

Database
—Number of deals modeled
—Types of deals modeled

Vendor
—Other products
—Financial stability
—Leading edge technology

Support Staff
—Training
—Conferences
—Experience
—Support desk
—Availability

Section III

CREDIT ANALYSIS

CHAPTER 5

The Default and Loss Experience of Whole-Loan CMOs

Thomas Gillis
Managing Director
Standard and Poor's

During the early development of the whole-loan CMO market, most transactions were sold privately. Issue volume and loss experience on those early transactions (in the late 1970s and through the early 1980s) are thus unknown. Even with emergence of the public whole-loan market, investors and analysts continue to complain about scarcity of information. Loss information is particularly poor. There is no central repository that collects loss data, making any loss study problematic.

We can, however, piece together enough data, however imprecise, to look at the loss behavior of whole-loan CMOs. In the analysis that follows, we review loss information on 1,117 whole-loan pools selected from the Standard & Poors data base.

Since the market's inception, S&P has rated approximately 2,237 issues, representing over $282 billion of whole-loan mortgage securities. Our analysis includes only those first-mortgage pools securing whole-loan CMOs issued publicly, rated by S&P, and outstanding as of December 1993. Actual loss data are used where available. Otherwise, a loss is assumed to be the difference between the original credit support provided and the current credit support outstanding.

LOSS EXPERIENCE

CMO loss experience is a function of the foreclosure and loss experience on the loans securing the CMOs. If all the mortgages pay, the CMO will pay. If mortgages default and losses are incurred, those losses will be covered by a third-party credit enhancement or allocated to the appropriate classes of the CMO.

Because credit protection and subordinated classes are barriers against most losses, the loss experience at the loan level can differ significantly from the loss experience of the securities supported. Since most senior classes are rated either AA or AAA, these classes receive the greatest amount of credit protection. Credit protection for senior classes rated by S&P has averaged 10.5%.

A simple rule of thumb for assessing credit protection is to convert it into foreclosure protection. Credit protection of 10% translates into a range of potential default scenarios: from 100% of loans being foreclosed upon and incurring on average a 10% loss to 10% of loans being foreclosed upon and incurring a 100% loss. The typical loss incurred on a mortgage will approximate 30% to 40%. At an average loss of 40%, credit protection of 10% will guard against 25% of the loans in the pool being foreclosed upon.

Exhibit 1: Breakdown of Loan Pool Level ($Millions)

Year	Number of Pools	Total $Amount	Total Losses	Loss as% Initial $Amt.
1986*	113	9,988.0	85.291	0.85
1987	100	10,300.5	102.007	0.99
1988	101	8,920.6	92.891	1.04
1989	107	12,156.3	108.833	0.90
1990	110	16,741.3	126.986	0.76
1991	152	31,519.3	184.795	0.59
1992	248	64,671.4	85.973	0.13
1993	186	42,073.3	11.450	0.03
Total	1,117	$196,370.7	798.230	0.41
* Includes transactions issued prior to 1986.				

LOSS ANALYSIS

Our analysis compares losses at the loan pool level and not the security level. Since securities often represent less than 100% of the unpaid principal balance of the loans securing the issue, the analysis would not be an accurate measure of losses at the security level. Most whole-loan CMOs are multiclass securities, with the subordinate class, which is in a first-loss position, generally retained by the seller.

The 1,117 pools of mortgages surveyed had approximately $196 billion in original principal amount. The pools had an average balance of $176 million. To date, losses total $798 million, averaging $715,620 per pool, representing 41 basis points. These pools are protected with approximately $20.6 billion of credit support, an average of 10.5% per pool. Exhibit 1 provides a breakdown by year of security issuance.

Any loss analysis performed for mortgages needs to be conducted on the basis of the origination year. As Exhibit 1 indicates, mortgage losses are a function of time. The losses increase over time, with the newest pools experiencing the lowest losses. This is a normal occurrence, given the nature of mortgages. A foreclosure on average takes a year to complete, making any losses in the first year unlikely.

Likewise, as the mortgage amortizes, losses become more remote after a certain passage of time, generally five to seven years. This is commonly referred to as the *loss curve*. The loss experienced on the 1993 book can be attributed to inclusion of seasoned mortgages in pools sold in 1993. S&P's surveillance of outstanding losses will measure a transaction's performance using as a proxy the default curve in Exhibit 2.

Exhibit 2: Residential Default Curve

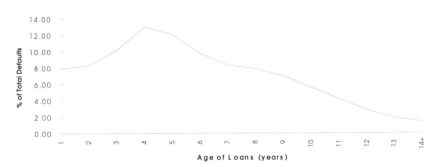

Using this curve, we can equate the losses experienced for pools originated over different years. By assuming each pool's future losses follow this curve, we can project the total loss that will be incurred over the life of the transaction.

While the curve provides a useful way to compare pools originated in different years, it too has its shortcomings. Each pool has its own loss curve, which can vary substantially from another. Pools with little seasoning render the use of the curve less reliable. Likewise, the more years a pool has seasoned beyond its origination date, the more weight can be placed on the loss curve analysis. The loss curve is a conservative approach, pushing more losses out into the future than may actually occur.

Exhibit 3 tabulates losses projected for the life of the pools sold each year, assuming the pools all follow the same pattern of loss as determined by the default curve in Exhibit 2. As Exhibit 3 indicates, losses approximating 1.5% of the initial principal balance have remained fairly steady over the years. The 1992 and 1993 book of transactions is less reliable, because there has not been enough time yet to judge its ultimate performance. The stability of the historical loss performance, in spite of the rolling regional housing recession that has affected the nation over this period, is a testament to the inherently strong credit quality of a fully amortizing mortgage.

While comfort can be taken in the consistency of the averages, individual transaction can perform quite differently. In Exhibit 4 the number of pools per loss category is provided by year. The table is segmented by decade to detail the impact of recently originated deals, which are still early in their loss curves. Here we can see a very tight distribution with less than 18% of the deals experiencing more than $1 million in losses. For loan pools originated in the 1980s, the distribution widens somewhat, but only marginally.

Such information can provide a useful benchmark in determining the adequacy of credit protection for investors in subordinate classes of whole-loan CMOs.

Exhibit 3: Actual versus Projected Losses

Year	Actual Losses		Projected Losses	
	Dollar (000)	Percentage	Dollar (000)	Percentage
1986*	85,291	0.85	110,317	1.10
1987	102,007	0.99	146,890	1.43
1988	92,891	1.04	152,003	1.70
1989	108,833	0.90	211,783	1.74
1990	126,986	0.76	322,694	1.93
1991	184,795	0.59	700,276	2.22
1992	85,973	0.13	530,576	0.82
1993	11,454	0.03	145,533	0.35
* Includes transactions issued prior to 1986.				

Exhibit 4: Pool Losses

	Number of Pools with Total Losses not Exceeding					
	Zero	$500,000	$1 mil	$5 mil	$10 mil	>$10 mil
1986*	48	44	6	9	4	2
1987	18	47	12	21	1	1
1988	16	40	22	18	5	0
1989	14	30	20	42	1	0
Sub-Total	96	161	60	90	11	3
1990	26	33	12	33	6	0
1991	50	54	15	26	4	3
1992	158	58	9	21	2	0
1993	156	23	5	2	0	0
Sub-Total	390	168	41	82	12	3
Total	486	329	101	172	23	6
% Totals	43.51	29.45	9.04	15.40	2.05	0.54
80s Only	22.80	38.24	14.25	21.38	2.61	0.71
* Includes transactions issued prior to 1986.						

ABOUT THE DATA

Standard & Poor's data base, which is one of the most extensive in the industry, required some adjustments in order to produce this analysis. Reporting differences from one issuer to another and the complexity of the data make precise measurements not possible.

For purposes of this analysis, all loss comparisons are made on the pools backing the transactions and not the specific issues. Issuers offering one series backed by two distinct pools of mortgages are treated as two pools. Similarly, multiple series backed by the same pool of mortgages are treated as one pool. All second mortgage and bond insured transactions were eliminated. Other pools are eliminated because of the lack of timely information.

Precise loss data are available on only 43% of the pools, representing approximately 50% of initial pool balances. The loss data came from the fourth quarter 1993 for the most part. More recent loss data from March of 1994 was issued for the Resolution Trust Corporation's (RTC) issues, and from April of 1994 for transactions issued by Guardian Savings and Loan Association of Huntington Beach, California (Guardian). As proxy, the difference between initial credit support levels and current support levels is calculated. In almost every case where both are available, the change in loss coverage exceeds actual losses.

All losses are rounded to the nearest thousand. For senior/sub transactions, the subordinated levels are added to the certificate amounts to approximate the total pool size. The size of the sample, notwithstanding these adjustments, should be useful for analysis of the whole-loan CMO market.

The study captures the impact of the recent losses incurred on the Guardian issues. Guardian's transactions have experienced large increases in losses and represent a significant amount of the total losses reported in the study. From June 1993 to April 1994, losses for all Guardian issues increased from $16 to $66 million for its 28 issues. This represents 8% of total losses, while only accounting for 2.5% of the issues represented in the study. High levels of foreclosure and real estate owned will continue to translate into additional losses for the Guardian issues.

FACTORS INFLUENCING LOSS

Four major factors influence losses: economic, underwriting, loan to value, and payment structure. The economic factor is the most important of these. Appreciation and salary growth can more than offset any other negative associated with a mortgage loan. Likewise, falling property values and unemployment can cause losses on the highest-quality mortgage. Therefore, predicting future loss experience is as difficult as predicting future economic conditions.

It is within any given economic environment that any other factor has a role in determining relative loss experience. Underwriting is the most influential of these remaining factors. Conservative and diligent underwriting provides the best defense against future economic uncertainty. Loans underwritten to less stringent standards are more vulnerable to losses.

What constitutes a well-underwritten loan? The monthly payment should not exceed more than 30% of the mortgagor's salary. An important factor in the income tests is in the sizing of a mortgagor's monthly payments, which should always be calculated at the then-current market rate for fixed-rate mortgages. Adjustable-rate mortgages based on short-term indexes, buy-downs of fixed-rate mortgages, and graduated payment mortgages, because of their lower initial payments, overstate a mortgagor's ability to service the debt.

Income and employment should be verified, along with the source of the mortgagor's down payment. Last, but not least, is the mortgagor's credit history. Any lack of adherence from these standards weakens the ability and/or willingness of the homeowner to withstand periods of financial stress.

Equity in the home can offset all other factors in mitigating or eliminating the loss potential of a mortgage. However, this is more theoretical than practical in that LTVs of less than 50% are necessary to mitigate losses in the most dire economic environments.

Loan pools composed of only 50% or lower LTVs cannot be found in our 1,119 pool sample. Certainly higher LTV mortgages can be found in our sample, and represent additional risk.

High LTV mortgages reduce the primary safety feature of mortgages, which is asset protection. A 95% LTV provides a built-in loss feature if a mortgagor defaults before any significant appreciation occurs. The 5%, that is, equity is insufficient to cover foreclosure costs, guaranteeing a loss upon foreclosure. If it were not for the presence of primary mortgage insurance, there would be little incentive to originate these mortgages at all from a credit perspective.

Most pools will include a spattering of LTVs ranging from 95% to 60%. While concentrations of loans above 80% LTV are a definite indicator of risk, pools with weighted average LTVs of between 70% and 80% are not always useful in differentiating risk. The lower LTVs of loans originated under limited and no-document programs of the late 1980s turned out to be ineffective in deterring foreclosures.

Payment structures have a direct impact on future losses. Depending on the loan's payment structure, the chances of a default can be mitigated or increased. The traditional fixed-rate, fully amortizing mortgage is the safest payment structure.

The fully amortizing mortgage, along with insurance, was promoted by the Federal Housing Administration after the Great Depression to attract lenders who had left the market after incurring major losses on partially-amortizing and interest-only mortgages. These balloon mortgages can still be found in the market today. Balloon mortgages increase the risk of loss by adding the risk of refinancing to the normal risk that a mortgagor will default.

The fixed-rate, fully-amortizing mortgage is structured ideally with respect to a mortgagor's income. Adjustable-rate and graduated-payment mortgages, while fully amortizing, add the additional risk that the borrower will not be able to maintain income growth that is commensurate with a rising mortgage payment.

ASSESSING FUTURE LOSSES

Investors have little information about a whole-loan pool to judge the numerous factors affecting loss. Credit protection to cover potential risks is based on rating agency risk assessments for loan pools. Credit protection puts all pools on an equal footing, reducing unnecessary concern with the risk of any individual mortgage pool. Knowledge about the risk factors and related loss experience can only enhance the quality of an investor's decision, however.

Exhibit 5 indicates S&P's experience of measuring loss coverage with risk. While the amount of loss coverage has varied as a percentage of initial pool balances from a low of 7% to a high of 13%, coverage for projected total losses has remained fairly constant between approximately five to six times, excluding the 1992 and 1993 pool years. The 1992 and 1993 data are too early in their life cycle to be considered reliable. The 1990 year projects the lowest level of coverage for projected losses of 4.83 times, which is heavily influenced by Guardian's loss experience. Guardian's lossses account for 28% of all pools originated in 1990. When taking into consideration Guardian and other notable issuers such as ComFed and the RTC, the consistency of the ratio of initial loss coverage to projected losses becomes even more impressive.

Exhibit 5: Measuring Loss Coverage with Risk

Year	Initial Pool Balance (Mil)	Initial $Loss Coverage (Mil)	Initial Loss Coverage (%)	Projected Losses (Mil)	Ratio of Initial Loss Coverage to Projected Losses
1986*	9,988.0	738.4	7.39	110.32	6.69
1987	10,300.5	848.3	8.24	146.89	5.77
1988	8,920.6	775.8	8.70	152.00	5.10
1989	12,156.3	1,158.8	9.53	211.78	5.47
1990	16,741.3	1,557.2	9.30	322.69	4.83
1991	31,519.3	4,141.2	13.14	700.28	5.91
1992	64,671.4	7,741.4	11.97	530.58	14.59
1993	42,073.3	3,600.3	8.56	145.53	24.74

* Includes transactions issued prior to 1986.

CHAPTER 6

The Rating Agencies' Approach: New Evidence

Douglas L. Bendt
President
Mortgage Risk Assessment Corporation

Chuck Ramsey
Principal, Alex. Brown & Sons, Inc.
CEO, Mortgage Risk Assessment Corporation

Frank J. Fabozzi, Ph.D., CFA
Editor, Journal of Portfolio Management
Adjunct Professor, Yale University

The authors wish to thank Tom Gillis, Standard & Poor's; Peter Rubenstein, Donaldson, Lufkin, & Jenrette; Henry Haysson, Duff & Phelps; and Ken Rosenberg, Fitch, for commenting and reviewing exhibits relating to their agencies' criteria.

INTRODUCTION

Credit analysis of non-agency mortgage-backed securities relies upon an unusual combination of large-scale statistical aggregate analysis and micro loan-by-loan analysis. This combination arises from knowing that out of a pool of 1,000 newly originated mortgages, it is virtually certain that at least ten will be defaulted upon and go into foreclosure, but there is no way of knowing *which* ten.

The expectation that ten or more homeowners will default is based on studies of millions of mortgages conducted by private mortgage insurers, federal agencies, and the four major credit rating agencies. But not all of these studies are relevant to the default experience of mortgages collateralizing non-agency mortgage-backed securities.

For example, studies by private mortgage companies focus only on mortgage defaults on loans with high loan-to-value (LTV) ratios, as would those done on FHA/VA mortgages. And by definition, studies of mortgages that meet Fannie Mae and Freddie Mac standards are not relevant. That leaves studies by Standard & Poor's Corporation, Moody's Investors Service, Fitch, and Duff & Phelps.[1]

This chapter reviews the approach these agencies take in evaluating the loss potential of defaults of non agency mortgages and presents new evidence about additional factors influencing losses. Rating agencies need to evaluate the magnitude of potential loss of a pool of loans to determine the amount of credit support the issuer is required to implement to achieve the desired credit ratings. Their approaches consist of four parts: (1) frequency of default; (2) severity of loss given default; (3) pool characteristics or the structure of the pool; and (4) credit enhancement or the structure of the security.

FREQUENCY OF DEFAULT

Most homeowners default relatively early in the life of the mortgage. Exhibit 1 shows the effect of seasoning assumed by two rating agencies and the Public Securities Association.[2] These seasoning curves are based on default experience of so-called prime loans — a 30-year fixed-rate mortgage with a 75% to 80% LTV that is fully documented for the purchase of an owner-occupied single-family detached house. These characteristics describe the most common mortgage type generally associated with the lowest default rates.

---

[1] "Moody's Approach to Rating Residential Mortgage Passthroughs", *Moody's Investors Service Structured Finance and Research Commentary* (New York, NY: Moody's Investors Service, 1990); Standard & Poor's Ratings Group, *CREDITREVIEW* (New York: McGraw Hill, 1993); *Rating of Residential Mortgage-Backed Securities* (New York, NY: Duff & Phelps Credit Company, 1992); *Fitch Mortgage Default Model* (New York, NY: Fitch Investors Service, Inc.,1993).

[2] *Standard Formulas for the Analysis of Mortgage-Backed Securities and Other Related Securities* (New York, NY: Public Securities Association, 1990).

Exhibit 1: Assumed Default Frequencies

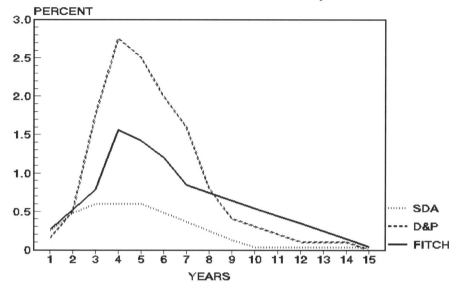

Loans with almost any other characteristic generally are assumed to have a greater frequency of default. Exhibit 2 summarizes the evaluation of these other risk characteristics among the four rating agencies.

Loan-to-Value Ratio/Seasoning

A mortgage's loan-to-value (LTV) ratio is the single most important determinant of its likelihood of default and therefore the amount of required credit enhancement. Rating agencies impose penalties of up to 500% on loans with LTVs above 80%. The rationale is straightforward. Homeowners with large amounts of equity in their properties are unlikely to default. They will either try to protect this equity by remaining current, or if they fail, sell the house or refinance it to unlock the equity. In any case, the lender is protected by the buyer's self-interest.

On the other hand, if the borrower has little or no equity in the property, the value of the default option is much greater. This argument is consistent with the long-held view that default rates for FHA/VA loans are much higher than for conventional loans.

Until recently, rating agencies considered the LTV only at the time of origination. Seasoning was an unalloyed good — if a loan did not default in the first three to four years, it deserved credit for making it past the hump. And many loans did not default because they were prepaid.

Exhibit 2: Effect of Required Credit Enhancement for AAA Levels

Category	Standard & Poor's	Moody's	Fitch	Duff & Phelps
Loan-To-Value: AAA				
Factors				
100	6.00	4.25	5.35	4.25
95	3.00	3.33	3.57	3.30
90	1.50	2.25	2.00	2.60
85	1.00	1.50	1.21	1.80
80	1.00	1.00	1.21	1.35
75	1.00	0.58	1.00	1.00
70	1.00	0.25	1.00	0.60
65	1.00	0.17	0.71	0.45
60	1.00	0.17	0.71	0.30
≤ 60		0.17	0.57	0.30
Seasoning	1. 50% of home price appreciation 2. 100% of depreciation 3. Variable, depending on term, mortgage type	1. Current LTV + qualitative assessments. E.g., for payment history		Partial adjustments for current LTV; varies by pool performance
Term				
15-year	0.73	0.65	0.85	0.70
20-year	0.88			
25-year		0.75		
30-year	1.00	1.00	1.00	1.00
40-year	>1.00	1.10		

Exhibit 2 (Continued)

Category	Standard & Poor's	Moody's	Fitch	Duff & Phelps
ARMS	See Table	1.20 - 1.60	1.05 - 1.60	1.20 - 1.40
Refinancings				
Cashout	90% 2.00 80% 1.20	1.25	1.10 - 1.25	1.10
No Cash	1.00	1.00	1.00	0.95
Reduced Documentation	LTV >90 2.00 80 - 90 1.50 75 - 80 1.20 60 - 75 1.10 <60 1.05	Limited 1.05 - 1.20 Poor/None 1.50	1.00 - 1.50	Alternate 1.05 Reduce 1.50 None 1.75
Non-owner Occupied				
Second Home	3.00	1.50	1.10	
Investor	3.00	2.50+	1.25	
Condo, Co-ops, Town-houses	Low-rise, 2-Family 1.20 Hi-rise, 3-to-4-Family 2.00	PUD 1.35 2-to-4 1.10	1.10 - 1.25	2-to-4 1.00 Condo 1.05
	High debt ratio 1.10			
Credit Proxies	Delinquencies: 2-to-5 1.10 6+ 1.20	≤ 8% 0.90 ≤9% 0.95 ≤10% 1.00 ≤11% 1.05 ≥11% 1.10+		1) interest rate above market 2) originators "score" A, B, C, D notes interaction of LTV & score

Exhibit 2 (Concluded)

Category	Standard & Poor's	Moody's	Fitch	Duff & Phelps
Mortgage Size/ House Price	>$400,000 1.2 >$600,000 1.6 >$1,000,000 3.0	Avg/low 1.00 High 2.00[1] Super High 2.50[2] Jumbo 3.00[3]	>$300,000 1.05 >$600,000 1.40 >$1,000,000 1.60	4x med 1.22 6x med 1.34 8x med 1.48 10x med 1.63
SEVERITY OF LOSS				
Foreclosure costs	13% balance + interest	25%+/loan balance	25%/loan balance	15%/sale price
Market Decline	34.5%[4]	25%	32 - 45%	40%[5]
POOL CHARACTERISTICS				
Pool Size	100 1.22 200 1.07	>500 0.95 <200 1.20		100 1.30 200 1.10 300 1.00 400 0.98 500 0.95
Geography	High zipcode concentrations penalized; wider areas on a case-by-case basis	Economic diversity: 0.9 - 1.3 Foreclosure time: 0.9 - 1.2 Zipcode concentration Adjustments for regional economic conditions	Impact of regional economies	Volatility varies by MSA 0.85 - 1.20 Concentration factor by state, MBA, zipcode

[1] 3 - 5 times med
[2] 6 - 9 times med
[3] 9+ times med
[4] Adjusted for jumbo ~ 1.5
[5] Adjusted by region

The recent declines in housing prices, increased volume of seasoned product, and greater emphasis on surveillance have made the *current* LTV the focus of attention. Seasoning now is as likely to be a negative for a pool as it is to be a plus. It is little comfort to own a pool of original 80% mortgages from California originated in 1990 because many of the borrowers will owe more than their houses are worth; their LTVs will exceed 100%. Moreover, the pre-payment option has been taken away for these borrowers.

Mortgage Term

Amortization increases the equity a homeowner has in a property, which reduces the likelihood of default. Because amortization schedules for terms less than 30 years accumulate equity faster, all the rating agencies give a "credit" of 15% to 35% — i.e., reduced credit enhancement levels, for 15-year mortgages. Conversely, mortgages with a 40-year term are penalized up to 10%. Adjustable rate mortgages that allow negative amortization are similarly penalized.

Mortgage Type

Fixed-rate mortgages are considered "prime" because both the borrower and the lender know the monthly payment and amortization schedule with cer-tainty. Presumably, the loan was underwritten considering this payment stream and the borrower's current income.

Both lender and borrower are uncertain about the future payment schedule for adjustable-rate mortgages (ARMs). Because most ARMs have lower initial ("teaser") rates, underwriting usually is done to ensure that the borrower will be able to meet the monthly payment assuming the rate adjusts up to the fully indexed rate at the first reset date.

Beyond that first date, however, there is uncertainty both about the future stream of payments and the borrower's ability to meet higher pay-ments. Future payment schedules for other mortgage types such as balloons and graduated payments are known, but uncertainty about borrowers' income still exists. All non-fixed-rate mortgages carry penalties of 5% to 100% or more.

Transaction Type

Mortgages taken out for cash-out refinancings are considered riskier than mortgages taken out for purchases, chiefly because the homeowner is reduc-ing the equity in the home. In addition, the fact that the homeowner is taking out cash may be an indication of *need*, which could indicate shakier finances, and the homeowner's monthly payment will increase. On the other hand, a no-cash refinancing — in which the rate is reduced — lowers the monthly pay-ment and speeds the rate of amortization, so there are no penalties.

Documentation

"Full" documentation generally means that the borrower has supplied income, employment, and asset verification sufficient to meet Fannie/Freddie standards. "Low," "alternative," or "reduced" documentation means at least one form was not supplied, perhaps, for example, because the borrower is self-employed. In this case, because the income stream is likely to be more volatile, the borrower is more likely to default.

"No" documentation loans generally are made as "hard money" loans — i.e., the value of the collateral is the most important criterion in the lending decision. Typically, lenders require larger down payments for these type loans. Guardian Savings and Loan in California — seized by the RTC for insolvency — had been a major proponent of this type of program. Its collateral was put into RTC 91-9, which has a 40% serious delinquency rate, despite an average LTV of 65%.

Occupancy Status

Property owners obviously have a greater vested interest in not defaulting on a mortgage on a house in which they live. Thus, mortgages for second homes or rental property are penalized.

Property Type

Generally, single-family detached houses are the most desirable properties because they are larger, more private, and include more land. Moreover, the supply of condominiums or townhouses is more likely to become overbuilt in a local area with the addition of a single large project, potentially increasing the volatility of prices and the length of time needed to sell a property.

Mortgage Size/House Price

Most mortgages are sold into non-agency mortgage-backed securities because the dollar amounts exceed the agency conforming limits (currently $203,150). The rating agencies make the strong presumption that higher-valued properties with larger mortgages are much riskier; they impose penalties of up to 200%.

Creditworthiness of the Borrower

Although loan originators place a great deal of emphasis on borrowers' credit histories, these data are not available to the rating agencies. The Fair Credit Reporting Act restricts access to such information to parties involved in a credit extension decision.

As a result, the agencies use credit proxies such as the debt-to-income ratio, the mortgage coupon rate, past delinquencies or seasoned loans, or originators' "scores" (A, B, C, or D).

SEVERITY OF LOSS

In the case of default, foreclosure, and ultimate property sale, lenders incur two costs: (1) direct foreclosure costs, and (2) market decline. These costs may be mitigated to the extent there is equity in the property, i.e., lower LTVs will reduce the severity of loss.

Direct foreclosure costs: Once a lender begins the foreclosure process — often as soon as a borrower becomes 60 days delinquent — it begins to incur significant direct costs.

Unpaid interest: The lender stops accruing interest on the mortgage as income, instead adding it to the unpaid balance of the loan.

> Cost = coupon rate of the mortgage per year

Property taxes: The lender becomes responsible for paying taxes to preserve its first lien position.

> Cost = up to 2% or more of the house price annually

Management fees: The property must be maintained so as to preserve its value for sale.

> Cost = average 6% of the house price annually

Legal fees: Variable

Market decline: When a house is sold out of foreclosure, the lender is unlikely to obtain market value. Potential buyers know that the seller is distressed and know the size of the mortgage on the property. One common bidding strategy is to bid for the amount of the outstanding mortgage, figuring it is the seller's obligation to cover the out of pocket costs. The price received on a foreclosure sale depends greatly on local economic conditions and future housing prices, both of which are unknown at the time a rating agency is evaluating a loan. The range of assumed losses is 25% to 45%.

POOL CHARACTERISTICS

Rating agencies draw upon general portfolio theory that diversification reduces risk and concentration increases risk. They typically consider two characteristics of the overall pool composition in setting credit enhancement levels: (1) size of the pool, and (2) geographic composition/location.

Pool Size

Pools with fewer than 300 loans are penalized by three of the four rating agencies, while larger pools are credited. The rationale is that smaller pools are not sufficiently diversified to take account of (unspecified) desirable statistical properties.

Geography

The first kind of geographic consideration is again a question of diversification: "too many" loans concentrated in a single zip code or small local area. For example, a lender might finance an entire subdivision, townhouse development, or condominium project that might be exposed to a common, special risk such as a single plant closing or an environmental hazard.

The second kind of geographic consideration is generally broader in scope, such as a pool with a high concentration in Southern California that is exposed to risks not of a single plant but of a single industry. In special cases such as Boeing in Seattle, the risk is both industry- and company-specific.

CALCULATING CREDIT ENHANCEMENT LEVELS

Pool characteristic risks are cumulative; that is, if a loan has two or more adverse characteristics, the factors are multiplied to determine the relative degree of the frequency of default. Then one calculates an expected loss equal to the discounted probability of default times the expected loss severity. After performing these calculations on a loan-by-loan basis, the overall pool characteristics are taken into account.

Credit enhancement levels are determined relative to a specific rating desired for a security. Specifically, an investor in a AAA-rated security expects to have "minimal," that is to say, virtually no chance of losing any principal. For example, Standard & Poors requires credit enhancement equal to four times expected losses to obtain a AAA rating.

Lower-rated securities require less credit enhancement for four reasons. First, the loss coverage ratio is lower. Second, some of the factors may be less stringent. Third, the base case frequency of default may be lower. And fourth, the severity of loss may be less.

NEW EVIDENCE

Default rates calculated from a data set comprised of mortgages securitized by major issuers of non-agency MBS are particularly relevant in setting factors for the frequency of default. The discussion is based on analysis of more than 500,000 such non-conforming mortgages.

Exhibit 3: Delinquency Rates by Current LTV Range

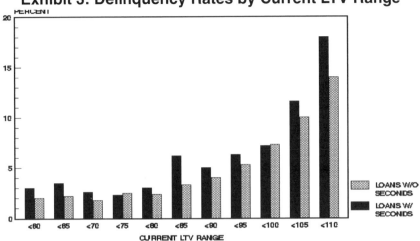

Loan-to-Value Ratio

With current LTV now the measure, assessment of risk needs to extend above 100%. Exhibit 3 shows that delinquency/default rates for mortgages with LTVs continue to rise. Approximate rates for 105% and 110% are 7.5 and 10, respectively, compared with 5 at 100%.

Exhibit 3 also shows that delinquency rates are higher for first mortgages whose borrowers have taken out second mortgages or home equity lines of credit even if their combined equity positions are identical. That is, if homeowner A has an 80% first mortgage, and homeowner B has a 65% first with the same coupon rate as A and a 15% second, homeowner B is a poorer credit risk. This heightened risk probably is a result of homeowner B's higher monthly payment.

As a special case of homeowners with seconds, consider borrowers who take out secondary financing as part of a purchase transaction. For example, the seller of the house — an individual if the house is a resale, the developer/builder if the house is new — may lend the buyer all or part of the down payment to facilitate the transaction. Exhibit 4 shows that the foreclosure rate for such transactions is nearly triple the rate of all transactions.

Mortgage Term

Recent experience with 15-year products has been exceptionally good, suggesting that previous credits were not generous enough. With the increasing popularity of 15-year mortgages as a liability management tool — to time the mortgage payoff either with retirement or children entering college, for example — a credit of as large as 50% seems appropriate (based on Exhibit 5) compared with the current range of 15% to 35%.

Exhibit 4: Delinquency Rates for Loans With and Without Silent Second Mortgages

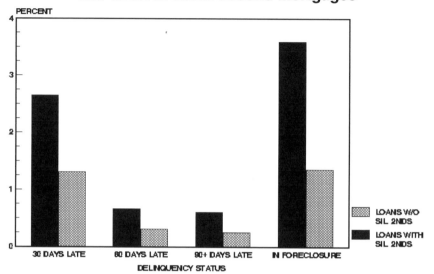

Exhibit 5: Ratio of Current Delinquencies
15-Year versus 30-Year Fixed Rate

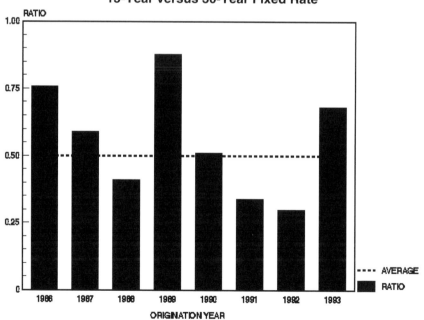

Exhibit 6: Ratio of Current Delinquencies
ARMS versus 30-year Fixed Rate

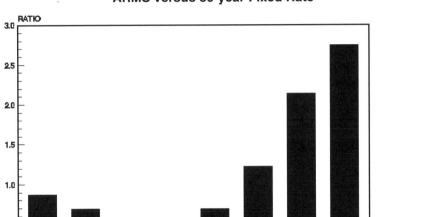

Mortgage Type/Borrower Credit

Although ARMs are considered riskier than fixed-rate mortgages, seasoning can have an adverse effect on mortgage holders and their ability to prepay. Consider homeowners who took out mortgages in 1990. A holder of the most popular ARM based on the one-year Treasury bill would have paid about 9% initially, and about 7% currently. In contrast, a fixed-rate mortgage would have cost about 10% in 1990 and about 7.75% currently.

If neither has refinanced, who's the better credit risk from this point forward? Exhibit 6 suggests that the ARM holder is the better risk because that borrower has not had an incentive to refinance, while the fixed-rate holder has had the incentive but failed to do so either because of a lack of equity or credit history deterioration. In either case, this borrower could not qualify for a new mortgage and is more of a risk.

This relationship suggests a formula for calculating credits/penalties by mortgage type:

$$\text{Fixed-rate mortgage} = \frac{\text{mortgage coupon}}{\text{current coupon}}$$

$$\text{ARM's} = \frac{\text{current rate}}{\text{initial rate}}$$

For ARM's, this formula has the additional feature of explicitly increasing the penalty as the rate rises in the future.

Exhibit 7: Ratio of Current Delinquencies
Cashout Refis versus Purchase Transactions

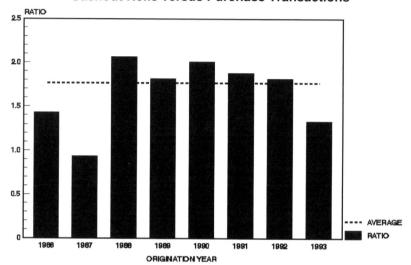

ORIGINATION YEAR

Transaction Type

Cash-out refinancings have performed abysmally in recent years, primarily because those still in existence were taken out at or near the peak in prices in California. However, there is no reason to think that the lending mistakes of California could not be repeated in other hot markets such as Seattle. Exhibit 7 indicates that the penalty for cash-out refinancings should be 100% compared with the rating agencies' maximum of 25%.

No-cash refinancings are currently not penalized by the rating agencies, although, Exhibit 8 shows significant "appraisal bias" for refinance transactions for which the appraiser has no purchase price as a guide. The extent of the bias is measured by noting that almost all the appraised values are higher than a property value estimated from indexing the previous sale price of the property to trends in property values in the same zip code; no such bias is present in Exhibit 9, which shows comparable data for purchase transactions for which the sale price is available to the appraiser.

This bias probably makes its effect felt in homeowners acting according to their "true" (read: higher) LTV. Thus, instead of penalizing refinance transactions directly, it would probably be more effective to raise the stated LTV at origination by 5% to 10% to reflect this bias. The impact on the required credit support would then be greater for relatively high LTV loans.

Exhibit 8: Evidence of Appraisal Bias
Refinance Transactions

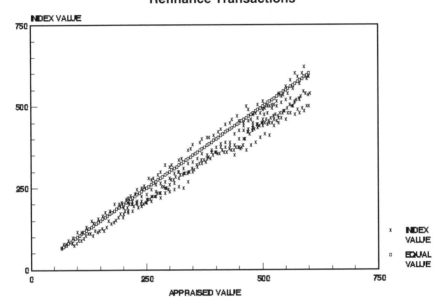

Exhibit 9: Evidence of Appraisal Bias
Purchase Transactions

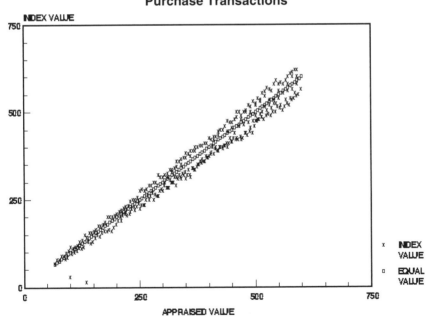

CHAPTER 7

The Rating of Securities Backed by B and C Mortgages

Andrew B. Jones

Group Vice President

Duff & Phelps Credit Rating Company

OVERVIEW

B and C mortgage lending is at the forefront of developments in the mortgage market. B and C loans, which are loans to borrowers with impaired credit histories, are not new to the marketplace, but until recently, only a small portion of these loans entered the securitized marketplace as a distinct product.

B and C loans include both first-lien and second-lien mortgages. The focus of this chapter is the development of the first lien sector of this marketplace. B and C lending also includes loans designated as A– (A minus) quality, which are made to borrowers slightly riskier than A borrowers. (The term A– or A minus is used sparingly herein.)

As the refinancing boom of 1992-1993 concluded, and as rising interest rates have dampened origination volume, many mortgage originators have begun to turn to the B and C market as a source for new loans. While B and C lending is a viable and active portion of the marketplace, it is unlikely that volume in this area will alone be able to counteract the decline in volume from 1992 and 1993 origination levels.

From a credit perspective, the unique qualities of B and C loans include characteristics that both increase and decrease risk relative to A loans. According to current guidelines, B and C mortgage pools generally require more protection or credit enhancement than a comparable A pool in order to achieve the same rating. Yet many B and C transactions have been structured in a manner that satisfies both the issuer's need for effective execution and the investor's need for adequate protection.

Defining B and C Lending

Private-label mortgage-backed securities generally represent interests in A loans. These mortgage loans are made to borrowers with excellent credit histories. The decision to lend is based primarily on the borrower's ability to pay and secondarily on the value and adequacy of collateral.

By contrast, B and C mortgage loans are made to borrowers who have some derogatory information in their credit histories. This derogatory information can include 30- or 60-day delinquencies on mortgage and credit card debt. Because of a reduced ability to pay, such borrowers typically qualify for loans only at higher rates and with higher down payments than borrowers with better credit histories. Borrowers with a preponderance of delinquencies or with defaults or charge-offs may fall under other categories such as D.

B and C lending programs are distinguishable from "hard money" lending, which is based solely on the value of the underlying collateral with little or no assessment of the ability of the borrower to meet the monthly payment schedule.

History of B and C Lending

While B and C loans have been characterized as a new mortgage product, this view is not necessarily accurate. B and C lending describes nothing more than traditional mortgage lending to risky borrowers. Traditionally, credit has been available to borrowers of different credit qualities, but the less creditworthy the borrower, the higher the rate and points, and the more collateral or equity is required.

B and C loans have included purchase money mortgages, as well as home equity loans either in a first-lien or second-lien position. These allow homeowners to cashout the equity in their homes for debt reconsolidation or other purposes.

The B and C terminology for borrowers of different credit grades began in the early 1980s. Because the terms were developed by individual lenders rather than by a national group or trade association, the terms were never standardized. As a result, one institution's B loan could be another institution's C loan.

Securitization

B and C loans typically do not conform to FNMA or FHLMC guidelines because of borrower credit history or other loan characteristics, even though the size of the loan may be within agency guidelines. Therefore, these loans can be securitized only in the private-label MBS markets.

B and C loans have been securitized for several years. They appear in securitizations of fully-amortizing home equity loan transactions dating back to the late 1980s. Securitized home equity transactions may include a mixture of A minus, B, and sometimes C product, including both first and second liens. Issuers in the B and C home equity sector have included Advanta, the Money Store, Long Beach, Conti Mortgage, and United Companies, among others.

In recent years as interest rates declined, many B and C lenders refinanced existing borrowers, including sometimes their own customers. In the case of the refinancing of second liens, the lenders often offered to refinance the existing first lien together with the second. In this manner, they retained existing customers and improved their overall lien position. Correspondingly, in the securitized market, an increasing percentage of first liens appeared in home equity transactions.

GROWING INTEREST IN B AND C MORTGAGES

In the late 1980s, issuers with B and C first liens began to securitize these loans in separate transactions from second liens. Other originators of B and C loans also began to look to the securities market for capital to grow their businesses.

The last few years have witnessed a dramatic increase in the securitization of B and C first liens. The growing interest in B and C loans is expressed by investors and issuers alike, and, of course, by the borrowers who seek financing.

Investors

Investors have experienced increased interest in B and C securitizations. They are comfortable with the credit features of the transactions and are focusing on other unique features of these loans.

1. Through appropriate credit enhancement levels, B and C loans can be securitized to produce securities rated as high as AAA, thereby satisfying investment credit guidelines.

2. Investors are attracted to an expected prepayment profile for B and C loans that differs from prepayment experience on A loans. Prepayments in full are expected to be lower, even in a declining interest rate environment, because these borrowers cannot qualify as easily as an A borrower for refinancing. Further, refinancing generally can be done only through another B and C lender; given that B and C borrowers are charged more points, it takes a larger drop in interest rates to offset the cost of refinancing in the case of a B borrower compared to an A borrower. In addition, curtailments are low on B and C product, because the borrowers by nature have little excess disposable cash. Finally, some B and C loans have prepayment penalties, typically in the first five years of the loan term, which makes refinancing more expensive for the borrower.

3. Loans under B and C programs have unique characteristics that can be passed through to investors in securitized transactions. For example, investors with a preference for a LIBOR-based security may be interested in securities backed by LIBOR-based adjustable-rate mortgages from B and C programs.

Originators

B and C loans are attractive to originators (including both retail originators as well as programs that acquire loans through mortgage brokers) for several reasons:

1. From a lender's perspective, including a portfolio lender, the additional risk of the borrowers can be offset by higher mortgage rates, higher points, and lower LTVs.

2. The development of securitization of these loans has provided originators with expanded access to capital with which to generate
   more loans.

3. There are more options on structuring transactions for higher-cou-
   pon B and C loans than for lower-coupon A loans. Because the
   rate on the loans can exceed the coupon on rated securities by a
   wide margin, the interest spread can be made available to new
   classes of investors, used as alternative credit support, or
   retained by the originator.

4. The demise of many financial institutions (for example, the insolvency and liquidation of many thrifts) has removed sources of
   credit for B and C borrowers. The result is a vacuum to be filled
   with new entrants into the marketplace.

Borrowers

The 1980s witnessed regional boom and bust cycles, resulting in periods of
high borrower defaults, followed by periods of tightened credit guidelines. Borrower interest in B and C loans is therefore increasing for two reasons:

1. The demand by borrowers for B and C loans is strong. In recessionary times, more borrowers have suffered dislocation and temporary unemployment, resulting in derogatory entries on their
   credit reports. Therefore, some former A borrowers are now B
   and C borrowers.

2. Finally, some lenders and third-party credit enhancers tightened
   their guidelines in the late 1980s. As a result, many former A borrowers fall outside the revised criteria.

SPECIAL FEATURES OF B AND C MORTGAGES

There are several unique features of B and C loans that set them apart from
traditional A loans.

First, the underwriting guidelines establish a credit profile that differs
markedly from A credits. By definition, B and C borrowers carry greater debt
burdens and are more likely to become delinquent. As a result, not only do
they have inferior credit histories, but they also pay higher mortgage rates
than A borrowers, adding to their debt burden. Correspondingly, permissible
debt-to-income ratios for B and C borrowers are higher than for A borrowers.

In order to counteract this risk, the guidelines require a borrower to
have more collateral in the form of equity in the home. Therefore, the under-

writing of B and C loans is particularly dependent on the accuracy of the appraisals at the time of origination. These considerations are explored in the review of underwriting below.

Second, the delinquency and loss experience on B and C loans is very sensitive to the quality of servicing. Because the borrowers are expected to be delinquent more often than A borrowers, collections must be more diligent than for A loans. These special considerations are reviewed in the discussion of servicing below.

Review of Underwriting Considerations

For every program issuing securities rated by Duff & Phelps Credit Rating Co. (D&P), D&P reviews the loan underwriting process. The review begins with an understanding of the underwriting guidelines and is enhanced with an on-site review of the originator.

Overview of underwriting guidelines: D&P's evaluation of underwriting guidelines for B and C programs reflects D&P's understanding of the fundamental differences between guidelines for A programs and guidelines for B and C programs.

Underwriting guidelines generally address (1) the value and adequacy of the real property as collateral for the loan, and (2) the ability of the borrowers to meet their payment obligations. B and C programs often put less emphasis on a borrower's ability to pay than do A programs. Rather, the primary focus for B and C programs is the assessment of the value and adequacy of the mortgaged property as collateral. Nonetheless, although the collateral value is the primary focus, loans are not made if the borrower has insufficient ability to make the monthly payments.

Borrower quality — guidelines describing credit grade: B and C guidelines include two types of criteria: first, descriptive guidelines that sort borrowers according to a scale of credit quality, and second, guidelines that limit the characteristics of a loan so as to counteract the particular risk of the borrower, the property, or other terms of the financing.

Underwriting guidelines address the borrower's ability to pay, focusing on credit history, debt-to-income ratios, and verification of income and assets. Program guidelines group borrowers' credit histories into categories. The A minus loan category may reflect payment data such as only one mortgage payment 30-days delinquent in the last year, a few 30-day late payments on consumer debt, and no prior bankruptcies. By contrast, a C designation may allow on existing mortgage debt several 30-day delinquencies, or a combination including one 60-day and one 90-day delinquency during the last year, derogatories on consumer debt, and a bankruptcy more than one and a half years prior.

Exhibit 1: Sample of Underwriting Guidelines

Loan Quality	Mortgage Credit	Other Credit	Debt-to-Income Ratios
A	1 × 30 last 12 months	Excellent credit	38
A-	1 × 30 last 12 months 2 × 30 last 24 months	Minor derogatories explained	45
B	4 × 30 last 12 months 1 × 60 last 24 months	Some prior defaults	50
C	6 × 30, 1 × 60, 1 × 90, 3 × 60 last 24 months	Credit problems	55
D	30 – 60 regularly, 2 × 90 last 24 months	Significant credit problems	60

Debt-to-income ratios are typically higher than for A lending programs. Nonetheless, many B and C borrowers are accustomed to tight budgets and have already exhibited an ability, although imperfect, to carry heavy debt burdens. Many B and C programs permit less risky borrowers to forgo the submission of some items of documentation for their applications.

Exhibit 1 sets forth a sample of underwriting guidelines. These do not necessarily represent the guidelines of any one program, but rather a combination of some of the more common specifications. While many market participants have asked D&P to help standardize the market through a set of prescribed guidelines, D&P, as a third-party observer, has chosen to let the market evolve and to assess each program on its merits.

Many guidelines specify discharge and date terms for each grade of borrower, if a borrower has filed for bankruptcy previously. The borrower's bankruptcy case must have been discharged at least 5 years prior for A-level credit, 3 years for B, 18 months for C, or 12 months prior for D credit.

Guidelines counteracting risk — LTV and accurate appraisals: Loan-to-value ratios (LTV) represent the ratio of the size of the loan to the value of the real property collateral, measured as the lesser of purchase price or appraised value. LTV is inversely related to the homeowner equity in the property. LTV guidelines are another aspect of assessing the adequacy of collateral. LTV guidelines, in combination with accurate appraisals, protect the lender and/or the investors in the security from loss in the event of default. LTV guidelines for B and C loans are generally lower, and therefore more conservative, than for A loans.

For example, the maximum LTV on B and C loans is typically lower than for A loans. Few B and C quality programs permit LTVs above 80%, while 80% LTV loans are a staple in the A lending programs. In addition, the average LTV of a typical B and C quality pool is approximately 65%. This is significantly lower than for A-quality loans, for which LTVs often average in the 70% to 75% LTV range.

Exhibit 2: Maximum LTV Ratios

(Assuming Full Documentation)

Loan Quality	Max LTV Single-family/Owner-occupied (purchase/refi)	Max LTV Vacation/Investor (purchase/refi)
A	80/75	75/50
B	75/70	70/NA
C	70/60	65/NA
D	65/NA	60/NA

Underwriting standards also provide that maximum permissible LTVs decline as the loan's risk increases. Inferior credit history, reduced documentation, or risky property or loan types can each reduce a lender's permitted LTV for a given borrower.

The presence of second liens is relevant in evaluating LTVs. If second liens currently exist behind the securitized first liens, the combined LTV must be reported to the rating agencies. Some guidelines permit the origination of subsequent second liens, but only up to specified combined LTV caps. While the presence of the second lien does not change the calculation of the potential loss to the first-lien position, it does increase the likelihood of a default and must be factored into the rating agency's assessment.

Exhibit 2 demonstrates how the maximum permissible LTV drops for worse credits and for riskier property types (e.g., vacation homes or investor properties) or loan type (e.g., refinancing). LTVs are lower than those presented here in the case of alternative, limited, or reduced documentation.

The importance of LTV ratios means that accurate and reliable appraisals are essential to the success of the program. Appraisals typically are made by an independent fee appraiser, then reviewed by trained in-house appraisers employed by the originator. These reviews are either desk reviews of the appraisal or drive-bys of the property, but are rarely full appraisals.

For new programs, typically every appraisal is reviewed. For subsequent transactions, reviews are made of significant samples. If, however, unacceptable variances appear, a larger portion will be reviewed.

D&P reviews the underwriting department of the originator, the background of the in-house appraisers, and the quality control measures taken to ensure reliable appraisals. For example, it is prudent for the originator to track by appraiser the variance between original appraisals and any reappraisals, either during file audits or by comparison to appraisals on defaulted mortgage properties.

Underwriting philosophy / Targeted borrowers: For each rated program, D&P conducts an on-site review to assess the originator's ability to originate sound loans.

D&P meets with management to obtain a business overview and to explore the particular business niche of each lender. B and C lending is more of an art than a mechanical process; therefore, the experience of the underwriters and their lending focus are significant. A review of underwriting guidelines does not explain entirely the quality of the underwriting. For each program, D&P seeks to understand the philosophy behind the program, with an understanding of the targeted borrowers and the reasons for lending.

For example, some programs focus on particular borrowers such as those with poor consumer credit histories but with good mortgage payment histories. A borrower who habitually pays the mortgage lender first may be a good mortgage credit risk, even if the credit history on other types of receivables is poor.

Another example is the A "turndowns." This focus may arise because an A program cannot accommodate potential customers who fall just outside of the existing guidelines. Lenders would rather lend at terms covering the risk than have to turn customers away.

A third example is lending to B and C borrowers, but only in those cases where the loan "makes sense." Some borrowers may have no access to mortgage credit and may have limited consumer credit at high rates. For these clients, it may be beneficial to arrange a first-lien cash-out refinancing to consolidate debts or pay for a child's education.

A fourth example is lending to borrowers who have encountered financial hardship in the recent recession but who have improved their financial condition — perhaps someone unemployed for a period of time who has just obtained secure employment. Another example is an individual once burdened by high medical bills that have subsequently been paid. In many cases, the originator focuses on only those borrowers who can establish that the cause of their poor credit history has been remedied.

Understanding each program's approach to developing its niche in this marketplace allows D&P to evaluate the appropriateness of the underwriting guidelines to each lender's objectives.

Quality control: To ensure that loans conform to program guidelines, programs must have quality control procedures, including preclosing reviews, post-closing audits, and monitoring loan performance by broker. D&P meets with the quality control personnel to discuss the procedures to assure compliance with guidelines.

Third-party underwriting: For most programs, there is typically some form of re-underwriting of the loans. The goal of re-underwriting is twofold: first, to determine if the originator is adhering to its written guidelines, and second, to verify the characteristics of the mortgages being securitized. For new programs, 100% of the loans may be subject to a re-underwriting; in more established programs re-underwriting may be on a sample basis.

The requirement for re-underwriting generally stems from the underwriter's and issuer's obligations to disclose the terms of the transaction accurately. Rating agencies generally rely on the data presented to them, and in the absence of any evidence to the contrary will assume the information is accurate. Further support may be derived from the accountant's letter, which verifies on a sample basis the characteristics of the loans as set forth in the disclosure.

Servicing Considerations

For B and C programs, it is critical that the servicer has strong operations and procedures to maintain contact with delinquent mortgagors. Although proper servicing is also important for A loans, it is even more significant in the B and C area because the loans will not perform well without diligent collections.

On-site reviews: D&P conducts an on-site review of the servicer in each transaction D&P rates. To assess the quality of a servicer's collections, D&P meets with management and determines the background and qualifications of the personnel. The collections personnel must have experience in these particular types of loans. Collectors with backgrounds in home equity lending and consumer finance may also be well-suited for collecting on B and C loans.

Collections: Since borrowers under B and C programs by definition have already exhibited a tendency to become delinquent, it is important that the collector make special efforts to keep the borrower current. Methods to maintain borrower performance include:

1) Contacting the borrower prior to the first payment date to remind the borrower about the payment, to verify source of funds, and to specify where the payment is to be mailed (the goal is to remove any excuse a borrower may have for not making the first payment).

2. Building a relationship with the borrower (some originators offer guidance or counseling to help borrowers budget their expenses, ensuring that the ability to pay becomes a reality).

3. Making telephone contact with delinquent borrowers quickly, as soon as five to ten days after the due date.

4. Tracking chronic late payers, determining the cause of the lateness, and remedying the situation to prevent further delinquencies.

5. For those loans that do not cure, starting foreclosure proceedings promptly, including sending a notice of default when the payment is 45 days past due (or sooner).

D&P assesses the systems of the servicer to determine that the systems meet industry standards for the B and C sector. For example, collections are typically done through computer-based systems, calls are usually initiated by automatic dialing systems, notes of each call are tracked by loan, and the efficiency of collectors is monitored individually.

Loss mitigation: D&P also focuses on the foreclosure department and related operations. The principal way to mitigate losses is to avoid the acquisition of the real estate whenever possible. The most successful originators are those that succeed in bringing a delinquent borrower current, including curing a loan for which foreclosure proceedings may have already been initiated.

Loss mitigation can take the form of modification of a loan. In this case, if the terms of the loans are materially changed, the loan is required to be repurchased under the transaction documentation. Loss mitigation may also include forbearance, but loans in forbearance must be treated on the books as delinquent, and D&P will question why any serious delinquencies have not yet entered foreclosure status.

In the event it is necessary to foreclose and liquidate a property, the servicer must liquidate the property promptly. The importance of the initial appraisal is key, as well as the expertise of in-house and other appraisers who are advising on the disposition of property. D&P recognizes that it is often in the interest of servicers, on behalf of investors, to sell at a price low enough to ensure a speedy sale. The benefits of achieving a higher price can be quickly offset by accrued interest if a sale is delayed.

To evaluate the servicer's foreclosure process, D&P determines the average time to foreclose and liquidate a property. D&P also evaluates the percent of the servicer's portfolio in non-paying and paying bankruptcy status to ensure that bankruptcy levels are normal, giving consideration to regional differences. D&P also questions any experience with cramdowns, which are exceedingly rare.

Advancing and back-up servicing: Advances for delinquent mortgagor payments are typically made by the servicer. The trustee acts as a back-up in the event the servicer is unable to service the loans or make advances. Trustees must correctly price their obligation to become back--up servicer.

If the servicer of record is unable to perform servicing, the servicing must be pulled immediately and transferred to a capable institution. Delays in the collections effort are particularly problematical in the B and C context, because any interruption of diligent collections will cause delinquencies to soar. When the long-term financial viability of the servicer is difficult to assess, D&P will require a third party to act as a "hot" back-up servicer.

D&P'S APPROACH TO EVALUATING B AND C MORTGAGES

D&P determines the protection or credit enhancement required for a rating by (1) applying its analytical model to evaluate the risk of each loan in a pool backing a security, and by (2) adjusting the model's output by factors addressing qualitative considerations such as originator and servicer quality.

D&P's Analytical Model

In D&P's analytical model, the credit enhancement level for a desired rating reflects each loan's credit enhancement requirement, which is calculated by multiplying the loan's balance by a base level of credit enhancement and by a series of factors corresponding to the particular characteristics of the individual loan or the transaction as a whole.[1]

With respect to credit enhancement levels, D&P's analysis assumes a housing price decline stress test, as high as 40% for AAA securities, recognizing that historical losses for programs are generally lower than the losses expected under adverse economic scenarios. By applying housing price decline stresses, D&P ensures that the rated securities are protected against a depressed economy.

Several factors that contribute to credit enhancement levels are especially important in evaluating B and C loans.

1. *LTV factor.* The fact that LTV ratios are generally lower for B and C programs results in a benefit (credit enhancement is reduced). Despite the fact that low LTV could indicate that the borrower did not qualify at a higher LTV and is therefore a riskier borrower, the low LTV is designed to offset this risk, providing protection against the severity of the loss in the event of default.

2. *Interest rate factor.* The interest rate or coupon factor, which increases credit enhancement for above-market note rates, reflects the fact that high-coupon loans accrue more interest during foreclosure and liquidation, resulting in higher losses.

---

[1] The individual loan factors are set forth for the D&P Triple-A model in "Rating of Mortgage-Backed Securities," p.11.

3. *High-margin factor.* For adjustable-rate mortgage (ARM) programs, D&P pays special attention to the loan margins. If the
margins are unusually high, it is an indication that the originator is counteracting risk with less emphasis on low LTVs and
more emphasis on rate. While this may work for a portfolio
lender, it does not help an investor in MBS. This is because
the benefit of the higher rate is not passed through to holders
of regular classes in MBS structures but rather is typically
stripped off. Therefore, since the factor counteracting risk does
not benefit the MBS investor, D&P may require additional
credit enhancement.

4. *Loan purpose factor.* The D&P model's benchmark loan is a purchase money mortgage, for which the value of the mortgaged
property is the lesser of the actual sales price or the appraisal.
The loan purpose factor will result in increased credit enhancement for any loan for which the value of the mortgaged property is based solely on appraisal, as is the case with regular
refinancings and cash-out refinancings. Cash-out refinancings,
which constitute a substantial portion of B and C loans, are
refinancings that are used to pay off the existing mortgage and
provide the borrower with additional cash secured by the property. Cash-out refinancings are common in areas with housing
price appreciation. The amount of appreciation is typically
measured by the appraisal. The risk therefore derives from the
absence of any actual sales price to corroborate the appraisal.

5. *Time-to-foreclosure factor.* The time-to-foreclosure factor adds
credit enhancement for those states where the process to foreclose is lengthy and thereby increases the amount of interest
that will accrue on any defaulted loans. California, where many
B and C programs are active, has an average foreclosure period
of four months, which is less than the national average, and
base credit enhancement levels are adjusted downward accordingly. Other states with shorter than average foreclosure periods
also lead to lower credit enhancement. Conversely, B and C
lending will incur greater losses in areas where foreclosure periods are longer, as in many states in the Northeast.

6. *Location-specific factors.* Location-specific factors adjust credit
enhancement based on characteristics of the Metropolitan Statistical Area (MSA) where the secured properties are located.
D&P collects housing price information by tiers of housing.

Many B and C lending programs focus on borrowers with homes in the lower and middle tiers, which historically have exhibited less price volatility than the upper tiers. The location-specific factors increase credit enhancement for loans secured by properties with values that are high for the MSA in which they are located. In addition, there is an adjustment reflecting loans located in MSAs with below average or above average housing price volatility.

Qualitative Considerations: Originator/Servicer Factor

The originator/servicer factor addresses a specific program's guidelines and performance and reflects the extent to which that program is riskier than the generic private-label A programs. This factor is multiplied against the model output along with other factors reflecting aggregate pool considerations (pool size, geographic concentration). The originator/servicer factors vary from 1.25 to 2.50, and incorporate an understanding of the guidelines, the borrower mix, and the originator's delinquency experience.

1. *Comparing guidelines.* The relative risk of loans is reflected by the differences in the guidelines describing the borrower's credit (e.g., debt-to-income ratios). Each program uses the B and C quality designations in a slightly different manner; therefore, one program's B product could be the equivalent of another's C product. While D&P does not establish industry guidelines, D&P nonetheless compares program parameters to determine, for example, if one program's B loan is riskier than that of another program.

2. *Borrower quality mix.* In the case of each transaction, D&P analyzes the guidelines and the loan-by-loan characteristics of the mortgages to determine the percentages of the pool reflecting different degrees of borrower quality. The more the pool is represented by risky credits, the higher the originator/servicer factor.

3) *Delinquency history.* B and C loans not only exhibit higher delinquencies than A loans, but they also are more sensitive to the quality and aggressiveness of the servicing. This risk is reflected in the servicing factor. For each program, D&P looks at historical delinquency and loss performance when available (preferably on a static pool basis). Lack of performance history may result in a higher factor, at least until enough history for that particular program has been obtained to justify a lower factor.

Exhibit 3: Sample Credit Enhancement Levels

	Sample B/C Transaction	Sample A Transaction
AAA	10% to 15%	7% to 12%
AA	6% to 9%	4% to 7%
A	3% to 5%	2% to 4%
BBB	2% to 3%	1% to 2.5%

CREDIT ENHANCEMENT STRUCTURES FOR B AND C LOANS

The Senior-subordinate Structure

The credit quality of the highest-rated class, the senior class in a senior-subordinate structure, is supported by credit enhancement in the form of subordination of other classes. The aggregate principal balance of these subordinate classes equals the percentage amount that the rating agency requires to cover losses. Subordination means that losses on mortgages in the pool are allocated to the subordinate classes before the senior.

Exhibit 3 presents sample credit enhancement levels by typical B and C pools. Actual credit enhancement levels are governed by the individual pool's characteristics and the quality of the particular originator or program.

These levels represent the amount of subordination required for securities representing the remainder of the pool to achieve the corresponding rating. Sample credit enhancement levels for a sample A-quality 30-year ARM transaction are provided for comparison.

As evident in Exhibit 3, the risk characteristics of B and C loans generally outweigh the factors counteracting the risk, leading to higher credit enhancement levels than for A product despite lower average LTVs.

Credit Tranched Structures

The numbers in Exhibit 3 represent the credit enhancement necessary to achieve the corresponding rating assuming a simple two-class senior subordinate structure, with only one senior class and only one subordinate class. Most residential mortgage-backed securities (MBS) are structured into multiple classes, each class subordinate to the ones before it. These subordinate classes include classes rated at different categories on the rating scale, from AAA to as low as BB, B, and even CCC. Losses on the underlying mortgage pool are allocated first to an unrated class (the "first-loss" class) until the class is completely written off, then to the next most junior and lowest-rated subordinate class, and so on through the classes. This series of subordinations, or "credit tranching," can result in the leveraging of losses into classes of very small sizes.

In transactions with highly leveraged subordinate classes, there is a disproportionate effect on smaller classes if losses exceed levels used to assign ratings to the classes. This possibility creates a credit concern that must be addressed by the rating. Ratings that do not address this issue expose investors to securities without the support necessary to counteract that risk. The leveraging feature, common in many MBS transactions, requires extra credit enhancement behind smaller classes as well as adjustments to preserve class size.

Variance Of Actual Losses

A source of concern about concentrations of excess losses in smaller classes is that for lower ratings there is a greater potential variance between the rating assumptions and actual events. It is highly unlikely that actual economic events will deteriorate to an AAA scenario. On the other hand, it is possible that economic events in the future may be worse than economic expectations backing a BB stress.

Ratings address more than the likelihood or frequency of loss on a security. They reflect, in part, how severe the loss may be on the security if one were to occur. For highly rated securities, the likelihood of loss is so minor, and the harm in the event of a loss is so small, that the distinction between the frequency of loss and its severity is minimal. For lower-rated securities, the likelihood of a loss increases so that it is important also to evaluate the likely severity of any loss that may occur.

Investors taking into account both the likely frequency and severity of a loss on a security should be indifferent between two securities with the same rating. In order to be indifferent, investors should expect a lower frequency of default of the security when the severity of the potential default increases because of a small class size.

Concentration Ratios And Concentration Multipliers

Duff & Phelps recognizes that the leveraging of losses makes a class riskier, all other factors being equal, because leveraging dramatically increases the severity of loss. In order for the leveraged class to achieve the same rating as the unleveraged class, it must have more credit support to reduce the chance of the excess loss occurring, as well as to reduce its severity. The additional credit enhancement necessary is determined by first quantifying the extent of the leveraging, as measured by the concentration of potential losses.

The degree of concentration (the "concentration ratio") is calculated as the ratio of the size of a leveraged class together with all classes senior to it divided by the class's balance. A quick rule of thumb to approximate the concentration ratio is to divide 1.00 by the class size (for example, a 0.25% class is 100/0.25%, or 400 times concentrated).

Exhibit 4: Concentration Multipliers by Rating Category

Rating	Concentration Ratio				
Category	25x	50x	100x	200x	400x
AAA	1.01	1.02	1.04	1.08	1.15
AA	1.03	1.06	1.11	1.23	1.45
A	1.05	1.09	1.19	1.38	1.75
BBB	1.08	1.15	1.30	1.60	2.20
BB	1.12	1.24	1.49	1.98	2.95
B	1.15	1.30	1.60	2.20	3.40
CCC	1.19	1.38	1.75	2.50	4.00

Examples of Duff & Phelps's concentration multipliers are presented in Exhibit 4. For subordinate classes with potential concentrations of excess losses, the required level of subordination equals the product of the appropriate multiplier and the level of support under the D&P analytic model (adjusted by qualitative factors).

Applying The Concentration Factor

Exhibit 5 sets forth examples applying the credit enhancement methodology reviewed above. Panel 1 shows the scale of credit enhancement levels assumed to be required for a simple two-class transaction. Any of the unleveraged two class structures outlined in Panel 2 would be acceptable to Duff & Phelps, whether a 90%/10% senior/subordinate split that would create a class rated AAA and an unrated class (Alternative 1), or the 99.25%/0.75% split, which would create a class rated BB and an unrated class (Alternative 5).

If concentration of excess losses were not a problem, the structure shown in Panel 3 would be the optimal structure. Every class has at least as much subordination as would be required for the senior bond in a two-class structure. This structure is called the "frequency-driven" optimal structure because, if the credit enhancement levels have been set in order to control only the frequency of default for each rating category, class size can be determined by taking the difference between the credit enhancements for each rating category. The frequency of a write-down on each class is equal to the frequency of a write-down on the comparably rated class under Panel 2.

The problem with the structure in Panel 3 is the concentration factor. Many classes are roughly 50 times concentrated, and the most junior classes are over 100 times concentrated. Because severity of possible loss should be considered when evaluating a security, there must be credit enhancement adjustments to offset the concentration. If Duff & Phelps were to rate this structure, its ratings would be those appearing in the last column of the panel. Except for the first class, all the ratings are lower than the frequency rating appearing in the second column.

Exhibit 5: Comparison of Frequency-Driven Structures to the Duff & Phelps Approach

Panel 1: Credit Scale

AAA	10.00%
AA	6.00%
A	3.00%
BBB	1.50%
BB	0.75%

Panel 2: Unleveraged Two-Class Structures

	Alternative 1 AAA Senior	Alternative 2 AA Senior	Alternative 3 A Senior	Alternative 4 BBB Senior	Alternative 5 BB Senior
	Senior Class: Class A				
Size	90.00%	94.00%	97.00%	98.50%	99.25%
Subordination	10.00%	6.00%	3.00%	1.50%	0.75%
Rating	AAA	AA	A	BBB	BB
Concentration	1.0	1.0	1.0	1.0	1.0
	Subordinate Class: Class B				
Size	8.00%	6.00%	3.00%	1.50%	0.75%
Subordination	0.00%	0.00%	0.00%	0.00%	0.00%
Rating	Unrated	Unrated	Unrated	Unrated	Unrated
Concentration	NA	NA	NA	NA	NA

Panel 3: "Frequency-Driven" Structure (FDS)

Class	FDS Rating	Size (%)	Subordination (%)	Concentration	D&P Rating
A-1	AAA	90.00	10.00	1.0	AAA
M-1	AA	4.00	6.00	23.5	AA-
M-2	A	3.00	3.00	32.3	A-
B-1	BBB	1.50	1.50	65.7	BBB-
B-2	BB	0.75	0.75	132.3	B+
B-3	NR	0.75	0.00	NA	NR

Panel 4: Duff & Phelps Structure

Class	Rating	Size (%)	Subordination (%)	Concentration (Ratio / Multiplier)
A-1	AAA	90.00	10.00	1.0 / 1.00
M-1	AA	3.50	6.25	26.7 / 1.03
M-2	A	3.00	3.25	32.2 / 1.06
B-1	BBB	0.75	2.25	129.6 / 1.40
B-2	BB	1.00	1.25	97.25 / 1.49
B-3	UR	1.25		

Note: Credit enhancement levels and class sizes are rounded to 25 basis points.

For Duff & Phelps, offsetting the concentration would result in the optimal structure that appears in Panel 4. Optimal in this case means that as much of the transaction is structured into the highest rating categories as is possible. Numerous other structures, perhaps excluding some rating categories in favor of others, are possible. Credit enhancement is increased slightly for every offered class other than the AAA class: 0.25% for the class rated AA, 0.25% for the A, and so on.

Because traditional ratings on subordinate corporate debt consider both frequency and severity, investors assume that subordinate MBS ratings do also. Because the frequency-only nature of some ratings is not disclosed, investors are not necessarily pricing these securities accurately. The use of frequency-only ratings not only exposes investors to more credit risk, it also distorts capital reserve requirements. One example of this is how the frequency-only system allows marginal speculative-grade debt to be mis-rated as investment-grade.

The D&P approach to rating subordinate MBS, incorporating the severity implications of leveraging, is consistent with traditional subordinate debt ratings and reflects the concerns of investors and regulators more accurately than a frequency-only system.

Super-Senior Structures

In some transactions, the most senior class is structured with more credit enhancement than is necessary to achieve an AAA rating. Nonetheless, AAA is the highest rating that D&P assigns. These levels may be demanded by an investor who is more familiar with non-credit-sensitive MBS (e.g., agency certificates). Sometimes the structure arises from the desire to produce a large mezzanine class that is locked out of prepayments.

In super-senior structures, the second most senior class may be structured with an AA level of credit support. If the senior class protection is in excess of the AAA requirement, it leaves a mezzanine that is sufficiently large not to have a significant leveraging problem.

Comparing Structural Alternatives

Although D&P primarily rates transactions in a senior-subordinate format, several other options are available to issuers, including third-party credit enhancements. Each form of credit enhancement has its advantages and disadvantages.

Advantages and disadvantages of the senior-subordinate structure:

Advantages: Securities issued in a senior-subordinate format are subject to downgrade generally only if the credit quality of the collateral deteriorates dramatically, whereas other types of enhancement may bring into question the credit quality of third parties. Another perceived advantage of the senior-subordinate structure is that in some cases the first-loss piece is retained by the originator. This offers the originator a strong incentive to maximize proceeds on foreclosure and to collect diligently.

Disadvantages: Lower rated classes of bonds can be sold only at a discount. For transactions not rated by D&P, investors may find the leveraging of losses in some classes to be unacceptable.

Advantages and disadvantages of third-party credit enhancement: Third-party credit enhancement includes surety bonds and pool policies (pool insurers, however, are not yet active in this sector).

Advantages: Bond insurers and pool insurers provide another layer of third-party underwriting. A second advantage is that insurance allows all the bonds to be sold. Finally, all bonds can achieve an AAA rating.

Disadvantages: From a credit perspective, the credit quality of an individual transaction depends on the credit quality of the bond insurer. The transaction therefore becomes subject to event risk, such as the financial strength of the guarantor or its re-insurers. Also, poor performance of other transactions insured by the same bond surety company, thereby lowering the company's credit quality, will adversely affect the securities, even if the collateral is performing as expected.

Advantages and disadvantages of spread account structures: Spread accounts are reserve funds that build up over time with deposits monthly of excess interest (mortgage coupon less security coupon, servicing fees, and trust expenses). Spread accounts may be used in conjunction with either subordination or third-party credit enhancement.

Advantages: Use of excess spread can help diminish the amount of subordinate classes required.

Disadvantage: Cash-flow funded spread accounts are prepayment-sensitive. Because rating agencies stress the interest cash flows under onerous prepayment assumptions, the result may sometimes be a transaction less efficiently priced than a transaction where the excess interest strip is sold.

TRANSACTIONS CURRENTLY RATED BY D&P

D&P currently rates transactions that include significant amounts of B and C loans.

D&P has rated several issues by Greenwich Capital Acceptance, Inc., representing interests in LIBOR adjustable-rate mortgages originated by Long Beach Bank, located in California. Long Beach pools typically include B and C loans, as well as A minus loans. Long Beach services the loans.

D&P has also rated several issues by DLJ Mortgage Acceptance Corp., also representing interests in LIBOR adjustable-rate mortgages originated or acquired by Quality Mortgage USA, Inc. and serviced by LOMAS Mortgage USA, Inc.

Loans of B and C quality are expected to have delinquency rates well above market averages. Without proper servicing, these loans would suffer losses above market averages. However, in the case of each of these transactions, D&P has concluded that the servicer has the expertise and capability to service the loans properly.

CONCLUSION

D&P expects the securitization of B and C loans to grow, albeit not at a pace that will fill the void left by the end of the refinancing boom. As new programs enter the market, D&P will monitor several areas of concern.

Are new programs stretching the risk parameters of loans such that the overall quality of this sector of the marketplace will be affected? Is increased competition among originators preparing the way for a wave of prepayments? Are programs expanding nationally as able to judge the adequacy of collateral as regional players?

These and other questions are areas that D&P will explore as the market develops.

CHAPTER 8

A Credit-Intensive Approach to Analyzing the Subordinate Classes of Whole-Loan CMOs

Edward L. Toy

Director: Private Placements
Teachers Insurance and Annuity Association

From 1987 to 1993, generally accepted estimates are that issuance in the whole loan mortgage-backed market grew from roughly $11 billion to $100 billion. Of those totals the amount that relied on a senior-subordinate structure increased from 30% to 48%. Unlike agency securities, whole-loan CMOs do not benefit from any kind of government guarantee. Investment decisions must, therefore, necessarily rely on different criteria.

The analysis of investment opportunities in the whole loan mortgage market can be divided into two principal components: fundamental and technical. While aspects of the two components inevitably overlap at times, this chapter focuses on fundamental analysis.

WHY CREDIT ANALYSIS IS IMPORTANT

While historical experience in the mortgage market has generally been very good, it is nonetheless true that borrowers do default on their loans and losses do occur. Without the benefit of a guarantee from FNMA, FHLMC, or GNMA to cover such losses, investors must rely on the quality of the underlying collateral and other forms of credit enhancement like subordinate securities, cash reserves, and pool insurance or guarantees. Subordinate securities represent only a small portion of the overall pool and other forms of credit enhancement rarely represent a significant percentage of the pool either. A careful fundamental approach to the analysis of the collateral will lead to a basic understanding of a mortgage pool's underlying quality and an ability to forecast its future performance on the basis of reasonably rational criteria. Alternatively, developing a basic understanding of the relevant risk areas will permit the setting of logical standards for making comparisons between competing investments or avoiding certain pools altogether.

While such a credit-intensive approach is important generally, it is critical for investors in the subordinate classes. These are the at-risk securities that have a greater likelihood of being impaired. In a senior-subordinate structure, the subordinate classes, or B-pieces, act as internal credit enhancement for the senior, or class A, securities. Depending on the quality of the collateral, the subordinate classes in total will account for between 5% and 8% of the structure.

Generally, the subordinate layer is further tranched into several subclasses. The result is very small layers with gradually smaller levels of subordination to support the given certificate. The most junior security, referred to as a first-loss piece, may be no larger than 25 basis points or 0.25% of the pool. The actual size and credit quality of the subordinate classes will be determined by the rating agencies analyzing the pool, but market acceptance of different subordination levels is also an important influence.

Analyzing a pool from the credit side is more important to B-piece investors because if the pool experiences defaults and losses on foreclosure, the subordinate classes will be allocated those losses sequentially, beginning with the lowest class, or first-loss piece. The senior bonds in any structure are allocated losses only after the subordinate classes are completely eliminated. Since the subordinate classes are allocated all of the first losses even though they represent only a small percentage of the overall structure, the subordinate classes are subject to a great deal of "negative leverage." This negative leverage will continue to be quite substantial until the pool experiences prepayments. With prepayments first allocated to the senior bonds in the typical senior-subordinate structure, gradually the subordinate classes will represent an increasing percentage of the remaining pool, thus reducing the negative leverage.

As even a relatively low level of losses can impair the value of the subordinate certificates, it is obvious that any investor considering such an investment must first develop an opinion about the likelihood of losses exceeding the level of subordination supporting the security. Even an extremely well-underwritten pool should be expected to experience some losses during its life. If the proposed investment is one of the lower classes or first-loss pieces, where little or no actual support exists in the structure, protection from losses will depend more on equity in the underlying collateral.

If one continues to assume some nominal level of losses, the emphasis shifts somewhat for these lowest classes to the timing for the losses. This is because until defaults and losses are actually experienced, even the lowest classes continue to receive a share of the interest and principal cash flow that is being generated by the pool.

A credit intensive approach to the analysis of mortgage pools will result in a strong base for estimating the likelihood and timing of experiencing losses on a pool.

THE ORIGINATOR/UNDERWRITER

The credit-intensive part of whole-loan analysis must begin with the seller of the underlying mortgages, or the entity on whose underwriting standards and abilities any investor relies. This may be the actual originator and underwriter of the mortgages. Or, it could be a conduit that is purchasing mortgages from various sources and re-underwriting those mortgages before combining them into a pool.

In this latter case, the underwriting standards of the actual originators are not relevant, because the conduit, even if it purchases packages of mortgages in bulk, will pick and choose out of that package, throwing out mortgages that do not fit its underwriting standards. The conduit will also dictate underwriting standards to its sellers so that the weeding out is not extensive. In some situations, the underwriting criteria referred to may also be underwriting guidelines of the mortgage pool insurers, to the extent a conduit program or dealer relies on pool certification by a pool insurer to package transactions. In some rare situations, the pool could involve a combination of all three. In most situations, the originator/underwriter is also the servicer or master servicer of the pool.

Historical Performance

Review of an originator begins with a basic and fairly simple quantitative approach with respect to its historical performance. Delinquency information is reviewed. Besides delinquencies, the review should include foreclosure data and segmentation of the total delinquency data into 30-, 60-, and 90-day delinquencies. Each of these should be analyzed in absolute dollar terms and as a percentage of the originator's servicing or master servicing portfolio. Generally speaking, only a fraction of 30-day delinquencies turn into unresolvable defaults. Therefore, while any delinquency may be problematic, the delinquencies of 60 to 90 days and 90 days or greater are more important.

One should view with some degree of suspicion low overall delinquency statistics, but high levels of serious delinquencies, either compared with the overall numbers or compared with other originators. This may indicate a definitional oddity that simply does not report delinquencies until they become more serious. Alternatively, a sudden increase in 30-day delinquencies, as a percentage of the overall portfolio, may be an indication of future problems. Just as for a straight corporate issuer, some degree of trend analysis can be quite revealing.

Finally, loss experience on foreclosures is also important. To the extent that an underwriter is more aggressive with respect to approving borrowers and debt-to-income levels, much of this can be offset with tighter underwriting of the collateral or enforcing tighter loan-to-value standards, resulting in lower loss levels. Of course, higher loss levels may indicate a lax underwriting approach, as opposed to just being aggressive. Housing price volatility does tend to increase with size, especially among jumbo loans. Most originators try to offset this somewhat by imposing tighter loan-to-value ratios with increased loan size, or alternatively by limiting loan size for higher loan-to-value ratios.

In looking at performance statistics, it is important to factor out distortions, both positive and negative. One factor that has led to performance statistics looking better than reality is high origination levels in a low interest rate environment. A large influx of new mortgages into a servicing portfolio will make the numbers look better than they actually are by increasing the denominator in the equation. Unless underwriting of the borrowers has been unusually weak, it would be surprising to see many newly originated mortgages going delinquent in the first year or two.

Generally speaking, one would not expect the typical mortgage pool to experience any significant defaults until the third or fourth year after origination (the "standard default curve"). Thus, in a high origination pattern, the delinquency and default numbers, which constitute the numerator in the equation, would initially stay relatively low. The easiest way to factor out this distortion is to take the current delinquency information but use the prior year's portfolio balance as a denominator, or, alternatively, use the average of the two years.

On the other side, when we see somewhat higher delinquency data, it is helpful at times to take a closer look at the reasons instead of making the automatic judgment that the underwriting is poor. For example, many originators in the late eighties were aggressive in pushing limited documentation programs to build volume. Since limited documentation loans tend to show higher defaults over time, the poor experience of these "low-doc/no-doc" mortgages may inflate the default numbers.

Current origination patterns emphasize full documentation underwriting and only permit limited documentation loans in selected situations. The shift for some originators has been from highs of 60% or 70% of originations to less than 20%. On top of this shift, today's limited documentation loans for most originators are themselves of better quality. In any case, it is only fair to note when applicable that the current profile of originations has a different breakdown and adjust historical numbers accordingly.

There are also several ways of taking a static pool approach that will reveal the true quality of the underwriting. Static pool analysis focuses on breaking down the originator's performance by origination year. The most common approach is to take the total number of loans originated in each year and determine how many loans became delinquent within 6, 12, and 18 months of origination. It can be equally informative to develop a foreclosure curve for each origination year and compare the accumulation pattern for those years. Static pool analysis is useful because overall portfolio numbers are affected by the addition of new loans and the prepayment of older loans.

Underwriting Criteria

The basic quantitative approach, of course, only gets us part of the way. Second is a thorough review of the underwriting criteria itself. While unforeseen problems can always occur, leading to a default on a mortgage, participants in the mortgage market know that certain types of loans have a higher probability of going into default. Also, loss severity can vary depending on the loan category. It would be easy simply not to make those loans, but that could also seriously limit an originator's ability to generate product. Therefore, originators set up different underwriting criteria to compensate somewhat for the additional risk of default. The task for investors is then to look at what adjustments exist for currently known risk areas.

There are four common areas of concern: documentation type, loan purpose, property type, and occupancy type. The relevant issue first is how the originator compensates for these risk areas. The most common methods are limitations on loan size or maximum loan-to-value ratios.

For example, if we accept the fact that cash-out refinancing mortgages have historically shown a higher probability of default, one would expect the maximum allowed loan-to-value to be lower, say 75%, as opposed to general restrictions for other loan types that may go as high as 90% or 95%. Also, if the usual maximum loan size is $1 million, the maximum loan size for cash-out refinancing loans might be as low as $650,000. Besides establishing specific standards to minimize known risk factors, the underwriter should also have rules that limit the possibility of loans that have cross-over risk, such as including cash-out refinancing mortgages that are also limited documentation loans. This kind of cross-over would compound the likelihood of default on the loan.

Third, and perhaps most important when reviewing originators, is the basic issue of quality control. The key is whether the establishment of underwriting criteria is a dynamic process under constant review and evaluation. The better originators will have set procedures for reassessing their approach. Many will take a regular sample of their servicing portfolio and re-underwrite the loans, looking for trends in defaults or losses.

This will likely go as far as including another appraisal. If there is a material change in the appraised value, this will be deemed suspicious, especially if the original appraisal is relatively recent. The result could be a conclusion that a given appraiser is aggressive or unreliable, and therefore no longer qualified for that originator's loan underwriting.

As discussed earlier, originators will make certain loans, notwithstanding the fact that they are recognized as having higher risk characteristics. The originator's quality control policies should include an ongoing review of the actual default rate and loss severity of such loans. If the originator concludes that the numbers are higher than expected, this should lead to adjustments for allowed loan-to-value ratios and loan sizes.

For the conduits, the statistical analysis is also key to tracking discernible patterns for defaults coming from a given mortgage originator. If a given originator shows a higher than average default pattern, that should result in the originator being put on notice, or possibly being deleted from the approved pool of originators. Generally the conduit will first look to working with the originator to determine and correct any underwriting problems.

Since in most situations the originator is also servicer or master servicer, the originator's servicing capabilities and procedures should often also be a subject of discussion during due diligence. There are several areas to focus on, such as capacity and efficiency of the servicing operation. One simple approach to getting a quick read on this is to review in some detail the mechanics of the servicing operation, specifically the procedures in place for dealing with delinquencies. For example, how quickly does the servicer react to a delinquency to get payments flowing again?

Given the substantial growth of some servicing portfolios, capacity utilization and efficiency are important issues, just as in any service-intensive industry. Many servicing operations have turned increasingly to various levels of automation to improve the effectiveness of a given group of service representatives. Just as an added level of review, it can be informative to see how and where loan files are maintained, including how much is computerized.

THE COLLATERAL

To the extent an originator/servicer passes this kind of detailed review, analyzing individual pools of collateral becomes a much more mechanical exercise. The process of reviewing individual pool characteristics can result in a sea of statistics. The easier approach is to use any anomaly as a red flag warranting further review. While it might not be possible to correct the problem by changing the constitution of the pool, any investor should at least recognize, and presumably be compensated for, pools that carry higher risk components. There are several key points that require emphasis.

Loan Type

One overall factor to be considered is loan type. The mortgage market is dominated by basic 30-year fully amortizing fixed-rate mortgages. Using that as a benchmark, there are other loan types that have tended to show different performance characteristics. Fifteen-year mortgages, another basic product type, have proven to be higher-quality collateral over time. This is because a shorter term requires higher debt service requirements. Borrowers who choose this option are, therefore, higher-income individuals who can afford to make those payments. Also, the more rapid amortization of principal results in a faster build-up of book equity. It is also true that pools of 15-year mortgages tend to have lower loan-to-value ratios to begin with as these borrowers generally bring more equity to the transaction.

One key characteristic for both of the mortgage types is that they are fully amortizing. On the opposite extreme are balloon mortgages. While there are undoubtedly many reasons for borrowers choosing a balloon mortgage, one significant one is the inability to meet higher debt service requirements under a fully amortizing one. This lower level of financial flexibility, when combined with a slower amortization of principal, results in loans that are inherently riskier. Beyond the increased likelihood of default during the life of the loan, pools that include balloon mortgages also face the potential problems that may arise in refinancing the larger final payment. The borrower's ability to do so will depend on the actual size of the balloon, the direction of home values and interest rates during the interim, and changes in the borrower's creditworthiness.

One last major product type is adjustable-rate mortgages, or ARMs. The principal concern surrounding ARM products is the potential for "sticker shock" whenever the rate adjusts. This is particularly true with the first adjustment because the initial coupon is usually an especially low teaser rate offered to entice the borrower into choosing that option. There is also the possibility that in underwriting the loan, the originator used a lower initial debt service requirement to qualify the borrower, rather than one that is more realistic for the longer term. The risk of a substantial increase in debt service, and therefore the risk of default, however, exists whenever there is a rising interest rate environment.

Geographic Concentration

The one pool characteristic recently requiring the most attention is geographic concentration. Given the historical balance of originations, this has most often evolved into a question of California concentration. Since most whole loan packages consist almost exclusively of jumbo products, and California accounts for a very large percentage of jumbo loan originations, many pools have also been formed with exposures to California loans of 60% to 70%, and even higher. Notwithstanding the many arguments about the size and diversification of the California economy, that kind of pool concentration in most cases is imprudent.

Some have rationalized that if an investor's overall portfolio of mortgage securities is lighter in California exposure, say, 20% on average through all the individual pools, it should be possible to take a pool that is higher because the overall portfolio concentration is still low. Even though portfolio considerations are important, this logic is faulty, because the strength or weakness of one pool has no direct impact on other pools in the portfolio.

For the logic to prove out, a certain scenario would have to be true. When one pool, because of its higher California concentration experiences some difficulties, thus weakening or expending credit enhancement levels; and other pools, given their lower concentrations, maintain their credit enhancement levels or perhaps even experience improvements with loan prepayments; the first pool would have to be able to gain access to the latter's improved positions. This is, of course, not the case, since all pools are distinct legal entities with no direct link. An indirect link might occur in the marketplace to the extent that market prices for the lower concentration pools could improve at the same time that the market prices for the higher concentration pools deteriorate. This is not a very reliable link. An analogous argument is to believe that owning an IO and PO, but of different coupon collateral, represents a perfect interest rate hedge.

Unfortunately, even the most detailed and thorough economic analysis cannot fully substitute for simple diversification. Until it actually occurred, few believed that home values in California could decline as far as they did between 1990 and 1993. And if one were to rely heavily on historical experience, one would have expected defaults in California to be only a fraction of the national average. Defaults in 1993, in California, were much closer to, and in some areas of the state exceeded the national average.

This is not to say that California is the only state to be on the watch for in terms of heavy concentrations, although the focus inevitably moves there because the state accounts for so much of the jumbo loan originations in the United States. Any concentration in any one state is not wise because that pool is vulnerable to the specific economic circumstances of that state. Over time, we have also experienced varying levels of concern about the Northeast, especially Massachusetts and the tri-state area surrounding New York City. Also, lest we forget, one of the most oft-referred to disaster scenarios is, after all, the "Texas Scenario."

Geographic dispersion goes beyond just looking on a state-by-state basis. Further limitations are important since maintaining a 10% concentration maximum in California is good only to the extent that all those California loans are not located in the same zip code. A very large percentage of California's jumbo originations come in the Los Angeles area and its surrounding counties. Rules of thumb have thus evolved in terms of concentrations within individual five-digit zip code areas, three-digit zip code areas, and county concentrations. Economics notwithstanding, it is always good to know that a large percentage of a pool's loans are not within five miles of the most recent earthquake's epicenter.

One factor that has provided some limited relief on the California factor is the divergence between northern and southern California. While both are subject to the same state government influences, the size of the state and the differences in economic drivers mitigate higher California exposures with some north-south diversification.

Of some greater difficulty is looking at cross-border concentrations. Suppose a pool has 20% of its loans in Maryland and 20% of its loans in Virginia. A 20% limit might be deemed acceptable, but this profile would mean 40% between two neighboring states, plus whatever might be located in the District of Columbia. The combination is actually a relatively small geographic area. A more detailed look might also show that in fact all 40+% of the pool is located within a very narrow geographic corridor between northern Virginia and Baltimore.

This is not to say that some exceptions could not be found with more detailed analysis. It might be possible to be more comfortable with a pool that has a somewhat higher California concentration if one finds that the loans in California were underwritten to tighter standards. Beginning in 1992, many originators in fact began to hold California underwriting to tighter standards, either by management focus or outright policy. If we could break down a pool between California loans and non-California loans, this differential might become readily apparent. In one pool, for example, we might be willing to go somewhat higher if the California loans had generally lower loan-to-value ratios, especially if the differential between the California loans and the pool in general increased with increasing loan sizes. There might also be greater comfort if a larger percentage of the California loans fell into the more attractive categories of single-family detached, owner-occupied, primary residence, rate/term refinancing mortgages with full documentation packages.

Other Collateral Characteristics

Geographic dispersion is not the only area that requires detailed analysis. Other collateral characteristics warrant careful review. These include documentation type, loan purpose, property type, and occupancy type.

Documentation Type: In documentation type, a significant difference generally exists between full documentation and different limited documentation programs. A full documentation package includes a significant amount of paperwork, verifying data that the borrower has supplied about employment history, income levels, and net worth. When an originator agrees to omit some of this documentation, the potential exists that not everything is as it appears.

There are times when some amount of flexibility in documentation requirements is warranted and does not materially change the risk profile. A simple example is requiring written employment verification from someone who is self-employed.

The one form of documentation that has proven to be critical in complete underwriting is asset verification. Most will agree that having invested a substantial amount of real equity in a home is one of the prime deterrents to borrower default. To be comfortable that some amount is actually being invested by the borrower, even if the loan includes a relatively high loan-to-value ratio, originators check to see that the borrower actually had assets equal to the downpayment for at least some period of time prior to closing. This avoids late discovery that the borrower also borrowed the down payment. In that case, not only does the borrower have little or no equity invested in the property, the debt-to-income ratio is also higher, further increasing the risk of default.

Whenever written asset verification, or some other important documentation is omitted, the loan is referred to as a limited or low documentation loan. Limited documentation loans have historically shown higher incidences of default, although the differential from full documentation loans tends to vary with the originator. This is because some originators focus on other forms of verification, at least on an oral basis to compensate for the missing documentation. When verification of facts is completed through other written means, and there is at least written asset verification, loans are categorized as alternative documentation loans. An example would be accepting W-2 forms in lieu of tax returns. Generally, alternative documentation loans are seen as performing the same as full documentation loans.

Loan Purpose: Concern about default also varies substantially depending on loan purpose. In most situations, there are only three basic categories: cash-out, or equity refinancing mortgages, rate/term refinancing mortgages, and loans to fund actual purchase of a home.

Cash-out loans are seen as much riskier than purchase loans or rate/term refinancing mortgages. A cash-out loan is in direct conflict with a prime deterrent of default. Rather than putting real equity into a home, the borrower is taking out equity. The risks of a cash-out refinancing mortgage are especially pronounced when the borrower is self-employed. Often this could mean the borrower is starting a new business, trying to expand an existing business (both risky), or trying to shore up a failing business.

While the riskier nature of cash-out refinancing loans seems readily apparent, the differential between purchase and rate/term refinancing loans is less distinct. In a rate/term refinancing transaction, the borrower can be accomplishing any one of a number of goals. The borrower could be reducing the remaining term of the loan from a 30-year to a 15-year mortgage. This will result in an accelerated amortization of the loan, thereby increasing the book equity and reducing the loan-to-value ratio. The borrower could also be keeping the same term but reducing the interest rate and therefore the monthly debt service requirements. The reduced cash requirement should mean additional financial flexibility for the borrower, therefore reducing the chances of running into cash flow problems. It also could enable the borrower to prepay a portion of the loan with the extra cash, again reducing the loan-to-value ratio at an accelerated pace. The one counterweight to these positive traits is that the appraised value in this case is not based on an arm's-length transaction, but will depend solely on comparables.

Property Type: While other factors are seen as more significant drivers for default rates on a pool, one other characteristic that can have a significant impact on recoveries when defaults do occur is property type. Property types can be broken down into very detailed categories. Generally the type recognized as cleanest is single-family detached housing. These loans are considered more desirable because they are somewhat easier to realize value on and are also less subject to loss in value due to external factors.

Second on the list is residences that are part of planned unit developments, but for which the common or shared facilities are considered de minimis. An example of not de minimis common facilities would be a golf course.

In this case, the value of the residence itself is heavily dependent on the attraction of the golf course.

Miscellaneous other types are: two- to four-family homes, townhouses, condominiums, and coops. Of these, coops are considered the worst because the asset is not actually real estate, but a share ownership. There is more volatility in values for these latter categories. Loss severity can also be somewhat higher because more time may be required for resale after foreclosure, especially in a weak real estate market. During this time the servicer will in most cases advance interest on the remaining principal amount, but the servicer will then have priority for recovery of these advances from the proceeds of liquidation, thereby increasing the loss on principal to the pool.

Occupancy Type: Most properties can be defined as primary residence, secondary residence (or vacation home), or an investor-owned property. Given the overriding desire to maintain one's home, there is no question that the best occupancy type is primary residence. Vacation homes and investor-owned properties where the owner does not occupy the property for most of the year, if at all, can create difficulties because the borrower can more easily rationalize walking away from the property.

Loan-to-Value and Loan Size

Throughout the discussion of important factors that drive default rates, there has been one recurring theme — loan-to-value. This, in conjunction with loan size, is the simplest aspect of collateral analysis because these are simple numbers with little room for judgment. There is little disagreement that loan-to-value is a prime determinant of default risk. There are two reasons for this. First, a large equity investment represents a substantial incentive to continue one's mortgage payments. Second, to the extent an income problem does arise, a lower loan-to-value provides significant cushion for either the borrower or the servicer to sell the home at a price sufficient to cover the remaining principal outstanding.

For these reasons, a key consideration in any mortgage pool is the weighted average loan-to-value and the number of loans with loan-to-value ratios greater than 80%. Most pools of 30-year mortgages have weighted average loan-to-value ratios between 70% and 75%. Most pools of 15-year mortgages have weighted average loan-to-value ratios between 65% and 70%. Any pool higher than the norm should then be considered somewhat riskier.

More difficult is the extent to which the pool consists of some very low loan-to-value mortgages and some very high loan-to-value mortgages, resulting in a normal weighted average. The situation is slightly muddied by the fact that most loans with loan-to-value ratios in excess of 80% are insured down to 75% by primary mortgage insurance. While these loans are a theoretical equivalent to a 75% loan-to-value, their likelihood of default will not be driven by the existence of insurance. Therefore, investors need to decide on how comfortable they can be relying on insurers on which little if any analysis has been done.

To the extent that analyzing loan-to-value ratios is relatively straight-forward, the question of loan size is also not very complicated. The simplest aspect of this factor is that the smaller the loans in a given pool, the greater the diversification for the given pool size. Larger loans, to the extent they become delinquent, will have a proportionately greater impact on the health of the overall pool. Generally speaking, higher-priced homes also tend to experience greater price volatility during cyclical swings in real estate values. The risk is also markedly greater when the price of the home is significantly above the median price for homes in the geographic area. In that case the resale process is almost certain to take significantly longer, and the likelihood of needing to accept a price that is closer to the median at resale is high.

Seasoning

One factor that can be used, on occasion, to offset some of the risk factors discussed is seasoning of the loans in the pool. The greatest likelihood of default is generally viewed to be in the early years of the loan, more specifically in years two through six. Few borrowers will default in the first twelve months of a loan. Also, after the first few years, default frequency tends to decline rapidly. This phenomenon has several explanations. The most important is the build up of book equity in the home through amortization of principal. When borrowers have more invested in the home and have more flexibility in the selling price they can accept because of their lower mortgage balance, it would be unusual for a problem to arise. A more intangible factor is the increased emotional commitment to the home.

Relying on seasoning can, however, be dangerous. To the extent an investor is considering a more seasoned pool, or a new pool that includes some more seasoned products, it is important to review in greater detail where and when those mortgages were originated. One may find that the loans were made at the peak of the market, and that home values in the area have dropped dramatically since then. This would clearly offset many of the perceived benefits of seasoning. It could also prove important to analyze the timing of the originations with changes in the originator's underwriting criteria since many originators go through cycles where underwriting standards are loosened or tightened to meet certain management objectives.

SUMMARY AND CONCLUSION

The two questions of availability of information and actual benefits that can be realized inevitably must be dealt with. As to the latter issue, the potential benefits are clearly much greater for the lower rated classes in the typical senior-subordinate structure. Assuming subordination levels stay relatively robust, this level of detail has only limited value to the AAA investor. It can have some impact on potential resale prices, but only in the extreme case of an unusually constituted package will a pool actually sustain losses sufficient to impair the senior class. This may happen when there are extremely heavy state concentrations or very high levels of limited documentation loans when originators chased after market share and pure production to sustain growth in overhead.

The analysis is much more important for the subordinate classes. Especially in the early years of a pool, it does not take much in the way of delinquencies and foreclosures for stop-loss levels to be triggered. The blockage of payments, even on a temporary basis, can have a significant impact on realized yield. Further, with the very thin layers of subordination, any concentrated problem can very quickly eliminate supporting securities through allocation of actual losses in the pool.

The only way investors have of limiting this potential, since it cannot be completely eliminated, is to focus on quality of the mortgage underwriting and quality of the collateral. Alternatively, if investors are prepared to take those risks, they should be in a position to look for higher potential returns.

As to the amount of effort required, let alone the ability to access information, much of the work on originators can be done up-front in anticipation of future investment opportunities. A substantial amount can be turned into a formulaic exercise. Only where there have been substantial changes in underwriting approaches at a given originator does the process become more time-consuming.

A good collateral summary on a specific pool from a dealer will also answer the majority of questions about the characteristics of the pool, at least enough to reveal anomalies requiring further analysis. Therefore while the detail can seem daunting at first, the credit analysis side of the mortgage market is nothing that a good fundamental analyst cannot handle.

CHAPTER 9

Evaluating Subordinate Mortgage-Backed Securities

Mary Sue Lundy
Senior Vice President
Fitch Investors Service, Inc.

The author would like to thank Greg Raab, Peter Cardinale, and Byron Klapper for their assistance and helpful comments.

With the onset of the 1990s, an evolution reshaped the speculative-grade, private-label mortgage-backed securities market. The use of pool policies as credit enhancement has lessened. Replacing it as a measure of investor protection is the senior/subordinate structure.

In 1993, over 80% of private-label transactions used this dual structure, up from 48% the previous year. Pool policies, by contrast, declined, accounting for just over 10% of new-issue volume that year.[1]

Use of the senior-subordinate structure to replace pool policies is the result of three concurrent market forces. First, pool insurers raised prices on pool policies to reduce their concentration in Southern California. Second, liquidity improved in the market for subordinate securities. Third, investors were attracted by the higher yields obtainable from subordinate mortgage-backed securities.

In response, issuers began to segment subordinate securities based on credit risk and to seek ratings on the individual subordinate tranches. Because ratings on non-investment grade securities (BB, B, CCC) are sensitive to moderate declines in current economic conditions, it is not appropriate for rating agencies to use a "worst case" scenario analysis, designed to stress high investment-grade securities. Instead, more realistic stress scenarios need to be developed to reflect the impact of current and expected regional economic changes on residential housing market performance.

The ability to forecast and use economic trends to project regional foreclosure rates and market value trends represents a significant advance in analyzing subordinate mortgage-backed securities. Credit enhancement levels should account for the expected economic activity as well as the potential volatility of the various regions.

Fitch recently introduced new rating criteria based on an evaluation of economic volatility/stability in 43 regions and its potential impact on future foreclosure rates and market values. This chapter outlines the rating methodology for calculating the required loss protection for non-investment-grade mortgage-backed securities.

REGIONAL APPROACH TO MORTGAGE ANALYSIS

Mortgage performance varies across the country. Foreclosure rates may be rising in Southern California, while declining in Atlanta. Chicago's economy reacts differently to changes in unemployment than does Houston's. New England's housing demand can't be relied upon to predict the

---

[1] "Conduits, Mortgage Companies and Senior/Sub Structure Dominate Private-Label MBS Market in 1993," *Inside Mortgage Securities* (January 28, 1994), pp. 3-5.

direction of single-family home prices in Florida. Only recently have analysts begun to take these factors into account in assessing mortgage-backed securities.

The evaluation of subordinate mortgage-backed securities requires criteria that recognize how moderate changes in regional economic performance affect mortgage performance. This has been achieved by Fitch's development of a series of econometric models in conjunction with the WEFA Group.

Fitch's approach segments the U.S. into 43 distinct metropolitan, state and multi-state regions. This segmentation reflects the similarity of the underlying economies, the geographic proximity of the regions to each other, and the geographic distribution of the jumbo mortgage market, where the demand for mortgage-backed securities ratings are the greatest.

The econometric models project foreclosure rates and housing prices in each of the 43 regions. The models are based on a series of statistical analyses that determine the current and historical correlation of foreclosure rates and market value trends with six key regional economic indexes. They are: (1) unemployment rate; (2) employment growth rate; (3) personal income growth; (4) housing starts; (5) sales of existing homes; and (6) number of households (as a measure of demand for housing). The unique combination of these indicators in each region provides the foundation for forecasting foreclosure risk and changes in housing values, which in turn drive credit loss projections.

FORECLOSURE RATES

Fitch's research concludes that one of the primary determinants of foreclosures is the unemployment rate. Unemployment results in a serious disruption of personal income and few households can continue to make mortgage payments after a primary income provider becomes unemployed.

If a borrower begins to have financial difficulties in a healthy housing market, the home can be sold, avoiding foreclosure proceedings. If, on the other hand, the housing market is declining, the borrower is more likely to default. Foreclosure risk is compounded for borrowers with high loan-to-value ratios (or nominal down payments), since these borrowers have little or no equity, offering little incentive not to default.

A measure of market depth, home sales per household, is also included in the foreclosure models. Even if some current equity is retained, an owner may still be subject to foreclosure if a willing buyer cannot be found quickly enough.

Some of the regional models include a measure of labor market depth, employment per household, further capturing the effects of local economic opportunity. A family that requires the income from both spouses is particularly susceptible to defaulting if one or both wage earners is suddenly unemployed.

HOME PRICES

The unemployment rate is one of the primary drivers behind single-family home prices. As unemployment increases in a region, indicating economic distress, after a lag of roughly one to three quarters, single-family home prices tend to decline. Home sales per household, a measure of market depth, personal income per household as a measure of savings, and total employment as a measure of labor market depth all determine the effect an increase in unemployment will have on home prices.

STRESS SCENARIOS

Once the relationship of the economic drivers to foreclosure rates and single-family home prices is determined, projections based on progressively more pessimistic scenarios are developed. For each region, historical volatility of each of the underlying economic drivers is analyzed by calculating the standard deviation from the trend for each variable over the past two decades.

The stress scenarios are developed by increasing the pressure on the underlying economic drivers by one, one and one-half, and two standard deviations over eight quarters, held at that level for four quarters, and then gradually returning to the base case. The change in the underlying economic drivers and their relationship to foreclosures and home prices for each region determines the potential impact on each region's real estate market.

Forecasts are quarterly over a five-year period, with each forecast updated as new economic data become available. The five-year window is consistent with the historical peak default period for residential mortgage loans. Estimates are also made to capture potential foreclosures after the five-year period.

This methodology offers a consistent approach across regions, enabling comparability of pessimistic scenarios. It does not assume one scenario for the U.S., but was developed with the recognition that each region reacts to different macro stimuli, and therefore will respond differently depending on local economic conditions.

Exhibit 1: Houston Foreclosure Rate Forecast

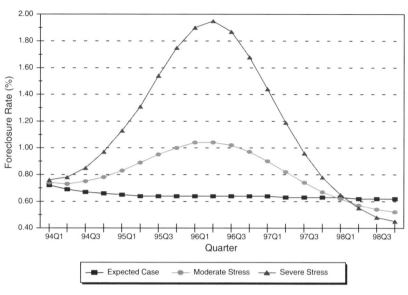

As a result, foreclosure rates and single-family home prices in histori-cally volatile regions, whether up or down, exhibit large changes under the various stress scenarios, while well-diversified regions exhibit relatively little change. This is highlighted in Exhibits 1 and 2. Exhibit 1 indicates the baseline forecast of foreclosure rates, as well as one and two standard deviations from the baseline for Houston, while Exhibit 2 depicts the same for Chicago.

Examining unemployment (Exhibits 3 and 4), it is apparent that, although both regions have similar unemployment rates under the same stress scenarios, the foreclosure rates for each region diverge dramatically. This attests to the diversification of Chicago's economy relative to Houston's.

LOAN-BY-LOAN ANALYSIS

The rate of foreclosure and loss severity vary with the individual character-istics of mortgage loans. Key factors impacting performance are: the sea-soning of mortgage loans relative to the historical default period, the loan's original loan-to-value ratio, the loan purpose, occupancy, documentation, and loan type.

Historically, borrowers do not default within the early years of the loan. This reflects prudent underwriting standards that ensure that borrowers generally have adequate savings to see them through. Foreclosures histori-cally increase in the second and third years, peak in the fourth year, and then tail off over the fifth and sixth years.

Exhibit 2: Chicago Foreclosure Rate Forecast

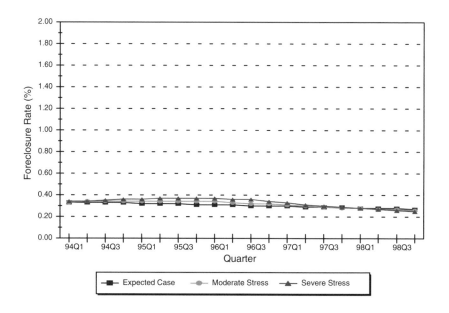

Exhibit 3: Houston Unemployment Rate Forecast

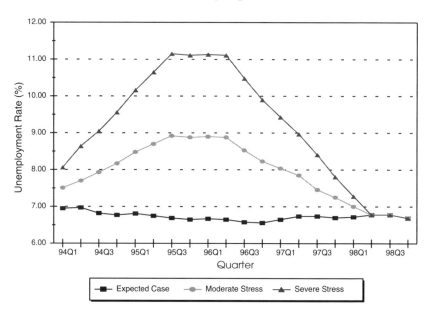

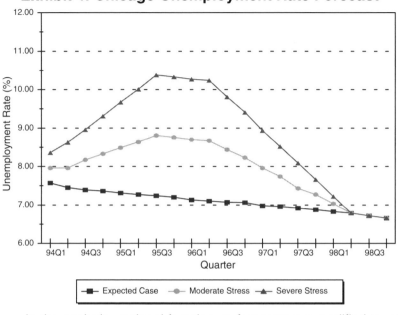

Exhibit 4: Chicago Unemployment Rate Forecast

Legend: ■ Expected Case ● Moderate Stress ▲ Severe Stress

In the analysis, regional foreclosure forecasts are modified to reflect the age of each mortgage loan. For a new mortgage, the forecast is adjusted to reflect the increasing probability of foreclosure up to the fourth year. For a seasoned loan, the foreclosure rate curve will shift based upon the age of the loan. A one-year seasoned loan, for example, will enter the peak foreclosure period in three years, while a two-year seasoned loan will peak in two years.

Foreclosure forecasts are also modified to reflect the loan's original loan-to-value ratio, loan coupon, occupancy, documentation, and loan type. In addition, if the loan is seasoned, the original appraised value is adjusted to reflect any change in home price between origination of the loan and the time the security is issued. Any decline in value will directly reduce the original appraised value, while price appreciation is discounted by 50%.

The home price forecast is adjusted for loans on properties other than single-family residences, including condominiums and townhomes, as well as for homes larger than those represented by the median home price. Non-single-family detached homes as well as large homes have historically suffered larger market value declines in deteriorating markets.

The loss severity, assuming the borrower defaults, is equal to the quarterly home price forecast less 15% in foreclosure costs, 10% in carrying costs (principal and interest advanced by the servicer while the borrower is delinquent), and a quick sale penalty of 12.5%, reflecting that less money is typically realized on a distress sale. Any recoveries due to claims under a primary mortgage insurance policy will be added to the recovery amount.

Exhibit 5: Expected Losses

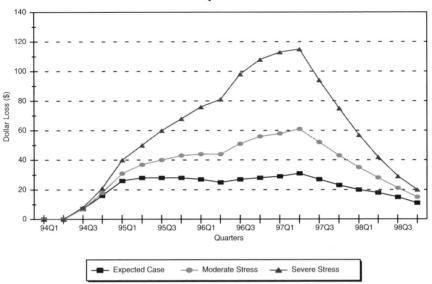

The total credit enhancement is the foreclosure percentage (a measure of the probability that the loan will default) per quarter multiplied by the quarterly loss severity, summed over a five-year period plus an estimate of losses anticipated to occur after the five year period. This number is calculated for each loan in a pool and then summed to attain the total credit enhancement needed.

The expected or baseline forecast approximates the CCC rating level while the mild and severe stress scenarios approximate the B and BB rating levels, respectively.

Exhibit 5 shows the expected loss per quarter for a newly-originated loan secured by a property in San Francisco with an original loan-to-value ratio of 80% (0.371) as well as the loss under mild (0.61%) and severe (1.03%) stress scenarios. All credit enhancement levels are further adjusted to account for origination and servicing practices of the individual issuers.

CHAPTER 10

Evaluating Residential Subordinated Tranches

John N. Dunlevy, CFA, CPA
Director and Senior Portfolio Manager
Hyperion Capital Management

INTRODUCTION

The senior/subordinated structure is now the most popular type of credit enhancement in whole-loan CMOs. According to *Inside Mortgage Securities,* the market share of the senior/subordinated structure rose from 51% in 1992 to 83% by the end of 1993.

Issuers have favored the senior/subordinated structure both because of its improved execution levels and investor concerns about other types of credit enhancement. Third-party credit enhancement, such as corporate guarantees, letters of credit, and pool policies, have fallen into disfavor due to concerns over downgrades and the general shortage of AAA credit enhancement providers.

Investors have been increasingly drawn to residential subordinated structures for several reasons:

- Yield advantages versus comparably rated corporates.
- Excellent mortgage credit story.
- Improving structural protection.
- Excellent call protection with limited extension risk.

In this chapter, we evaluate four important factors to consider when evaluating subordinated securities. First, we discuss approaches to performing collateral analysis. Second, we discuss structural analysis. Next, we show some common methods of stress testing. Finally, other factors such as special hazard, bankruptcy, and fraud risk are analyzed.

COLLATERAL ANALYSIS

The first step in determining the relative value of investing in subordinated tranches is a detailed analysis of the deal's collateral. The collateral represents the raw material from which the deal's final structure is produced. In a typical deal, the collateral might consist of 100 to 400 loans, while for a Re-REMIC structure (a structure created by using tranches from previous deals as collateral) the number of loans constituting the collateral pool could be 1,000 to 5,000. Regardless of the complexity of the structure or the number of loans involved, the steps involved in a collateral analysis are similar.

Risk Factors

The factors to examine during a review of a deal's collateral include:

- Loan type: (fixed/adjustable).
- Loan-to-value ratio.
- Property type: (single-family, condominium).
- Loan purpose: (purchase, refinancing, equity-take out).
- Loan term: (30-year, 15-year).

- Geographic diversification.
- Seasoning of loans.
- Occupancy status.

Because many of these factors are discussed elsewhere in this book, we highlight only some important features for analyzing subordinated tranches.

Historical analysis of static-pool data has shown that fixed-rate collateral is considerably safer than adjustable-rate mortgage (ARM) collateral. Hence, the subordinated market for deals backed by ARMs is still largely undeveloped. Therefore, this chapter's discussion focuses on fixed-rate mortgages.

A key variable in any analysis of mortgage loans is loan-to-value (LTV). This ratio provides important information about a borrower's credit quality and net equity in a property. When analyzing a disk or tape of loan pool information what is particularly important is the pool's dispersion of LTV, not its weighted average LTV. Further, it is important to know the issuer's policy on pool insurance coverage for loans in excess of 80% LTV.

Another variable to examine is the percent of a pool that does not represent single-family detached homes. Single-family homes as the largest and most desirable segment of the housing market and have historically shown the best resale performance. Condominiums, townhouses, and planned unit developments do not enjoy the same record of relative price stability.

Loan purpose is another category that should be carefully examined. A potential investor should closely examine the exposure, number of loans, and individual LTVs associated with equity-take out loans (also called cash-out refis). The main risk associated with these loans is that the loan may be initiated to increase a borrower's leverage. This can be problematic particularly since no market transaction is evident to confirm market value; that is, these loans are made solely on the basis of an appraisal.

Loan term is another important segment in collateral analysis. Currently, however, most pools backed by 15-year mortgages are separated from those backed by 30-year mortgages. This is the case because 15-year mortgages amortize much faster than 30-year loans, and therefore present less risk due to rapidly declining LTVs. As shown in Exhibit 1, the LTV ratio is considerably different over time for these two mortgage terms.

A final important consideration is geographic diversification. Pools with the lowest level of default risk have consisted of mortgages distributed over a wide geographic area. Many investors have become particularly concerned about their levels of California exposure. This actual level of exposure should be further divided into a pool's exposure to northern and southern California. Many investors analyze a pool's exposure by zip code and overlay these zip codes by California region or county. Within California, as in the rest of the country, geographic diversification limits risk. Recent estimates show that between 50% and 60% of all non-agency borrowers are in California.

Exhibit 1: Loan Balance, Market Value, and LTV Ratio for 30-year and 15-year Mortgages for Selected Years*

	30 Year			15 Year		
	Year 0	Year 3	Year 7	Year 0	Year 3	Year 7
Loan Balance	240,000	237,003	231,677	240,000	215,080	170,786
Market Value	300,000	300,000	300,000	300,000	300,000	300,000
LTV Ratio	80.0%	79.0%	77.2%	80.0%	71.7%	56.9%

* Assumes an 8% mortgage rate, full amortization, and 0% housing inflation.

Issuer Analysis

Another important consideration in analyzing collateral risk is the credit risk originating with the issuer and servicer. In this analysis we focus on the following factors:

Issuer	Servicer
• Underwriting guidelines.	• Written policies.
• Credit approval.	• Cash management/systems.
• Quality control.	• Collection procedures.
• PMI Policies.	• Property management record.
• Delinquency/loss history.	• Historical track record.
	• Financial strength.

In our discussion, we focus only on the factors that are particularly important in the analysis of subordinated tranches.

Exhibit 2 highlights the industry's largest non-agency MBS issuers. Of particular importance are the issuers underwriting guidelines and delinquency/loss history and the servicer's ROE and collection record. In terms of underwriting guidelines, we think that full documentation or alternative documentation (when underwritten by a reputable originator/issuer) should be emphasized. Limited and no documentation loans have consistently shown a record of higher delinquencies and realized losses. Full documentation originations should fulfill the following criteria:

- Independent property appraisal.
- Credit check.
- Verification of income (VOI).
- Verification of deposit (VOD).
- Verification of employment (VOE).

Exhibit 2: Largest NonAgency MBS Issuers ($Billions)

Rank	Issuer	1993	1992
1.	Prudential Home	$27.2	$16.9
2.	Residential Funding	13.0	11.9
3.	GE Mortgage Cap.	8.0	2.9
4.	Ryland/Saxon	7.4	6.5
5.	Countrywide	6.2	0.0
6.	Chase Mortgage	4.8	5.6
7.	Citicorp/Citibank	4.3	5.8
8.	Capstead	3.4	4.4
9.	Bear Stearns	2.9	1.1
10.	Securitized Asset Sales	2.5	0.0
	Others	18.8	34.4
Total		98.5	89.5

Source: Inside Mortgage Securities

Another factor to consider is the issuer's policy on *compensating interest*. Mortgage borrowers are required to make mortgage interest payments in arrears for the number of days that the mortgage is outstanding in the previous accrual period (1 month). Scheduled mortgage payments thus include 30 days' interest on the previous month's balance. However, when mortgagors fully prepay a mortgage, they are required only to pay interest on the number of days the loan was outstanding, not for the entire accrual period. The lender/servicer therefore receives less interest than was scheduled, creating an *interest shortfall*. In a CMO structure, interest shortfalls are allocated pro rata among the different classes. Some issuers do, however, reimburse investors for this shortfall, by paying compensating interest. Exhibit 3 shows the policies that apply among the larger issuers.

The value of this compensating interest will vary with the position of a bond class within a CMO structure and the degree of prepayments experienced by the collateral pool. Compensating interest is discussed more fully in the structural analysis section of this chapter and in Chapter 3.

Rating Agency Analysis

The rating agencies determine the appropriate amount of credit enhancement for a given pool of collateral. For example, Standard & Poor's (S&P) developed its rating standards through analysis of the Great Depression of the 1930s and the regional recessions of the 1980s (such as in Houston, Texas). S&P's prime pool loss coverage statistics are shown in Exhibit 4. Exhibit 5 lists the criteria for a prime pool.

Exhibit 3: Compensating Interest Policies of the Larger Issuers

Issuer	1993 Rank	Pay Compensating?
Prudential Home	1	Yes
Residential Funding	2	No
GE Mortgage	3	No
Ryland/Saxon	4	Yes
Countrywide	5	Yes
Chase Mortgage	6	Yes
Citicorp/Citibank	7	Yes
Capstead	8	Yes

Exhibit 4: Standard & Poor's Prime Loss Coverage Statistics

Rating	Foreclosure Frequency	Market Value Decline	Loss Severity	Loss Coverage
AAA	15%	37%	47%	7.0%
AA	10%	32%	40%	4.0%
A	8%	28%	35%	2.8%

Exhibit 5: Criteria for a Prime Pool

300 or more loans
Geographically diverse
First lien
Single-family detached
Purchase mortgage
30-year term
Fully amortizing
Fixed rate
Full documentation
Owner occupied
80% LTV
Balances less than $300,000

Exhibit 6: Impact of LTVs on Base Loss Coverage for an AA Rating

LTV	Frequency Foreclosure	Severity Loss	Coverage Base Loss
50%	10%	0%	0.0%
60%	10%	12%	1.2%
70%	10%	28%	2.8%
80%	10%	40%	4.0%
90%	15%	29%[*]	4.4%
95%	30%	37%[*]	11.1%

[*]Assumes loans over 80% LTV are covered by Private Mortgage Insurance (PMI).

Source: Standard & Poor's

Application of an AA prime pool rating criteria is shown below:

Home price		300,000
Loan balance (80% LTV)	240,000	
Market value decline (32%)		-96,000
Market value at foreclosure	204,000	204,000
Loss at time of foreclosure	36,000	
Foreclosure costs (25% of loan)	60,000	
Loss	96,000	

Loss severity (96,000/240,000)	40%
Foreclosure frequency	10%
Loss coverage required ($40\% \times 10\%$)	4%

The credit enhancement levels shown above are for "prime pools" as defined in Exhibit 5. Adjustments are made to the prime pool loss coverage for a variety of factors. First, the pool's loan-to-value ratios will impact a pool's loss coverage significantly. For example, assuming an AA rating is still desired, LTVs will impact base loss coverage ratios shown in Exhibit 6. Further, once an AA-level of credit enhancement is determined, S&P then scales the base loss coverage up or down depending on the desired rating level as shown in Exhibit 7. In addition to LTV adjustments, a variety of adjustments are made from the prime pool loss coverage levels to adjust for documentation standards, geographic concentration risk, property values, and occupancy status.

Finally, rating approaches vary by agency. Moody's philosophy is that ratings on mortgage securities are comparable to other types of securities (i.e., corporate and municipal bonds). Therefore, from extensive analysis of bonds that it has rated, it determines expected credit losses in terms of yield impairment within each rating level. Fitch's approach is similar to S&P's, except Fitch places more emphasis on regional economics. Duff & Phelps, the newest entry in this market, has a rating philosophy most similar to Moody's

Exhibit 7: S&P's Adjustments to Base Loss Coverage

Rating	Factor Adjustment
AAA	AA Level × 1.75
AA	Established by model
A	AA Level ÷ 1.42
BBB	AA Level ÷ 2.00
BB	BBB Level ÷ 2.00
B	BB Level ÷ 2.00
NR	Sized to cover expected losses.

STRUCTURAL ANALYSIS

Structural analysis involves an assessment of the type of senior/subordinated structure, class tranching, methods of allocating losses, deal triggers, clean-up calls, and compensating interest.

Shifting Interest Structure

A number of variations on the senior/subordinated structure have been employed since the late 1980s, but the most popular structure is the *shifting interest mechanism*. The subordinated classes are designed to increase as a percentage of the total outstanding principal (during the early years of the transaction) and to lend additional credit support for the senior tranches.

In shifting interest structures, amortization and interest are allocated pro rata among all the deal's classes. Prepayments that would normally be allocated to the subordinated tranches are shifted to the senior tranches for a period of time. This is illustrated in Exhibit 8.

For example, for an initial period of five years, 100% of all prepayments on the mortgage pool are allocated to the senior tranches. After the initial prepayment lockout period, a smaller percentage of the pro-rata share of the subordinated tranche's prepayment is paid to the senior classes. A typical shifting interest structure is given in Exhibit 9.

In a shifting interest structure, the junior class has a claim not on a particular amount of class flow, but on a portion of the underlying assets. Realized losses act to reduce the lowest rated subordinated tranche outstanding, on a dollar for dollar basis. Hence, the *first-loss tranche* (also called the *unrated tranche*) will be reduced by losses until its principal balance is exhausted, then the next highest rated tranche will absorb losses, and so on.

Exhibit 8: Shifting Interest Structure

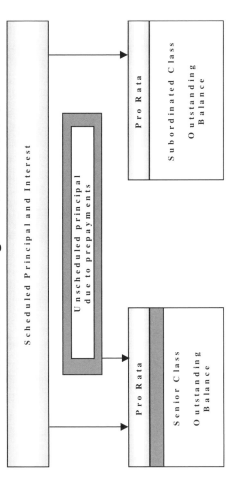

Exhibit 9: Typical Shifting Interest Mechanism Allocation of Cash Flows

	To Subordinated Tranches			To Senior Tranches			
Year	Pro Rata Interest (%)	Pro Rata Scheduled Principal (%)	Pro Rata Prepayment (%)	Pro Rata Interest (%)	Pro Rata Scheduled Principal (%)	Pro Rata Prepayment (%)	Additional Prepayment
1 through 5	100	100	0	100	100	100 +	100% of Sub.'s Share
6	100	100	30	100	100	100 +	70% of Sub.'s Share
7	100	100	40	100	100	100 +	60% of Sub.'s Share
8	100	100	60	100	100	100 +	40% of Sub.'s Share
9	100	100	80	100	100	100 +	20% of Sub.'s Share
10 and up	100	100	100	100	100	100 +	0% of Sub.'s Share

Class Tranching

Originators/issuers often sell their subordinated cash flows to Wall Street dealers on a competitive basis. Therefore, the issuer is not always sure how a dealer will end up structuring a pool's cash flows. Further, the subordinated cash flow are often sold separately from a pool's senior (AAA-rated) cash flows. A typical senior/subordinated structure will often look like that shown in Exhibit 10.

The dealer may consider whether to create a multi-tranche structure as shown in Exhibit 10 or the single-tranche "Moody's Structure." Exhibit 11 shows some of the information needed to create the single-tranche "Moody's Structure." In the example given in Exhibit 10, the dealer would have better execution using this Moody's structure.

The broker/dealer most often chooses the structure which will provide the best all-in execution. Dealers will sometimes go with the higher cost execution when there is a higher probability of successfully selling the B-pieces tranches.

It should be pointed out that the BBB bond in the multi-tranche structure is a very different bond from the Baa3 bond created in the Moody's structure. The single-tranche Moody's structures have been controversial since their introduction in 1993. Many investors argue that the Moody's structure is not of high enough credit quality to deserve the Baa3 rating since there is little protection (only the first loss tranche is subordinated in the structure) against a loss of principal.

For example, in the illustration in Exhibit 10, the BBB in the multi-tranche structure is supported by 2.00% of the structure, while the Moody's structure is protected by only 0.60%. Advocates of the Moody's structure argue that although the risk of loss is higher, it can withstand a higher degree of losses because its size (5.5%) is substantially larger than the multi-tranche structure (BBB is 0.60% of deal). An example is given in Exhibit 12.

Methods of Allocating Losses

Losses within a senior/subordinated structure are absorbed by the most junior tranche, although the timing and allocation of cash flow can vary within a deal structure. There are two traditional methods of allocating losses within a senior/subordinated structure: (1) the waterfall method, and (2) the direct write-off method. Exhibit 13 highlights the differences between these two methods.

Several distinctions should be made between the two methods. First, under the waterfall method, multi-tranche subordinated structures can be adversely affected with the accrual of interest payments.

Exhibit 10: A Typical Senior/Subordinated Structure

		Securities/Rating	Class size	Cushion provided by classes below
Pool of mortgage loans		Senior class (AAA/AA rated)	94.0%	6.0%
		B AA	2.0%	4.0%
		C A	1.0	3.0
	Junior classes	D BBB	1.0	2.0
		E BB	1.0	1.0
		F B	0.5	0.5
		G NR	0.5	0.0

Exhibit 11: Information for Determining Multi-Tranche or Single-Tranche Moody's Structure

Multi-Tranche Structure			Single-Tranche Moody's Structure		
Rating	Size	10-Year Spread	Rating	1Size	10-Year Spread
AA	8,333	135			
A	4,167	155			
BBB	4,167	195	Baa3	22,500	195
BB	4,167	425			
B	2,083	525			
NR	2,083	1,850	NR	2,500	1,850
	25,000	372		25,000	361

Exhibit 12: Comparison of Two BBB Bonds

Multi-Tranche Structure

Loss%	% Deal	Level of Subordination%	% Tranche Remaining
0.0	0.6	2.0	100.0
1.0	0.6	2.0	100.0
1.5	0.6	2.0	100.0
2.0	0.6	2.0	100.0
2.5	0.6	2.0	22.3

Single-Tranche Moody's Structure

Loss%	% Deal	Level of Subordination%	% Tranche Remaining
0.0	4.0	0.5	100.0
1.0	4.0	0.5	88.8
1.5	4.0	0.5	76.3
2.0	4.0	0.5	63.7
2.5	4.0	0.5	51.1

Source: Hyperion Capital Management

Exhibit 13: Comparison of Waterfall and Direct Write-Off Methods

Example		Month 1	
Collateral:	$200,000,000	Interest	$1,333,333
90% Senior:	180,000,000	Scheduled principal	200,000
5% Mezzanine	10,000,000	Prepayments	800,000
5% Subordinated	10,000,000	Recovery	100,000
8% Coupon		Total	2,433,333
		Realized Losses	150,000
		Reduction Mortgage Balance	1,250,000

Senior Bonds		
	Waterfall Method	Direct write-off Method
Interest	$1,200,000	$1,200,000
Scheduled Principal	180,000	180,000
Prepayments	800,000	800,000
Recovery	90,000	100,000
Unrecovered Senior	135,000	0
Total	2,405,000	2,280,000
Beginning Balance	180,000,000	180,000,000
Ending Balance	178,795,000	178,920,000
Change in Balance	-1,205,000	-1,080,000

Mezzanine Bonds		
	Waterfall Method	Direct write-off Method
Interest	$28,333	$66,667
Scheduled Principal	$0	10,000
Prepayments	0	0
Recovery	0	0
Unrecovered Mezzanine	0	0
Payment Unpaid Balance	0	0
Total	28,333	76,667
Write-down Principal	0	0
Ending Unpaid Account Balance	38,334	0
Beginning Balance	10,000,000	10,000,000
Ending Balance	10,000,000	9,990,000
Change in Balance	0	-10,000

Junior Class		
	Waterfall Method	Direct write-off Method
Interest	$0	$66,667
Scheduled Principal	0	10,000
Prepayments	0	0
Recovery	0	0
Total	0	76,667
Write-down Principal	45,000	150,000
Unpaid Interest	66,667	0
Beginning Balance	10,000,000	10,000,000
Ending Balance	9,955,000	9,840,000
Change in Balance	-45,000	-160,000

For example, in the example given in Exhibit 13, the mezzanine tranche receives only $28,333 of its scheduled $67,667 interest payment. Therefore a shortfall is created that must be repaid in later periods. If credit problems persist, the unpaid interest can amount to several months without any cash flow. This problem, which arises due to the payment of the senior's share of the loss in cash, can severely impact the liquidity of the tranche in accrual status.

These bonds have additional problems: (1) extension of average life and duration; (2) roll-up the yield curve; and (3) no interest on interest potential.

Under the direct write-off method, the senior bond is entitled to the proceeds of the liquidated property, and any loss is written off against the most junior tranche. In addition, all interest and scheduled principal are allocated on a pro-rata basis.

Of the major non-agency issuers, Prudential Home and Residential Funding Corporation (pre-August 1993) use the waterfall loss allocation method. The other major issuers, including Residential Funding Corporation (since August 1993), generally use the direct write-off method.

Deal Triggers

An important component to be considered when analyzing senior/subordinated tranches are the deal's "triggers." Triggers are step-down tests that allow the subordinated tranches to be reduced as a percentage of the overall deal. For example, as illustrated in Exhibit 9, the subordinated bonds, in the standard senior/subordinated structure, are locked out from unscheduled payments (prepayments) for five years. Following this lockout period, the prepayment protection gradually "steps down" until the subordinated tranches receive their full pro-rata share of prepayments in year 10.

During the initial five-year lockout period, the subordinated bonds delever, i.e., they grow as a percentage of the overall deal. These stepdowns allow the subordinated bonds to relever. This relevering can occur only if a series of tests (or covenants) are met. These tests address (1) total losses, and (2) total delinquencies (60+ days).

These tests are levels of credit performance required before the credit support can be reduced. The tests are applied annually after year 5, and monthly if a test is failed. Of the two tests, the loss test prevents a stepdown from occurring if cumulative losses exceed a certain limit (which changes over time). The delinquency test, in its most common form, prevents any step-down from taking place as long as the current over 60-day delinquency rate exceeds 2% of the then-current pool balance.

Exhibit 14: Average Life at Different Speeds and Step-Down Allowances*

	Prepayment Speed (PSA)		
	250	400	600
All Step-Downs Taken	10.9	9.4	8.2
No Step-Downs Taken	16.0	15.0	13.1

* Assumes 30-year fixed-rate loans, 8.5% gross WAC,
320 WAM, and 4.50% subordinated tranche.

Although most non-agency deals in the market will currently pass the loss test, the delinquency test could be a potential problem for many deals. As the loans season and enter their peak loss years, higher delinquencies can cause a deal trigger to disallow a step-down. This occurrence can lead to a significant extension in average life and a roll-up of the yield curve, as illustrated in Exhibit 14. This potential risk should be carefully considered when evaluating securities.

Clean-up Calls

Non-agency deals are usually subject to a 5% to 10% clean-up call; that is, the issuer has the right to collapse a deal if the deal factor is down to 0.05 - 0.10. As shown in Exhibit 15, the average life can vary significantly if run to the call date.

How does this option impact subordinated tranche holders? It has two major effects on B-piece investors. First, since most subordinated tranches trade at discounts to par, it has a positive yield impact on these securities. Second, since these calls will come into play before maturity, the duration and the average life of these securities will shorten. Since subordinated tranches are locked out from prepayments during the first five years, only the clean-up call can accelerate their payment.

Although most deals use a 10% clean-up call, that does not necessarily mean that these deals will be called. Reasons why many deals may not be called include:

1. Advances in computer technology allow servicers to continue to maintain pool servicing functions economically.

2. Adverse selection (last loans in a pool can be the least creditworthy) may prevent the repurchase of these loans.

3. Issuer of pool often retains economic interest in pool by controlling servicing function and/or by owning the IO-tranche.

Exhibit 15: Residential Funding 1993-27, Class M2

	225 PSA +100		300 PSA Base		600 PSA -100	
	Maturity	Call	Maturity	Call	Maturity	Call
Average Life	11.63	9.56	10.54	8.06	8.06	4.31
Modified Duration	6.86	6.33	6.53	5.62	5.62	3.53
Last Pay	6/23	11/05	6/23	4/03	4/23	9/98

Source: Hyperion Capital Management

During the prepayment spike of 1993, investors where shown how negatively convex these securities can be. That is, tranches which were trading above par, were being bid by dealers to their calls, despite the 5-year prepay lockouts and the lack of first-hand experience as to the likelihood of the call option actually being exercised.

Exhibit 16 shows the likelihood of a newly issued deal being eligible for call during the subordinated tranches' initial five-year lockout period. For both 5% and 10% clean-up calls, if prepayments speeds are 35% CPR or below there is no interruption of the scheduled five-year subordinated tranche lockout. If the deal prepays at 45% CPR for five years, the structure with the 5% clean-up call is unaffected, but the 10% call could be exercised in year 4. At very fast prepayment speeds (i.e., 55%-65% CPR or faster), the calls could come into play as early as the third year after issuance.

Although most deals are structured with the 10% call option, the 5% structures can have substantially lower option costs, while trading at the same yield spreads versus the Treasury curve.

Compensating Interest

Compensating interest is an important element to examine when evaluating a subordinated tranche. Compensating interest, which represents the interest shortfall caused by the borrower paying only interest through the date of the principal prepayment, can be reimbursed depending on the policy of the issuer. The value of this reimbursed cash flow is a direct function of the speed of prepayments on the mortgage pool. During a period of slow prepayments, the yield impact of compensating interest can be small, but this reimbursed cash flow can be substantial during periods of prepayment spikes.

For example, for a tranche with a long scheduled average life (such as a subordinated tranche), the value of compensating interest assuming a 15-day interest shortfall is as follows:

PSA Speed	Basis Point Value
100	2.0
225	4.5
600	9.0
800	13.8

Exhibit 16: Likelihood of a Newly Issued Deal Being Eligible for Call During the Initial Five-Year Lockout Period

	25%		35%		45%		55%		65%	
	5%	10%	5%	10%	5%	10%	5%	10%	5%	10%
Year	Call	Call	Call	Call	Call	Call	Call	Call	Call	Call
1	No	No	No	No	No	No	No	No	No	No
2	No	No	No	No	No	No	No	No	No	No
3	No	No	No	No	No	No	No	Yes	Yes	Yes
4	No	No	No	No	No	Yes	Yes	Yes	Yes	Yes
5	No	No	No	No	No	Yes	Yes	Yes	Yes	Yes

Source: Hyperion Capital Management

Investors should remember, however, that for issuers that do reimburse, compensating interest reimbursements are usually limited to the amount of servicing fee collected during the month. Therefore, during periods of fast prepayments, interest shortfall will also occur on pools of issuers that do reimburse for compensating interest.

The monthly breakeven prepayment rate for compensating interest reimbursement can be illustrated using the formulas in Exhibit 17. Therefore, for the illustration in Exhibit 17, if prepayments exceed 56.3% CPR in the first month, interest shortfalls will be present.

Breakeven rates can vary widely depending upon the servicing fees that would be passed through. For example, one of the top five non-agency issuers pays compensating interest only up to 12.5 basis points of its total servicing fee. In the illustration given in Exhibit 17, assuming that the available servicing fee is only 12.5 basis points of total 50 basis points collected, the breakeven prepayment rate drops from the hefty 56.3% CPR to 18.3% CPR.

Although it's always better to be reimbursed, investors must be sure to understand the issuer's policy and its associated value at different prepayment levels.

SUBORDINATED TRANCHE STRESS TESTING

After getting comfortable with a deal's collateral and structure, the next step is to perform stress testing to evaluate the adequacy of a tranche's credit protection.

Exhibit 17: Illustration of Monthly Breakeven Prepayment Rate for Compensating Interest Reimbursement

Deal size: $185,000,000
Gross WAC: 8.00%
Servicing fee: 50 basis points
Deal factor: 1.00

1) $\text{Monthly interest paid} = \dfrac{\text{Current face} \times (\text{GWAC} - \text{Servicing fee})}{12} = \dfrac{\$185,000,000 \times (0.08 - 0.005)}{12} = \$1,156,250$

2) $\text{Available servicing} = \dfrac{\text{Current face} \times \text{Servicing fee}}{12} = \dfrac{(\$185,000,000 \times 0.005)}{12} = \$77,083$

3) $\text{Minimum principal bal.} = \dfrac{12\,(\text{Interest paid} - \text{Available Servicing})}{\text{GWAC} - \text{Servicing Fee}} = \dfrac{12\,(\$1,156,250 - \$77,083)}{(0.08 - 0.005)} = \$172,666,720$

4) $\text{Minimum factor} = \dfrac{\$172,666,720}{\$185,000,000} = 0.9333$

5) $\text{Monthly breakeven prepay rate (SMM)} = (\text{Old factor} - \text{New factor}) = (1 - 0.9333) = 6.67\%$

6) $\text{CPR} = 1 - (1 - \text{SMM})^{12} = 1 - (1 - 0.0667)^{12} = 56.32\%$

How Do Losses Occur?

Before we can perform meaningful stress tests for subordinated tranches, we must understand how losses occur. As shown in the flowchart in Exhibit 18, before a pool loss can occur a loan must pass from current status into 30-, 60-, and 90-day delinquency status before finally entering the foreclosure process. During this process, the servicer plays a very important function.

It should be pointed out that the servicer will commonly advance (principal and interest) to bondholders all the way through foreclosure. These advances, which will be reimbursed once the property is liquidated, will be paid before any pool losses are calculated.

The servicer also will work to prevent any losses from occurring to bondholders. The servicer will attempt to minimize losses, once a loan becomes delinquent, by:

1. Contacting borrower and seeking to bring the balance current.
2. Providing borrower with new loan schedule (to bring balance current).
3. Encouraging owners with equity to sell the property.

If any of these strategies are successful, the servicer has prevented a delinquent loan from resulting in a pool loss.

The best defense against pool losses adversely impacting the subordinated tranches is homeowner's equity in the property. That is, the homeowner's down payment or actual perceived equity in a particular property is the first line of defense against default. Defaults rationally occur only when a negative equity condition exists. Otherwise the homeowner would sell the property to prevent default.

Empirical studies on homeowners in negative equity situations show that only a small portion of this universe will default. Statistics show that it requires a period of severe borrower stress (i.e., divorce or unemployment) coupled with a negative equity condition to result in significant levels of default. Mortgage borrowers have resisted default in most negative equity situations due to: (1) the social stigma of losing one's home; (2) fear of tarnishing credit rating; and (3) the ongoing need for housing. Furthermore, negative equity/default conditions are not that common to begin with because of annual housing inflation, regular loan amortization, and improving debt coverage ratios with time (rising income versus fixed-debt burden).

As shown in Exhibit 19, a typical loan with a 75% loan-to-value ratio, assuming no housing inflation, will decline to 71.4% after five years and 66.1% after ten years. This occurs due to normal amortization of principal over the loan's 30-year life. If any improvement in housing values is assumed (i.e., 2% housing inflation) the loan-to-value ratio will decline to 64.7% after five years and 54.2% after ten years. Thus credit mortgage pools have a normal tendency to improve with time.

Exhibit 18: Flowchart of the Way Losses Occur

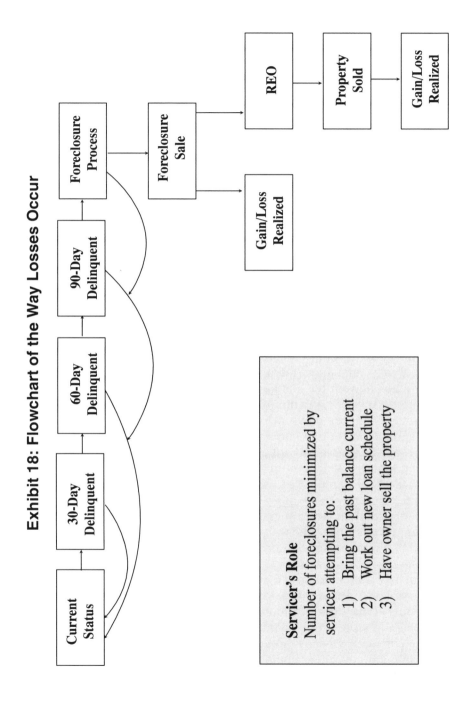

Exhibit 19: Impact of Principal Amortization and Housing Inflation on LTV

Principal Amortization: Impact on LTV

	Year 0	Year 5	Year 10
LTV	75.0%*	71.4%	66.1%

* Assumes gross weighted average coupon (GWAC) of 8.24% and 30-year weighted average maturity (WAM).

Housing Inflation: Impact on LTV

	Year 0	Year 5	Year 10
LTV	75.0%*	64.8%	54.2%

* Assumes gross weighted average coupon (GWAC) of 8.24% and 30-year weighted average maturity (WAM) and 2% housing inflation.

Timing and Extent of Losses

The most widely accepted loss curve is the Moody's curve. This loss curve, which is shown in Exhibit 20, highlights the expected timing of losses for 30-year collateral fixed-rate single-family pools. The shape of the curve highlights the fact that losses do not typically occur during the first year (since the foreclosure process can often last more than one year), but are typically concentrated in years 3 through 7. During these years the homeowner has not had substantial time to amortize principal or enjoy the benefit of housing inflation. This is in direct conflict with the longer part of the loss curve, where losses become quite rare due to seasoning and the build-up of homeowner's equity.

Most conservative investors will perform their stress testing assuming that the allocation of a pool's total losses will be front-loaded. That is, 100% of total losses will occur between years 2 through 4 or 2 through 6.

An important factor in making new subordinated investors comfortable has always been historical pool losses. Historical pool numbers reported in a deal prospectus can be misleading, however, and we do not advocate using these statistics. An important and unbiased measure of historical pool performance is static-pool statistics, as shown in Exhibit 21. These statistics represent all losses that have occurred on all Moody's rated pools during the particular year of origination. For example, all Chase fixed-rate pools originated and rated in 1990 have suffered 12 basis points of cumulative losses through the end of 1993.

Investors can use static pool data as a way of extrapolating the extent of total pool losses.

Exhibit 20: Moody's Loss Curve

Age	Losses	Cumulative
1	0.5%	0.5%
2	3.5%	4.0%
3	11.0%	15.0%
4	21.5%	36.5%
5	21% 13.5%	57.5%
6	13.5%	71.0%
7	11.5%	82.5%
8	7.5%	90.0%
9	7.0%	97.0%
10+	3.0%	100.0%
	100.0%	

Exhibit 21: Cumulative Loss Information on Moody's Rated Deals (%)

	1993	1992	1991	1990	1989	1988	1987
Chase	0.00	0.03	0.02	0.12	0.07	0.07	---
FBS	---	0.00	0.12	0.05	0.24	---	---
GECMS	0.00	0.00	0.25	---	---	---	---
Pru	0.00	0.14	0.01	0.13	0.97	1.40	---
RFC	0.00	0.04	0.35	1.32	1.74	0.50	0.35
Countrywide	0.00	---	---	0.00	0.14	---	0.00

Source: Kidder Peabody, and Moody's.

Exhibit 22: Default Rates (%) on FHLMC Purchased Loans 1975 - 1985

Origination Year	LTV				
	0-75	76-80	81-85	86-90	91-95
1975	0.04	0.11	0.32	0.33	0.94
1976	0.06	0.11	0.42	0.60	0.92
1977	0.09	0.22	0.66	0.80	1.89
1978	0.25	0.63	1.2	1.84	4.30
1979	0.50	1.25	1.75	3.29	7.43
1980	0.80	2.87	3.07	6.84	10.42
1981	1.01	4.81	5.00	11.45	12.03
1982	0.78	3.40	3.20	7.11	12.68
1983	0.33	1.43	2.75	4.19	8.21
1984	0.20	0.54	1.20	2.17	5.23
1985	0.09	0.49	0.67	1.09	3.48
Average	0.37	1.40	1.79	3.52	5.85
Factor vs. 0-75%	1.00X	3.78X	4.84X	9.51X	15.81X

Estimating Potential Pool Losses

In order to assess the potential risk of a non-agency pool, an investor has to address three key issues:

1. Amount of loans that will default (foreclosure frequency).
2. The amount of the loss on default (loss severity).
3. The timing of the loss.

First, for estimating defaults, FHLMC statistics over the 1975-1985 period show how important LTV is in determining default rates. These statistics are given in Exhibit 22. As shown in the exhibit, loans originated with LTVs between 81% - 85% defaulted on average 4.84 times as often as loans with LTVs below 75%.

Another common guidepost for estimating appropriate levels of foreclosure frequency and loss severity is the "Texas Scenario." This represents a statistical study, by LTV strata, of FNMA 30-year fixed-rate loans on properties in Texas originated in 1981-1982.

The cumulative default rates, which were compiled by Fitch Investors Service, as of April 30, 1989, are shown in Exhibit 23. Texas loans underwritten during this period are examples of the worst modern day housing market. Some salient points about these loans:

• This sample is a totally undiversified pool as 100% of the loans are from Texas with no zip code concentration limits.

Exhibit 23: Foreclosure Frequency and Loss Severity for FNMA 30-Year Fixed-Rate Mortgages on Texas Properties Originated in 1981-1982 (As of April 30, 1989)

LTV	% Defaulted	Loss Severity	Cumulative Losses
0-50%	0.7	0.0	0.00
50-60%	0.7	12.9	0.09
60-70%	1.6	25.9	0.41
70-75%	3.6	33.3	1.20
75-80%	8.1	37.5	3.04
80-90%	14.1	42.8	5.29
90+	24.1	50.0	12.05

Source: Fitch Investors Service.

- The loans included in the statistics in Exhibit 23 also represent a high concentration of condominiums and investor-owned properties.
- Low and limited documentation loans are included.
- LTVs above 80% are not protected by private mortgage insurance (PMI).

An important point to remember is that when a loan is covered by private mortgage insurance (PMI), the loss severity is usually limited to the equivalent loss on a 75% LTV loan. Most major non-agency issuers have a policy of requiring PMI on any loans underwritten in excess of 80% LTV. The insurance company will then be responsible for 25% LTV exposure on any losses on the loan. Therefore, in the Texas statistics cited in Exhibit 23, if the pools had been underwritten with PMI, the losses would have been lower.

As shown in the Texas statistics, loss severity for loans with PMI should not exceed 33.3%-37.5%. Other underwriters, such as Citicorp, with less than pristine track records have experienced historical loss severities of around 24%. In addition, Citicorp has had cure rates, for loans entering foreclosure, of around 50%.

There are two quick and simple methods to estimate what total losses will be on a pool. The first estimates expected losses using the Moody's loss curve. Assume a 1988 originated Pru-Home pool has had the following loss record:

Cumulative losses	1993 losses	Number of years seasoned
0.25%	0.15%	5

According to the Moody's loss curve, pools that are five years seasoned should have experienced 57.5% of the lifetime losses, and losses occurring during the fifth year should represent 21% of total lifetime losses. Therefore, the investor can get a range of losses based on this seasoned pool's actual performance:

Projected losses (cumulative) = 0.25/0.575 = 0.43%
Projected losses (5th year) = 0.15/0.21 = 0.71%

Under this method, estimated lifetime losses would range between 43 and 71 basis points.

Another popular method, illustrated in Exhibit 24, takes recent pool performance and estimates cumulative losses by assigning a probability factor to each category. In the exhibit, we are using Citicorp's estimated cure rates to calculate estimated pool losses. This example shows that loans in the 30-day delinquent category default approximately at a rate of 5%, while loans in foreclosure default 50% of the time. After coming up with a foreclosure frequency, we would apply a loss severity rate of 30%. The result is an estimated lifetime cumulative loss of 17 basis points.

This method, if used, should be updated often to reflect changes in loan categorization. That is, as a loan moves from 30 days to 60 days delinquent, the estimated losses will increase due to the lower assumed cure rate.

SDA Model

In May 1993, the Public Securities Association (PSA) came up with a benchmark default standard for evaluating the credit risk of non-agency MBS (see Exhibit 25). The model is designed along the same lines as the PSA's prepayment curve, which is used by investors to analyze prepayment risk in mortgage securities. Investors can use multiples of the SDA curve to stress test mortgage securities.

As shown in Exhibit 25, the SDA curve begins with an assumed default rate of 0.02% in month 1 and increases by 0.02% per month until it reaches a peak of 0.60% in month 30. This peak level default is maintained through the 60th month and then subsides monthly until reaching its constant level of 0.03% for the pool's remaining life.

An important point to remember is that the SDA default curve in any month is applied to the remaining balance of the performing loans at the end of the month. Therefore, the cumulative default rate over the life of the pool depends not only on the assumed monthly default rate but also on the prepayment assumption. This is illustrated in Exhibit 26. Note that the larger the assumed prepayment speed, the lower the cumulative default level for a given percentage of the SDA model.

The SDA curve's basic assumption of 100 SDA and 150 PSA produces cumulative default levels of 2.78% — which is high on a historical basis. Only high LTV loans have generally experienced this type of default levels. Most historical studies show that for loans with LTV ranging between 70% and 80%, the range of defaults have ranged between 0.5% and 1.5% which would equate to less than 50% SDA.

Exhibit 24: Estimating Pool Losses by Assigning Cure Rates by Delinquency Category

	Delinquencies (%)					
	30-Day	60-Day	90-Day	Foreclosures	REO	Total
Current (1)	2.05	0.77	0.53	0.14	0.10	3.59
Non-cured Default (2)	5.00	15.00	30.00	50.00	100.00	
Foreclosure Frequency (1) × (2) = (3)	0.10	0.12	0.16	0.07	0.10	
Loss Severity (4)	30.00	30.00	30.00	30.00	30.00	
Estimated Loss (3) × (4) = (5)	0.03	0.04	0.05	0.02	0.03	0.17

Exhibit 25: Annual Default Rate, 100% SDA

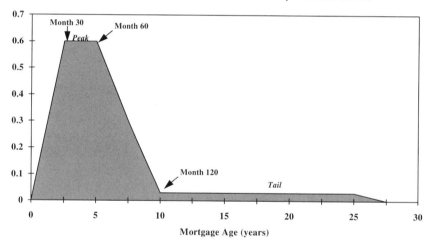

Exhibit 26: Cumulative Default Rates (%)*

	50 SDA	100 SDA	200 SDA
100 PSA	1.56	3.09	6.08
150 PSA	1.40	2.78	5.47
400 PSA	0.88	1.74	3.45

* Assume 30-year fixed loans with 360 WAM and 8% coupon.

Exhibit 27: Loss-Adjusted Yield Matrix
for Typical Unrated Subordinated Tranche

Scenario	Foreclosure (%)	Loss Severity (%)	Cumulative Loss (%)	CPR 15% Yield (%)	CPR 18% Yield (%)	CPR 21% Yield (%)
1	0.00	20.0	0.00	19.6	20.0	20.30
2	0.50	20.0	0.10	18.1	18.6	19.01
3	1.00	20.0	0.20	16.6	17.21	17.77
4	2.50	20.0	0.50	12.6	13.46	14.28
5	5.00	20.0	1.00	7.4	8.59	9.72
6	10.00	20.0	2.00	...	...	-5.11

Source: Hyperion Capital Management

To use the SDA model properly, the investor must provide input assumptions for:

• Loss severity level.
• Servicer advancing.
• Time to liquidation on defaults.

The final step in our analysis of a subordinated tranche is stress testing to determine the impact on credit-adjusted yield. The idea is to break the collateral into different groupings that can then be stressed in different ways. The most common grouping is by LTV ratio. That is, the loans are broken into LTV clusters and stressed at different foreclosure frequencies and loss severities. One method is to apply the Texas scenario to these LTV clusters. The idea, of course, is to insure that the security in question can survive these stress testings.

Stress testing also involves the testing of housing values. The idea is to calculate a credit-adjusted yield on the individual tranche. Therefore, the investor will need a model that can calculate the yield impact of losses, payment delays, and "trigger" events. Most investors, when calculating credit-adjusted yields, will assume a front loading of defaults and cumulative losses.

The final step is the production of a loss matrix, which will show the credit-adjusted yield under a variety of scenarios. Exhibit 27 is a loss-adjusted yield matrix for a typical unrated subordinated tranche.

OTHER RISKS

Losses can also result through: (1) borrower bankruptcy; (2) borrower fraud; and (3) special hazard risk.

Borrower Bankruptcy

When a borrower files for personal bankruptcy, there is a risk that a bankruptcy judge could reduce the borrower's mortgage debt. This debt reduction, called a *cramdown*, usually occurs only when the value of the borrower's home has fallen so that in the mortgage loan balance exceeds the home's market value. If a cramdown is ordered, the loan's terms can be altered by reducing the unpaid principal balance or the loan's interest rate.

A mortgage borrower can file for personal bankruptcy under Chapter 7, Chapter 11, or Chapter 13. A few cramdowns have occurred in recent years in settling Chapter 13 bankruptcy cases. Chapter 13 allows for restructuring or forgiving debts while letting borrowers retain their assets. However, the 1993 Supreme Court case of *Nobleman v. American Savings* ruled that a borrower filing under Chapter 13 cannot effectively reduce its mortgage debts.

In a Chapter 7 bankruptcy filing, a type of bankruptcy that generally involves liquidation of assets to make payments to creditors, cramdowns have also been disallowed under a Supreme Court ruling.

Finally, cramdown filings under Chapter 11 are more rare than those under Chapter 7 or Chapter 13 because of their cost and complexity. Jumbo loan borrowers are more likely to file under Chapter 11 because this section can be used only when the debtor's secured debt exceeds $350,000. According to *Inside Mortgage Securities*, during 1992 Chapter 11 filings represented only 0.35% of individual filings; 71.4% filed under Chapter 7, and 28.2% under Chapter 13.

The rating agencies determine the size of the bankruptcy carve-out, based on the collateral. For example, Standard & Poor's states that for securities backed by mortgages that exceed 75% LTV, issuers must have a bankruptcy reserve of $100,000 or have cramdown coverage equal to 12 basis points.

Borrower Fraud

Another potential risk to the non-agency investor arises from borrower fraud or misrepresentation during the application process. This type of risk is often not covered by the originator/conduit/sellers' representations and warranties.

Senior-subordinated structures provide a carve-out as protection against the risk of fraud. The risk of fraud losses is front-loaded. That is, borrowers who misrepresent their income, employment, or net worth will generally run into payment problems early in the loan's life. Therefore, fraud coverage is largest at issuance — around 2%, declining to 0% by the sixth year.

Special Hazard Risk

Special hazard risk deals losses can result from properties damaged by earthquakes, mud-slides, tidal waves, volcanoes, or floods. Such losses are excluded from coverage under homeowners' and private mortgage insurance policies.

Subordinated tranches absorb special hazard losses up to a predetermined capped amount that will decline as the mortgage pool amortizes. This "capped" amount is determined by the rating agencies. Standard & Poors requires a triple-A level of special hazard risk equal to the highest of:

- 1% of current mortgage pool balance.
- Twice the principal balance of the pool's largest loan.
- The principal balance of the highest zip code concentration within California.

Special hazard losses in excess of this capped amount are distributed among the senior and subordinated classes pro rata.

Historically losses from special hazards are quite rare because:

- Special casualty insurance is often required on homes in high risk areas (i.e., flood insurance in flood zones, and earthquake insurance along known fault lines).
- Damage caused indirectly by an act of God, such as water damage or fire caused by an earthquake, can be covered under standard homeowners' policies.

Another important factor is land value. In costly areas such as Southern California, the value of land can represent over 50% of the value of a single-family home. Thus, if a home is totally destroyed, the land value acts as a floor in terms of the loan's loss severity.

Finally, where damage to property caused by special hazards is uninsured, the homeowner can often get access to low-cost government funds to help rebuild. Therefore, special hazards have not historically resulted in significant losses. In addition, geographic diversification can help to limit a pool's risk to special hazard risk.

CONCLUSION

In this chapter we have discussed a method of analyzing subordinated CMOs. This started with a detailed review of a deal collateral, followed by an understanding of structural risk. We discussed tranche stress testing before finally considering other risks (such as bankruptcy, fraud, and special hazard).

Of course, deciding on whether to purchase a subordinated tranche is also a function of the following:

- Relative value opportunities versus alternative products.
- Portfolio considerations (i.e., applicable benchmarks).
- Client objectives and constraints.
- Liquidity considerations.

We believe that subordinate CMOs can provide an excellent opportunity to achieve a superior risk/return profile and yet maintain a reasonable degree of liquidity within a broadly diversified portfolio.

CHAPTER 11

Using Subordinate Mortgage-Backed Securities To Enhance Portfolio Returns

Eva A. Zeff, CFA
Portfolio Manager
The Oppenheimer Mortgage Income Fund
Oppenheimer Management Corporation

Richard M. Lerner
Senior Commercial Mortgage-Backed Security Trader
C S First Boston Corporation

INTRODUCTION

How can one portfolio manager outperform another in a world where everyone's portfolio is expected to look similar in duration and structure to an index, without taking "market directional duration bets" that have historically very little return stability? A few years ago a manager might have used derivative structures such as interest-only and principal-only strips or inverse floaters. Time has shown that our inability to predict prepayments and the course of interest rates has made this a risky course. As a result, many investors moved into the private-label mortgage market where triple-A-rated securities provide incremental returns over agencies without the structural complexity of derivative securities. That was a good game for a while, but the market has caught on, and these securities are now included in the indexes as well as in almost everyone's portfolio.

What is the proper strategy for the 1990s? One answer lies in subordinate securities with lower than triple-A ratings created from both single-family and commercial mortgages. These subordinate securities have far higher risk-adjusted returns than similar securities with comparable ratings, credit quality, and risk profile. An understanding of the historical behavior of these types of collateral, the rating agencies' approach to these securities, and the various structures that are employed to protect the subordinate investor allows a portfolio manager to reap the benefits of the incremental yields that these securities offer without taking undue market or prepayment risk versus an index.

We discuss the evolution, size, and scope of the subordinate mortgage-backed securities (MBS) market, describe the securities themselves, recommend how best to evaluate their risk and value, and review a number of different approaches for including them in a generic mortgage or bond portfolio.

EVOLUTION OF THE MARKET

Single-Family Mortgage Securitizations

The market for single-family subordinate mortgage-backed securities is the logical extension of the development of the corporate bond market in the United States and the growth and diversification of the U.S. mortgage market. As a new investment vehicle appears in the market, it is usually traded in a high-grade, low risk form.

In the corporate bond market, for example, it was not until the early 1980s that companies with sub-investment-grade ratings were able to access the capital markets. Now, the sub-investment-grade or "high-yield" corporate market is a large liquid market, and companies with ratings of BB or lower can readily raise public debt.

When the mortgage market was first evolving, the vast majority of securities issued were guaranteed by the government or its agencies, such as GNMA, FNMA, OR FHLMC. in 1986, according to *Inside Mortgage Securities*, there were $529 billion mortgage-backed securities outstanding, of which only $8 billion were not government guaranteed, but issued by private entities.

In 1986, large rated banks such as Travelers, Bank of America, and Citicorp began issuing securities backed by their residential mortgages, and the private-label mortgage market began to grow. By the end of 1993, there was $1.5 trillion of MBS debt outstanding, and $164 billion of that was privately issued. Because *private-label* MBS are issued by private entities and are not government guaranteed, issuers can elect to provide credit enhancement equal to, for example, 10% of the total pool value, whereby investors are protected from losses due to defaults on the underlying mortgage up to a dollar amount equalling 10% of the original pool and secure a triple-A credit rating from the rating agencies. Many of these issues were credit-enhanced using external techniques such as letters of credit, corporate guarantees, or pool insurance. Securitizations using external forms of credit enhancement, though effective, can run the risk of downgrade due not only to the quality of the underlying mortgages but also to downgrades of the corporate insurance provider.

Alternatively, an issuer could elect to use a form of internal credit enhancement, such as subordination of principal. This structure consists of two or more classes of certificates differing in the amount of credit risk each bears. If subordination is chosen by the issuer, 10% of the pool, for example, would be subordinate and rated lower than triple-A, and the remaining 90% could be issued as a triple-A-rated security. Because the credit support is provided internally, senior-subordinate structures have no corporate downgrade risk. Credit risk is due solely to the credit of the mortgages themselves, not external parties.

Subordinate MBS are often structured to meet specific investor preferences and issuer constraints. The resulting variety of cash flow and credit structures offers potential investors a wide spectrum of risk alternatives, from triple-A-rated publicly offered securities to high-yielding, unrated private placements.[1] The senior-subordinate structure is today's most commonly used credit enhancement form. In 1987, according to *Inside Mortgage Securities,* only 30% of all private-label deals were credit-enhanced using senior-subordinate structures. By the end of 1993, 83% of all private-label deals were structured in this manner.

---

[1] A subordinated security can earn a triple-A rating via an insurance wrap. At the other extreme, some subordinated MBS are "first loss" investments, whereby all losses on the collateral are applied first to the first loss class and no credit protection is available. First loss positions are sold at deep discounts and have yield quoted after a loss assumption.

Commercial Mortgage Securitizations

The commercial securitization market has undergone explosive growth in recent years. With the new risk-based capital rules and a stricter regulatory environment for insurance companies, banks, and thrifts, these institutions have reduced their investment activities in the commercial mortgage markets. In reaction to the S&L crisis and the severe losses that the plummeting real estate market caused the banking and insurance industries, government regulators have arguably become over zealous in their efforts to restrict investments by these entities in real estate-related products.

In the 1980s a large percentage of all money lent on commercial and multi-family real estate came from the S&L system. S&Ls were the "lender of last resort", and the bulk of their loans were on lower-quality properties. Due to the S&L failures and regulatory changes, this source of funds no longer exists.

Banks and insurance companies made up the bulk of the remaining lending, with insurance companies focusing on the high profile, top-quality assets, and banks lending on average-quality properties. New bank regulations make it extremely expensive for banks to hold commercial and multi-family whole loans, and as a result banks are severely limiting their investment in this sector. Insurance companies expect similar restrictive regulation and have recently made only small forays into the high-quality lending market. There is no longer a logical lender for anything but the highest-quality commercial assets. Securitization of commercial mortgage loans is being used to fill this gap.

The rapid growth of the commercial MBS sector was further facilitated by the Resolution Trust Corporation (RTC), which was created by the United States government to dispose of the assets of the bankrupt thrift industry. The RTC issued approximately $16 billion of commercial mortgage backed securities in 1992 and 1993, facilitating a liquid secondary market. The rating agencies, in response to the RTC's supply of product and the ever-increasing issuance of similar securities by private issuers, have established well-defined criteria for rating these securities, thus providing investors with a guide for assessing the credit risk profiles of these investments.

The subordinate commercial MBS market is now large, expanding, and well-entrenched. Actively traded securities are available in a wide spectrum of maturities, average life profiles, ratings, and property types such as multi-family developments and apartment buildings, hotels, office buildings, retail space, industrial and warehouse properties, and hospitals and nursing homes.

Due to the aforementioned regulatory initiatives, banks and insurance companies are diverting their capital from traditional real estate loans to the investment-grade securities of commercial securitization. This creates an unprecedented opportunity for the entrepreneurial investor who is not subject to strict government regulation to reap the benefits inherent in the excess returns available in subordinate and non-rated commercial MBS.

Today there are approximately $43 billion commercial MBSs outstanding, and the market is expected to continue growing. Estimates of production in 1994 range from $20 to $30 billion.

ADVANTAGES

The subordinate mortgage sector provides numerous advantages to the portfolio manager relative to other asset classes.

Higher Yields: Subordinate securities provide high base case and risk-adjusted yields. The returns on these securities can match those available from direct real estate and high-yield corporate bond investment, while providing greater liquidity and more predictable cash flows than those alternatives. In addition, comparably rated subordinate mortgage-backed securities currently provide higher yields than high yield corporate bonds.

Exhibit 1 illustrates the yield spread over Treasuries of both corporate and private-label mortgage-backed securities. For example, as of the date of the exhibit, BB-rated corporate bonds traded at +250 to Treasuries, while private-label commercial mortgage-backed securities with a similar rating traded at +475 to the Treasury.

No Corporate Style Event Risk: Real estate related securities are much less subject to downgrades due to events unrelated to their inherent value. For example, a AA rated corporation, through no fault of its own, might become involved in a takeover fight that will negatively impact its credit and performance, to the extent that subordinate mortgage-backed securities credit enhancement is provided internally. Credit performance is dependent only on the credit quality of the underlying mortgage pool, and not unpredictable external sources.

Call Protection (Prepayment Lockout): As interest rates declined over the past few years, homeowners rushed to refinance their home mortgages. These refinancings or "prepayments" have caused many agency and senior securitized mortgage-backed securities to underperform relative to call-protected fixed income alternatives. Over the same period, subordinated MBS performed extremely well. This is due in part to an initial "lockout" period (typically five years for fixed-rate mortgages) in which the subordinate classes receive zero prepayments; 100% of the prepayments on the mortgage pools are allocated to the senior certificates. After the initial prepayment lockout period, the subordinate certificates receive their pro rata share of the prepayments, or a smaller share (a partial lockout typically begins in year six). Subordinated certificates are primarily subject to credit risk; whereas senior certificates are primarily subject to prepayment risk.

Exhibit 1: Basis Points Over the Five-Year Treasury Bond as of June 30, 1994

	Corporate Bonds	Subordinated Private-label Residential Mortgages	Subordinated Private-label Commercial Mortgages
AA	50	160	125
A	70	180	155
BBB	100	210	205
BB	250	450	475
B	350	550	675

Greater Diversification and Lower Risk than Real Estate Investing: A single subordinated MBS investment can include thousands of underlying mortgaged properties of differing collateral and geography. By contrast, if one were to invest in real estate as an equity owner, one must be able to own, operate, and service each property, prohibiting the same degree of diversification.

With subordinate mortgage-backed security investing, there is no need for additional funds if the property experiences cash flow shortage, whereas with real estate investing, it is the responsibility of the equity owner to put up the additional cash flow needed to support the property and prevent a default. If a property were to go into foreclosure, the equity owner will likely lose the entire investment before a subordinated MBS investor experiences any loss. The "real first loss" position is the property owner. Subordinate securities can provide returns, similar to those expected by equity investors, but have fewer inherent risks due to these factors.

Growing Investor Base: With the stock market at a seemingly precarious point and volatility increasing in all markets, many investors are looking for a stable security that can produce returns significantly higher than those available in the traditional fixed-income market. In recent years, investors were flocking to hedge funds and emerging markets. At comparable yields, an investment in a diversified portfolio of well-underwritten U.S. real estate has less uncertainty associated with it than an investment in a third world country with political, currency, sovereign, and economic risks, as proven by recent downturns in the Latin American debt markets. Many portfolio managers, have recently reached this conclusion and have entered the subordinated MBS market at a rapid pace.

In addition, Real Estate Investment Trusts (REITs) are providing huge pools of capital earmarked for investment in real estate. This should have a very positive effect on the real estate market, in the way that mutual funds have impacted on the stock market.

Improved Mortgage Underwriting Policies Nationwide: Undisciplined underwriting practices were one of the primary causes of the real estate and thrift debacle of the late 1980s. Bankers, in their quest to compete in a hyperinflated real estate lending market, enticed developers with ever-larger loans based on inflated appraisals and small to non-existent down payments. Because real estate had done nothing but appreciate over the previous 20 years, lenders assumed these risky loans would be "bailed out" by ever-increasing rents and property values.

After the real estate crash, banks revised their underwriting standards and reverted to the more conservative, traditional underwriting practices that had prevailed before the fast eighties. Of the loans that were underwritten to the more conservative standards, most survived the recession, and (although there were very few issued) losses on securities backed these by well-under-written loans in the late eighties were deminimis.

DESCRIPTION OF THE SECURITIES

A mortgage-backed security (MBS) is a collection of individual mortgages, pooled together to make investment in them easier and safer. Because mortgages are loans to either individuals or partnerships that do not have investment-grade credit ratings, they can, and do, go into default. Mortgage lenders are entitled to take the mortgaged property if a borrower defaults.

To show how this works, let's look at a sample loan. Assume that a bank lends a couple $80,000 to purchase a $100,000 house. Since the loan amount is 80% of the value of the house, the loan is said to have an 80% loan-to-value ratio, or LTV. If our hypothetical couple defaults, the bank would take possession of and sell the house. Theoretically, the bank should be able to recover at least the $80,000 loan balance, since the house is worth $100,000.

The protection afforded the lender by the difference between the amount of the loan and the value of the property is called "overcollateraliza-tion from equity". In this case, the couple has $20,000 invested in the home. They are the first to lose. Equity is always the first to lose if the value of the property declines and a fault occurs. If a foreclosure sale recovers $80,000, the bank would be made whole. If the foreclosure sale recovers only $70,000, the lending bank would lose $10,000.[2]

Now, let's look at a simple hypothetical passthrough with no senior or subordinated class distinctions, backed by 1,000 loans all exactly the same as the $80,000 one above. The security would look like this:

Size	$80,000,000
Number of Loans	1,000
Average Loan Balance	$80,000
Average LTV	80%
Number of Investors	10

[2] In actuality, the loss would be higher due to missed payments and legal and selling expenses.

Exhibit 2: Expected losses for Benchmark Pools With Varying LTVs

LTV	Expected Loss (bp)
95.01 - 100.00	10.5
90.01 - 95.00	7.0
85.01 - 90.00	3.5
80.01 - 85.00	1.7
75.01 - 80.00	0.7
70.01 - 75.00	0.3
65.01 - 70.00	0.2
60.01 - 65.00	0.1

Source: Moody's Investor Service.

If our couple's loan was one of the 1,000 in this security, the $10,000 loss in our example would be split evenly among the ten investors. Each investor would have $8 million invested, and each would lose $1,000 of that investment. The diversification of the default risk among different holders and borrowers is a major reason for pooling mortgages.

It is unlikely that only one of the 1,000 loans in the security would default. Exhibit 2 illustrates that a security with this profile is likely to experience losses of 0.07% of the original balance. Although historical data suggest it is unlikely that our security would experience the loss of 10% of its principal, the rating agencies consider the likelihood of a security losing only $1 of principal as sub-investment grade. This explains the reason for credit tranching.

Let's return to the sample security. We have 1,000 loans totaling $80 million. If we create a senior-subordinate structure by issuing two classes of bonds, the majority (90%) of the bonds might carry an investment-grade rating of triple-A, based on the existence of 10% "credit" enhancement (the principal amount of the subordinate bonds). The subordinate bonds in this example would total 10% of the deal, will have less than triple-A ratings or be unrated, and offer commensurately higher yields.

To date, the highest loss experience on a single family pool of this sort has been 3.23%, and the median losses are much lower. If we split up the security by credit (senior vs. subordinate), the odds of the senior tranches experiencing any losses are low enough for the rating agencies to assign them a triple-A rating.

Exhibit 3: Senior-Subordinate Structure
for $80,000,000 Single-Family Pool

Tranche	Rating	Size	Principal Priority	% of Deal	Spread to Treasury
Senior	triple-A	$72,000,000	First	90%	+105
Subordinate	Not Rated	$8,000,000	Last	10%	+650

In Exhibit 3, if our couple's mortgage were to default, and the recovery is only $70,000, the entire $10,000 loss would be applied to the subordinate tranche. Subordinate mortgage securities exist to cushion their senior counterparts against credit losses in the mortgage pool. Senior bonds would not experience any principal loss unless the subordinate bonds had been exhausted due to losses. This would not happen until the pool of mortgages experienced a 10% loss across the board, or, in this example, an $8 million loss. Such a loss would be over 140 times the average loss experience of 7 basis points.

Often, the subordinated class as described above is further segmented into several subordinated classes in a hierarchy of credit (or loss) positions. The loss position determines the order in which the pool's losses are applied to the various subordinate classes.

A first-loss class is the portion of the security to first absorb principal losses on the underlying mortgage collateral. If default losses were to exceed the size of the first loss class, further losses are absorbed by the second-loss class. The absorption of losses continues on up to higher classes, as needed. The first loss position is not rated. Second loss positions and higher are usually rated.

Rating agencies determine how large each credit class must be in a securitization depending on the characteristics of the pooled loans and the historical performance of that asset type. For a standard single-family mortgage pool, a rating agency might require 6.25% subordination for a triple-A rating, but only 4.0% subordination for a AA rating. The yield spread demanded by investors is higher for lower rated classes, so it is expensive to issue these lower-rated classes. As a result, underwriters of MBS use the subordination structure levels from the rating agencies and create deals with multiple credit classes, one for each rating level. This is more economical than creating only one, unrated class.

Exhibit 4 is an example of a typical single-family senior-subordinate securitization and the credit support needed to achieve different levels of credit rating.

Exhibit 4: Credit Support Needed for a Typical Single-Family Securitization to Achieve Specific Credit Ratings

Rating of Class	Size of Class ($)	Size of Class (% of Deal)	Percentage Subordination Protecting Class*	Yield Spread To Treasury	Application of Losses
AAA	$75,000,000	93.75	6.25	+105	last
AA	1,800,000	2.25	4.00	+160	sixth
A	1,400,000	1.75	2.25	+180	fifth
BBB	1,000,000	1.25	1.00	+210	fourth
BB	360,000	0.45	0.55	+450	third
B	120,000	0.15	0.45	+550	second
First Loss/ Unrated	320,000	0.40	0.00	+700	first

* Credit enhancement.

THE RISKS

Investments in subordinate securities backed by commercial and single-family real estate share many of the same risks associated with other fixed-income products, such as interest rate, call, default, and liquidity risk. Subordinate classes are unique, however, in that they compensate the investor for their credit risk by providing incremental yield, while also providing inherent protection from most other risks associated with fixed-income investing. For example, rising interest rates can cause fixed-income portfolios to decline in value. Investing in already high-yielding instruments with improving credit stories (such as characterize today's real estate market) can be a natural defense against this occurrence.

Prepayment Risk: The plight of some investors in mortgage derivatives over the past year has been widely publicized. Many losses were caused by the unexpected refinancing or "prepayment" of single-family mort-gages backing these very complex investments. Although subordinate MBS have a limited degree of prepayment risk, most carry "lockout" peri-ods where they receive no prepayments at all.

Credit Risk: A subordinate MBS is a vehicle for taking credit risk in MBS and should be viewed by investors as an asset with leveraged credit risk. The subordinate class takes, to the extent of its principal balance, the credit risk for the entire pool so that if a subordinate class equals 10% of the pool's total principal it has ten times the credit exposure of the overall pool. Some comfort can be taken, however, in knowledge that the rating agencies use historical depression and recession stress tests as worst-case scenarios when rating subordinate classes. Securities with ratings as low as BB must still perform reasonably well under economic stress.

Liquidity Risk: As is true in all markets, the more a security differs from the liquid benchmark, the more liquidity risk an investor must assume. Because they represent a smaller percentage of the market than their senior counterparts, subordinate MBS are generally less liquid than senior MBS. A mortgage-backed security's liquidity is *inversely* proportional to its complexity, and directly proportional to its rating. A straightforward triple-A security will be more liquid than a complex BB subordinate class.

EVALUATING LOAN QUALITY

In order to minimize the risk of investing in private-label mortgage-backed securities, one examines the loan quality of the underlying mortgages. Here we overview the most significant factors affecting the quality of both the individual mortgage and the mortgage pool.

Single-Family MBS

Evaluating the cash flow characteristics of a non-agency single-family mortgage-backed security is not enough. A manager must also evaluate the pool's credit risk. As a first step, look to the rating agencies. The major national rating agencies, such as Standard & Poor's and Moody's, have a large staff dedicated to evaluating, rating, and maintaining continued surveillance of not only real estate securitizations but also the entire real estate market in general. These ratings continue to be based on historical default rates (not yet taking into consideration stricter underwriting standards in use today) so that credit enhancement often remains well in excess of the creditworthiness of high-yield "junk" investments.

Two newer agencies, Fitch and Duff & Phelps, have entered the market to provide competition through additional surveillance and market expertise. For every deal rated, a detailed analysis of the quality of the collateral is performed to determine creditworthiness of the underlying loans as well as determining the credit support needed to achieve a specific rating. Investors should do their own due diligence on the collateral pool, looking closely at loan characteristics to assess both credit quality of the pool and the quality of its cash flows. This will help determine value relative to competing securities.

The creditworthiness of a mortgage pool credit risk should be assessed on two levels: loan level and pool level.

Loan Level Credit Risk

In general, loan characteristics directly related to the borrower's equity provide the most insight into the loan quality and have the biggest impact on loss severity assumptions. These characteristics include the loan-to-value ratio at origination and the amortization schedule of the loan, but other considerations discussed below are also important.

Loan-to-value: Loan-to-value ratio, or LTV, is a strong indicator of credit risk. The LTV is the ratio between the market value of the mortgaged property and the dollar amount of the loan on that property. Loan-to-value provides information about how much equity the borrower has in the property. Lower LTVs are preferable to higher LTVs.

If, for example, a borrower has a down payment of $25,000 on a $100,000 home, the mortgage would be for $75,000, or 75% of the value of the property, making the LTV 75%. Historical data suggest a very strong correlation between the amount of equity a borrower has invested in a home and the probability of default. Higher equity implies that the borrower is less likely to default and walk away from a sizable investment. A lower LTV is also preferable because it makes a full recovery of the mortgage amount in a foreclosure sale more likely, if a default were to occur.

Although the foreclosure frequency is assumed to be higher for LTVs above 80%, high LTV loans are often required to carry private mortgage insurance (P.M.I.). PMI is an insurance policy paid for by the borrower, which covers losses in the event of default, synthetically lowering the LTV to 75% for the lender. Private mortgage insurance increases the lenders odds of recovering the loan balance in a foreclosure, but does not reduce the likelihood of foreclosure and its resultant disruptions in the timeliness of cash flows.

Exhibit 2 illustrates the expected losses for pools with varying loan-to-values. Loans with little equity built up or high LTVs (95.01 - 100.00), have the highest historical loss experience of 10.5 basis points. Loans with high equity and low LTVs (60.01 - 65.00) have a considerably lower loss experience of 0.1 basis points.

Amortization Type: Fixed-rate mortgages (FRM) that are fully amortizing with level monthly principal & interest payments are the least likely to default. Borrowers pay an identical mortgage payment each month, with a greater share of their payment going to reduce debt as the loan amortizes. This consistency makes it easy for borrowers to plan their mortgage payments as part of their monthly budgets, and the idea that each check brings a borrower closer to owning a home debt free makes writing that check more palatable.

Loans with negative amortization, where the debt owed actually grows over time, (such as graduated payment mortgages, GPMs), have more risk. Despite paying diligently every month, borrowers might find themselves deeper in debt than when they began. This makes default more likely, because it erodes the borrower's equity. If borrowers find they have little or no equity left in their home, it is easier to turn over the keys. The resultant increase in loan amount and the corresponding increase in LTV makes complete recovery in the case of foreclosure less likely.

For similar reasons, 15-year fixed-rate loans are viewed as less risky than 30-year loans, since the significantly faster amortization rate results in a faster debt reduction and more rapid growth in the borrower's equity. Fifteen-year borrowers also tend to be more creditworthy, because they qualify for and choose to make higher monthly payments.

Balloon loans are more risky than fully amortizing loans because they call for a large payment at maturity. If the financial situation of the borrower has deteriorated since the time the mortgage was originated, or the value of the property has dropped, the borrower may not qualify for a new loan to "take out" the balloon. This would force a foreclosure or restructuring of the mortgage. Because there never is a need for a bulk payment with a fully amortizing loan, these situations would not challenge the borrower's ability to meet their mortgage obligation.

Adjustable-rate mortgages (ARMs) are riskier than fixed-rate securities because of the possibility of upward adjustments in ARM coupons, which can cause "payment shock" as well as slowing of the amortization rate. "Payment shock" occurs when a family sees its monthly mortgage payment go from $500 to $650 because of upward movements in interest rates.

Exhibit 5 illustrates historical losses for both fixed- (FRM) and adjustable- (ARM) mortgages. In some cases, ARMs have experienced two to three times the losses that FRMs have experienced. For AA rating on a pool of ARMs, Standard & Poor's requires that loss coverage be 1.5 - 2.0 times greater than on a pool of fixed-rate mortgages, all other things being equal.

Loan Purpose: The motivations behind a borrower's application for a mortgage help to determine its relative risk. Mortgages used to refinance an existing mortgage are the least likely to experience credit problems. Refinancing usually reduce the borrower mortgage rate and reduce the size of the borrower's monthly payments, lessening the likelihood of default. Mortgages used to finance the purchase of a primary residence are also relatively low risk. Loans used to refinance existing debt that allow mortgagors to borrow more money than they previously borrowed are called "equity takeout" loans or "cash out refis". Equity takeouts result in higher LTVs and run a larger risk of default than do purchase or refi mortgages.

Exhibit 5: Non-Agency Mortgage Default Losses
Average Cumulative Pool Losses to Date by Loan Type (in basis points)

Origination Year	FRM	ARM
1989	49	58
1990	36	54
1991	9	26
1992	2	3

Database represents estimated 75% of all non-agency rated deals issued.
Source: C S First Boston.

Property Type: The relative liquidity and stability of occupancy trends for a type of property directly affect the ability of the asset class to withstand negative economic cycles. In recessionary environments, single-family detached properties usually experience the least declines in their market values for a number of reasons. People who own their own home are less likely to walk away from their property during times of economic duress. After years of planting gardens and cutting grass, it is very difficult for a borrower to lose a home and move into a rental property. As a result, mortgages on single-family detached properties are viewed as having the least risk. Condominiums and townhouses do not stand up as strongly in economic down times.

Occupancy: Mortgages on owner-occupied properties are considered the least likely to experience payment problems. In times of economic difficulty, a homeowner is more likely to continue to make payments on a primary residence, forgoing payments on other debts. Purchasers of second homes or investor properties, where mortgage payments are often generated by rental income, are more likely to default in economically adverse circumstances.

Loan Size: The larger the loan balance, the higher the risk of loss when a default occurs. This is due to generally lower liquidity of high priced homes, (relative to median prices in a given area). In times of economic weakness, there will be more buyers looking to purchase moderately priced homes than expensive homes. A million dollar house is worth a million dollars only if there is someone willing and able to pay that much for it.

Loan Documentation: Different mortgage originators require varying levels of documentation to verify the creditworthiness of a prospective borrower. The level of detail and reliability of the sources used in this process affect the projected creditworthiness of the resulting loan. Applicants to federal programs must meet strict requirements that include full documentation of all credit-related information such as verification of income and employment, net worth, outstanding debts, and property appraisals. Loans originated along these lines are called full-documentation loans and all else being equal have the least credit risk.

Some originators use standards that are less stringent than the agencies. Alternative documentation allows an underwriter to verify income and assets from sources less reliable than those used for full agency documentation. Originators of limited documentation loans usually verify either income or assets, but in many cases not both. A no-documentation loan demands no documentation of the borrower's creditworthiness, focusing instead on verifying the market value of the property.

Of course, each mortgage loan is characterized by a number of these and other factors which all interplay in the determination of credit worthiness. For example, a full documentation loan with an LTV of 70% appears to be low risk, but it may not be if it's on an investor-owned condo. Likewise, an 80% LTV mortgage on a second home may seem risky... but perhaps not if it's a refinancing from a 30 year into a 15 year, and is a moderate sized loan on a single family property with full documentation. By evaluating each underlying mortgage loan in the pool, and considering all of these (and other) risk factors, rating agencies assess the credit risk of the pool.

Pool Level Credit Risk

Besides loan-oriented risk factors, there are various risk factors that are relevant at the pool level.

Geographic Dispersion: Geographic concentration within a pool increases its exposure to localized economic and natural hardships, and decreases its creditworthiness. A loan package with loans from only one state or region is generally considered riskier than a pool of mortgages diversified across several different regions, although the actual economic diversity of different regions is also factored into the evaluation. Geographic dispersion limits the risk of dependence on one local economy.

Number of Loans: When there are a large number of loans in a pool, the investor's risks are more diversified, and the pool's actual performance will have a lower standard deviation than that asset class's expected performance. S&P will apply actuarial underwriting standards to pools with over 300 loans. Pools with below 300 loans are penalized in that additional credit enhancement is required.

Delinquency/Foreclosure Status: Unlike newly issued pools, existing private-label pools have actual delinquency and foreclosure experience. This information is available from the issuer, servicer, or trustee, depending on the particular pool, and is stated either in terms of number of loans or principal balance. Delinquent loans are reported as being 30, 60, or 90 days delinquent.

Exhibit 6: Moody's Loss Curve

Expected Distribution of Losses over Time

Year	Percent of Expected Losses
1	0
2	4
3	11
4	22
5	21
6	14
7	12
8	8
9	7
10	3
	100

Source: Moody's Investor Service

All other things equal, the most attractive pools are those with the lowest delinquency and foreclosure experience, for although past performance is no guarantee of future results, it can be an indicator of the quality of underwriting practiced by the loans' originators. However, investors should be aware that many issuers have tightened their underwriting standards over time. Investors should pay most attention to the 60- and 90-day delinquent categories, because even a slightly late payment can technically put a loan into the 30-day delinquent category, and therefore the 30-day category includes many observations that are unlikely to develope into defaults.

ESTIMATING LOSSES FOR SINGLE-FAMILY ANALYSIS

Historical delinquency and loss information is available for outstanding mortgage pools. Losses differ from delinquencies in that they represent actual realized losses, not potential future losses. Delinquent loans can resume paying as scheduled, and foreclosure sales sometimes produce enough cash to cover the outstanding mortgage balance. Losses represent dollars forgone; a dollar lost can never be recovered. When evaluating a mortgage pool, look at its specific characteristics, such as LTV, amortization type, documentation, and geographic dispersion, and compare it to existing pools with similar features. Assign loss assumptions that reflect this comparison and reflects your current outlook on housing prices versus the housing market that impacted historical losses.

It is assumed that some losses will occur in every pool. According to Moody's (Exhibit 6), very few losses will occur in the first two years. Losses are generally assumed to be concentrated in years 3 through 7, and tail off to negligible levels around year 10, based on historical experience.

Exhibit 7: Non-Agency Mortgage Default Losses
Cumulative Pool Losses To Date By Origination Year

Origination Year	Average Pool (%)	Median Pool (%)	Top 5 Issuers (Range:% -%)
1987	0.254	0.084	0 - 0.75
1988	0.471	0.147	0 - 3.23
1989	0.547	0.318	0 - 2.33
1990	0.443	0.080	0 - 1.92
1991	0.170	0.00	0 - 1.58
1992	0.019	0.00	0 - 0.38
1993	0.00	0.00	0 - 0.02

Database represents estimated 75% of all non-agency rated deals issued.
Source: C S First Boston.

When evaluating a mortgage-backed security, one should compare its loss experience to average and median loss experiences for similar pools, being careful to account for the relationship between actual losses, the pool's age, and Moody's loss curve model.

Actual loss experiences have been very low to date. Exhibit 7 depicts historical cumulative pool losses to date for the whole-loan market (shown as an average and median), and also the range of pool level losses experienced by today's top five, non agency MBS issuers.

A portfolio manager should remember that subordinate securities represent leveraged credit risk. A 2.3% loss experience is insignificant to a holder of a security with 5% subordination below it, but disastrous for the holder of a 3% first loss position.However, first loss classes are sold at very deep discounts and given assumed levels of losses, for this reason, the timing of losses is also of great importance to a first loss investor. The size of the subordinate investment, and the amount of protection below it, must both figure into an evaluation of a pool's credit risk. Since most pools will experience some losses, investors purchasing a first loss position should always do so factoring in a reasonable loss expectation. *The loss-adjusted yield is the important factor to look at, not the zero-loss scenario.*

This actuarial approach to underwriting is adequate for the evaluation of subordinate MBS backed by single-family mortgages. The homogeneity of the underlying collateral as well as the large number of loans in each pool make loan level underwriting unnecessary. Investing in commercial mortgage pools however presents different challenges.

COMMERCIAL MBS

When evaluating commercial mortgage securitizations many of the same factors used to evaluate single-family mortgages should be examined including loan-to-value, amortization type, loan size, documentation, geographic diversification, number of loans in the pool, and delinquency and foreclosure experience. In addition, because commercial real estate is, by definition, income-producing property, there are several additional loan level characteristics that an investor must evaluate.

Debt Coverage Ratio

The debt coverage ratio (DCR) indicates the amount of income a property produces relative to the contractual debt service. A debt coverage ratio of 2x indicates that the property is generating twice the income needed to make its regular mortgage payment. A debt coverage ratio of 0.9x indicates that the property is earning only 90% of the income needed to pay its mortgage. If a property is producing less income than it needs to pay its mortgage, the owner of the property must make up the difference by subsidizing the property's cash flow with alternative sources of income, or go into default. Since, by definition, commercial properties are not their owners' primary residences, the borrowers are much more likely to choose to give up the property than to continue to pump in more cash.

Property Type

All commercial income-producing properties are not created equal, and the market differentiates between each type's creditworthiness. A key factor in the underwriting process for commercial properties, as noted above, is debt service coverage. In order to determine the DCR ratio on a property, income and expenses related to running the property must be determined. The stability of the cash flows and the resulting net operating income (NOI) contribute directly to the creditworthiness of the loan.

A building that produces $1 million in cash flow one year can easily cover annual payments of $700,000 per year. On the surface, this would appear to be a good loan. Yet risks may become evident if you consider the source of the income. If, for example, an office building has one major tenant renting half the space for $40 per square foot, and that tenant moves out and is replaced by a new tenant at $20 per square foot, the resulting NOI, and DCR could fall dramatically. It is conceivable that it could fall below the $700,000 necessary to service the property's debt. The more stable the NOI on a property type, the easier it is to estimate future NOI, and hence the more creditworthy the loans on that property type.

Buildings leased for long periods to "credit" tenants with investment-grade debt ratings are the most predictable. Since the tenant has the ability to pay and has committed to making lease payments for a long period of time, the NOI on this type of loan is very stable. Multi-family properties are considered the next most stable. Although leases on apartments usually do not last longer than one year, apartment markets rarely run at less than 90% occupancy rates. There is also a very large pool of potential users of available space, unlike some other property types. NOI changes on multi-family properties usually occur more slowly than on other property types.

Commercial loans on property without credit tenants usually are more at risk in terms of cash flow of the individual tenants. Anchored regional malls with long-term leases to the anchors can ameliorate this risk. Strip retail shopping centers and office buildings are considered riskier. Industrial and warehouse properties are usually stable, but other risks such as environmental risk are associated with them.

Environmental Risks

Commercial and multi-family properties carry additional risks that are generally not significant for single-family properties and are not related to the property's ability to service its debt. Our country has increased its awareness of the impact that progress has had on our environment, and the legislative sentiment is currently hostile to owners of developed real estate. Property owners can be liable for the costs related to cleaning up any environmental problems found on their properties, regardless of fault. As a result, lenders must consider the environmental status of any property they lend on and the likelihood of its experiencing any future environmental problems.

For example, assume a lender provides a mortgage on a local strip mall with a gas station next door. If the gas station has underground storage tanks that have leaked oil and gas into the area's watershed, the owner of the strip mall could be responsible for removing the contamination. Since contaminated soil must be placed in specially regulated dumps that can be very costly, it is likely that this expense would be enough to cause the owner to default on the mortgage. If the lender then foreclosed on the property, the lender would be the new owner and must assume the previous owner's obligation to clean up the site.

The costs associated with a cleanup could exceed the economic value of the property. In order to avoid this scenario, originators of commercial loans contract with firms that are expert at detecting environmental risk. Their initial survey of a property is called a Phase One survey. When buying a pool of commercial mortgages, an investor must make sure that full environmental Phase One surveys have been completed on every property, and either any risks detected have been cleaned up or money has been placed in escrow to cover these expenses.

SPECIAL SITUATIONS IN COMMERCIAL MBS

The lower the credit rating of the security, the more detailed the due diligence must be. At the investment-grade levels (triple-A through BBB), the general analysis outlined above should suffice for investors. For commercial securities with subinvestment-grade ratings, far greater due diligence is warranted including property inspections, loan file examinations and appraisals. For first loss and very highly leveraged below investment-grade classes, real estate equity expertise is required, which is beyond the scope of this chapter. There are, however, unique opportunities where an investor can purchase lower-rated commercial securities without all the expense and time of massive equity-level due diligence.

Cash Reserve Funds

The RTC, in its eagerness to dispose of assets, structured many of its commercial real estate deals with cash reserves of 20% - 30% to absorb losses experienced in the pool. With that much protection, the deal would lose up to 30% of its principal before any bondholders lost their first dollar. To put it in perspective, 60% of the portfolio could default, and foreclosure sales could recover only 50% of the loan amount, and the bondholders would still be made whole. One would expect these bonds to be investment grade, but because of the lack of good historical data for commercial mortgage loss experience, the ratings agencies assigned ratings as low as BB.

Excess Interest

Because many of the underlying mortgage loans in securitizations have coupons that are much higher than the coupons on the various classes created in the securitization, the difference, or excess interest, is available. Sometimes the excess interest is sold as an IO strip. Other times a deal is structured such that the excess interest cash flows are used to pay down principal on lower-rated classes. Since excess interest from a $100 million pool might be used to help pay down principal on a $5 million class, the security is retired much faster than the underlying loans. As a result, some lower rated classes may mature before the underlying loans have even had time to default. The ratings agencies will not give full credit to these so called "interest apply" structures, so MBS with this feature sport ratings that probably overestimate their true credit risk.

Real Estate Equity Participant

Some deals are issued by non-governmental entities with significant real estate expertise. Sometimes, these issuers have enough confidence in their own underwriting to take a major equity stake or the first-loss bond position themselves. These issuers would receive no money until all of the bondholders are paid off. In these situations, investors can take additional comfort at the BB and B levels by the confidence implied.

STRUCTURAL FEATURES

The cash flow priorities in both single family and commercial mortgage backed security can impact the credit risk in a bond. Average life stability that results from a deal's structure, like agency collateralized mortgage obligations (CMOs), is still important in determining a security's relative value. There are other features that can protect subordinate investors from prepayments or losses that would otherwise negatively affect their returns. These include shifting interest, compensating interest, and special hazard insurance.

Shifting Interest

The shifting interest mechanism is found in many senior subordinate structures, and causes the senior certificates to absorb all prepayments in the early years of a pool's life. In a typical shifting interest structure, the senior class of a fixed-rate deal will receive 100% of the total prepayments for five years. For example, assume a $100 million pool were split up into a $90 million senior class and a $10 million subordinate class. If the pool were to experience $1,000,000 worth of prepayments during years 1 through 5, the senior class's balance would be reduced by the entire $1,000,000 of prepayments, not just its pro rata (90%) of $1,000,000. The subordinate class would receive no prepayments. This prepayment lockout causes subordinate MBS to take on PAC-like average life profiles.[3] In most structures, the subordinated class's share of prepayments begins at 0% in the first five years, and increases by 20% increments per year after that until a pro rata amount is reached.

   Exhibit 8 illustrates the average life profile of a sample security with a shifting interest structure. Under a considerable range of prepayment scenarios, the average life stability of the subordinate class remains stable when compared to its senior counterpart. For example, from 100 PSA to 500 PSA the senior security's average life changes from 6.8 years to 3.2 years, for a variation of 3.6 years. In contrast, the subordinate security is much more stable, shortening from 8.2 years to 6.9 years, for a difference of only 1.3 years.

Compensating Interest

Compensating interest reimburses investors for interest income lost due to prepayments that occur other than on the mortgage's payment date. If a loan is prepaid on the first of the month for example, the borrower owes interest only through the date of the prepayment. Yield analysis generally assumes that investors receive all prepayments on the payment dates, and that these prepayments are accompanied by interest through that date. A prepayment received by the servicer on the first will not include interest through the payment date, usually the 25th day of the month.

---

[3] Planned amortization class is generally regarded as the CMO class best protected from average life variability.

Exhibit 8: Average Life Profile of a Senior Versus a Subordinate Security

Model Prepayment Speed Assumption (PSA)	Average Life of Senior Security	Average Life of Subordinate Security
0	8.7	8.7
100	6.8	8.2
200	5.4	7.8
300	4.4	7.5
400	3.7	7.2
500	3.2	6.9
1,000	1.9	5.0

The restitution for lost interest, so-called "compensating interest", is paid by some servicers out of their fees. Because only some deals provide for compensating interest, investors should determine if the servicer of the deal pays all, part, or no compensating interest. The impact of not paying any compensating interest is usually nominal, ranging from 2 to 10 basis points, depending on the prepayment rate.

Special Hazard Insurance

Subordinate mortgage-backed securities are often subordinate with respect to not only credit-related default losses, but losses due to special hazard risks, (the most common being earthquake risk). Subordinate MBS can be used to absorb a specific amount of special hazard losses, perhaps 0.5% - 1.0% of the pool balance. Losses beyond that are due to special hazard, are usually absorbed by both the senior and the subordinates on a pro rata basis.

As always, we recommend that investors read the prospectus carefully and focus on all factors that can affect cash flows and overall performance.

CASH FLOW ANALYSIS

Once the collateral quality and structural characteristics of a deal are evaluated investors should conduct a cash flow sensitivity analysis focusing on expected and worst-case scenarios. Scenarios should be designed to stress the security for greater than expected prepayments and loss-rates within the context of historical data for the issuer and mortgage type, and given outlook. The manager should be comfortable with the performance of the bond in a reasonable worst-case scenario, and should be comfortable that the compensation for the additional risk is adequate.

If advanced modeling tools are not available to an investor, it is advisable to ask the investment bank structuring the security to provide any scenarios deemed necessary. Most modern deals are too complex to be modeled by the investor in a timely manner, and many deals will not be available on public market information system: such as Bloomberg or Passport, until after they have been seasoned for several months. The issuer should also have the most detailed and up-to-date information on the collateral and its historical performance.

SUBORDINATE MBS IN A FIXED-INCOME PORTFOLIO

How can a manager utilize their knowledge of the subordinate mortgage market to improve their portfolio returns? There are many ways in which subordinate mortgage-backed securities can be integrated into a generic mortgage or corporate bond portfolio. We discuss several strategies, and then illustrate how subordinated MBS can be used to enhance portfolio returns.

Minor Credit Rating Shifts

A low-risk way to enhance portfolio returns relative to an index is to buy securities similar in structure and duration to those in the index, but one notch lower in credit rating. A bond in an index with a triple-A rating would return yields of 40 to 80 basis points over comparable Treasuries. AA-rated securities with the same or better average life profiles provide spreads 80 to 100 basis points wider, while carrying minimally increased credit risk. A portfolio that matches its index in every other way will produce returns 80 to 100 basis points higher than the index in almost every scenario.

A manager need not do this with an entire portfolio, but it is a very effective way to enhance returns with minimal additional risk. The farther a manager diverges from the credit profile of the index, the higher the potential returns. As always, the amount of risk managers want to add is based on how much incremental yield is necessary to achieve their objectives.

Diversified Portfolio of High-Yielding Subordinate MBS

Portfolio managers of high-yield, lower-credit quality corporate bond funds should be natural buyers of subordinate mortgage-backed securities. Subordinate mortgage-backed securities can add the diversification of an asset class whose performance is not directly correlated to the fortunes of U.S. corporations lowering the volatility of the overall fund, while still maintaining attractive incremental yields. By investing a portion of their funds in highly leveraged, diversified first-loss or subinvestment-grade securities, high-yield managers can realize returns comparable or in excess of those available in their traditional markets.

The optimal strategy to employ when assembling a subinvestment-grade mortgage portfolio is to buy leveraged pieces from many different deals, issuers, and asset classes, to achieve the full effect of diversification. If we assume a typical first-loss or subordinate security represents 10% of a deal, a $50 million fund, invested in 50 different $1 million first loss or subordinate securities can provide diversified exposure to over $5 billion worth of mortgages.

Taking Advantage of New Structures or Undervalued Asset Types

The relative value technique of active portfolio management can be used within the subordinate security market to help significantly enhance returns. Just as there are situations in traditional markets where the price of a security relative to similar investments seems out of line, undervalued securities can also be found in the subordinate market. There are times when the spreads between rating levels in the mortgage market are much wider than the spreads between the same rating levels in the corporate bond market. Although triple-A-mortgage products traditionally trade wider than triple-A-corporate securities, the spread between triple-A and AA mortgage securities should be similar to the spread between triple-A and AA corporate securities. Because the subordinate MBS market is relatively new and there is a paucity of educated buyers, subordinated MBS currently trade cheap to not only sub-investment grade corporates, but also to senior investment grade MBS.

There are also occasions where a mortgage backed security will trade at a wider spread than other mortgage backed securities with comparable ratings. This can be due to structural or collateral deficiencies, but usually is caused by factors that should not affect the value of the bond. For example, a securitization backed by unusual or new asset types, such as mobile home parks or nursing homes. The rating agencies are usually even more conservative in their approach to newer asset types, and so demand higher levels of protection for the same ratings.

Because of the enhanced credit protection, one might think that these securities would trade at tighter spreads than more accepted asset types. The opposite is generally true. The first few securitizations of a new type of asset tend to trade at a yield concession to the market. As the investor base becomes educated about the product, that spread tends to contract. It is a good strategy to learn about new securitized products early and take advantage of opportunities in the early stages.

Exhibit 9 illustrates the value of learning about a product type early in the process. Notice how the spreads on the RTC BB-rated securities tightened over time. These classes in all three deals were almost similar in both structure and collateral quality, so that early buyers were handsomely rewarded for being the first to learn about this asset type and for realizing its relative value.

Exhibit 9: RTC Commercial Deal Spreads
from 10/30/92 To 3/30/93

	RTC Issue	1992-C8	1993-C1	1993-C2	1993-C1
	Closing Date	11/24/92	1/28/93	3/30/93	4/28/94
Spread:	AA	+275/7.6 yr.	+232/9/1 yr.	+185/9.9 yr.	Previously Issued
	A	+325/7.6 yr.	+325/7.0 yr.	+260/7.5 yr.	Previously Issued
	BBB	9.125%/3.4 yr.	Not Issued	9.75%/4.3 yr.	9.50%/4.6 yr.
	BB	13.25%/2.3 yr.	Not Issued	11.50%/1.5 yr.	10.50%/1.3 yr.

Integrating Subordinate MBS into a Fixed-Income Strategy

We have developed an example of a private-label MBS portfolio that invests in both agency and non-agency MBS. This portfolio is based on an actual portfolio that has outperformed the average mortgage fund by 312 basis points over the past 12 months and ended up in the top 10% of all mortgage funds for the one year period ending June 30, 1994. This was accomplished without taking any significant duration or prepayment risk and maintaining an overall investment grade rating on the fund.

Exhibit 10 provides summary data on both the private-label MBS portfolio and the Generic MBS Index. Exhibit 11 illustrates expected total returns for both the portfolio and the index over a one year holding period for unchanged and up and down 100 basis points scenarios. Note that the private-label MBS portfolio had a similar duration and a one-notch lower weighted average credit rating than the Generic MBS Index, yet outperformed it in all scenarios, including a credit stress scenario in which the spreads on all the subinvestment-grade securities were widened by 200 basis points.

CONCLUSION

The performance of the private-label MBS portfolio illustrates that subordinate mortgage-backed securities can help enhance yields and total return performance when intelligently integrated into a generic mortgage or corporate bond portfolio. Managers who take the time to understand subordinate mortgage-backed securities, will be rewarded with better performance without incurring undue risks.

Subordinate securities will continue to provide higher yields than alternative securities with similar risk profiles. The still maturing commercial markets will continue to afford entrepreneurial investors a myriad of opportunities for exceptional value, and those on the cusp of the learning curve will stand to reap the greatest rewards.

Exhibit 10: Private-label MBS Portfolio versus Generic MBS Index

Private-label MBS Portfolio Composition (June 30, 1994)

Security Type	Rating	Percent of Portfolio	Average Spread at Purchase
GNMA	AGY	16%	90
FNMA	AGY	17%	90
FHLMC	AGY	19%	90

Total Agency Holding: 52%

Single-family:	AAA - BBB	19%	153
Multi-Family:	AAA - BBB	5%	178
Commercial:	AAA - BBB	7%	191
Commercial:	BB	8%	525
Single-family:	BB	6%	475
Agricultural:	Unrated	3%	800

Total Non-Agency Holdings: 48%

Generic MBS Index: Portfolio Composition (June 30, 1994)

Security Type	Rating	Percent of Portfolio	Average Spread at Purchase
GNMA	AGY	30%	90
FNMA	AGY	33%	90
FHLMC	AGY	37%	90

Total Agency Holding: 100%

Exhibit 11: Private-label MBS Portfolio versus Generic MBS Index
One-Year Holding Period

		Effective	Total Return		
Sector	Rating	Duration	-100	Unchanged	+100
Private-label Portfolio	AA	4.00	10.77	7.80	4.51
Private-label Portfolio (Stress)	AA	4.00	9.46	6.22	3.76
Mortgage Index	Agency	4.00	6.43	5.91	3.52

Section IV

PREPAYMENT ANALYSIS

CHAPTER 12

Prepayment Analysis for Non-Agency Mortgage-Backed Securities

Douglas L. Bendt
President
Mortgage Risk Assessment Corporation

Chuck Ramsey
Principal, Alex. Brown & Sons, Inc.
CEO, Mortgage Risk Assessment Corporation

Frank J. Fabozzi, Ph.D., CFA
Editor, Journal of Portfolio Management
Adjunct Professor, Yale University

INTRODUCTION

Prepayment analysis typically has been limited to the value of the pre-payment option — determined chiefly by the gap between the mortgage coupon rate and the current mortgage rate and, to a lesser extent, the impact of loan age or seasoning along with macroeconomic variables such as GDP growth or the unemployment rate.

Analysts know that prepayment models ideally should discriminate between a homeowner's decision to refinance an existing mortgage — whether to obtain a lower rate or to obtain cash — and the decision to sell the property. Modeling these decisions accurately would require much more data, such as information on the homeowner's family composition, life style stage, and overall financial situation. Hence, the existing "three-factor" models are only proxies for the "real" model.

These model imperfections are not the result of any lack of creativity, but rather the limitations of the data released by Fannie Mae, Freddie Mac, and Ginnie Mae. The agencies release only aggregate information such as weighted average coupon/maturity (WAC/WAM) by quartile and geographic concentrations at the state level, average loan age, and average loan size. Moreover, prepayments are not reported by type.

Issuers of private mortgage-backed securities or non-agency MBS are much more forthcoming with data, generally releasing loan-level detail for the collateral backing their deals. These data generally are in a standard format such as the one developed by the Public Securities Association (see Appendix A). This detail makes it possible to do much more complete prepayment analysis to answer the following kinds of types of questions:

- Is the prepayment function for loans taken out to purchase a house different from the function for loans that refinance a previous mortgage?

- What is the effect of homeowners' equity and changing property values on prepayments?

- Do alternate documentation or low/no-doc loans prepay differently from fully documented loans?

TRADITIONAL AGENCY/NON-AGENCY PREPAYMENT COMPARISONS

Exhibit 1 shows that prepayments for non-agency MBS tend to be faster than "comparable" agency MBS. The quotation marks are necessary because some analysts control only for the WAC and the WAM of the pools being compared.[1]

Exhibit 1: Multipliers for Non-Agency MBS Prepayments Relative to Agency MBS Prepayments

Issuer	Multiplier
Capstead	1.45
Chase	1.90
Citibank	0.82
Prudential	1.58
Residential Funding	1.40
Ryland	1.18

Source: Bear Stearns and Co., "Prepayment of Whole Loan Securities," June 4, 1993.

Among the factors cited for the faster speeds are that:

1. Greater variation in loan composition, such as greater WAC dispersion can make WAC/WAM comparisons inadequate.

2. Larger loan sizes tend to prepay faster because the same size prepayment option in percentage terms is worth more in dollar terms.

3. More affluent borrowers tend to be more mobile.

4. California — traditionally a fast-prepaying state — is overrepresented in non-agency MBS.

Other analysts correct for some of these factors.[2] Adjusting for collateral diversity and geographic concentrations, Prudential finds the multipliers averaging about 1.5 except during the depths of the last recession, when non-agency securities prepaid *slower* than agency MBS.

ADJUSTED AGENCY/NON-AGENCY PREPAYMENT COMPARISONS

Rather than compare non-agency and agency prepayment rates, it would be preferable to make such comparisons on a loan-level basis. This analysis would effectively remove the effects of WAC/WAM discrepancies and dispersions, allowing the effects of other factors to be seen more clearly.

---

[1] See "Prepayment of Whole Loan Securities," Bear Stearns and Co., June 4, 1993.

[2] Prudential Securities, "Prepayments on Whole-Loan Securities," (1993).

Exhibit 2: WAC Dispersion and Prepayments
30-Year Fixed-Rate Pools
Freddie Mac: March 1994

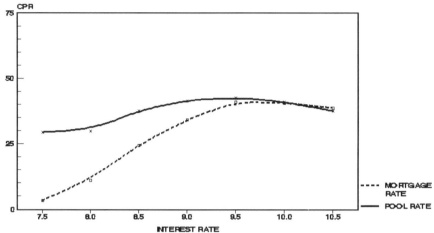

With agency data, such comparisons are normally impossible. The data provided by Dow Jones/Telerate's Advance Factor Service in Exhibit 2, however, clearly show the effects of analyzing prepayments by pool coupon compared to analyzing prepayments using the actual mortgage rate. Even if the pool coupon curve is shifted to the right by 75 basis points (the average servicing fee), the discrepancy is extremely large for low coupons, implying that the greatest impact of WAC dispersion is on future prepayments of relatively new collateral.

Exhibit 3 shows traditional prepayment curves for agency and non-agency collateral calculated from loan-level detail. The agency data are derived from Freddie Mac's loan file (also provided by Dow Jones/Telerate's Advance Factor Service), while the non-agency data are a composite of six of the ten largest issuers. Note that the average "multiplier" for the new-issue, lower coupons is about 2.5 — well above the range cited by other analysts —while multipliers for older, higher-rate collateral are about 1.5 — right in the middle of the range cited by other analysts.

The higher multipliers for the lower coupons are measuring the effects of the refinancing wave of the last two years. For example, the barriers to refinancing have been lowered substantially with the increasing popularity of no-points mortgages. Thus, the value of the prepayment option for jumbo borrowers has increased in dollar terms relative to the value of the option for agency borrowers, given the same size of rate decrease.

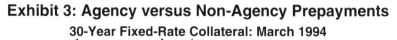

Exhibit 3: Agency versus Non-Agency Prepayments
30-Year Fixed-Rate Collateral: March 1994

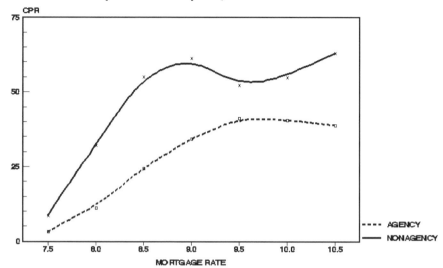

Although these data eliminate distortions in speed due to difference in WAC or WAC dispersion, differences in WAM could still account for some of the discrepancies in speeds. Exhibit 4 shows prepayment curves for non-agency loans of different years of origination. Prepayments for 1993 originations are lower than prepayments for 1992 originations for every coupon by some 25% to 40%.

OTHER FACTORS AFFECTING PREPAYMENTS

Besides coupon and seasoning, there are three major influences on prepayment rates for non-agency securities. In order of importance, they are (1) homeowners' equity; (2) transaction type (purchase versus refinance); and (3) level of documentation.

Homeowners' Equity

A homeowner's equity depends chiefly upon two major factors: (1) the initial down payment, and (2) changes in home prices. Together, these factors determine the current loan-to-value (LTV) ratio, defined as the current mortgage balance divided by current market value. Amortization and partial prepayments are of lesser importance.

Exhibit 4: Non-Agency Prepayments By Origination Year
30-year Fixed-Rate Collateral: March 1994

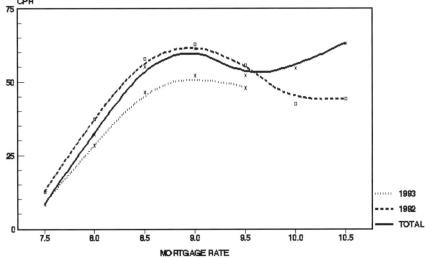

Homeowners with lower LTVs — greater equity — have more home financing choices. Most importantly, they could sell their houses to unlock the equity to use as a down payment on another house. Second, they could do a cash-out refinancing to unlock the equity even if they don't want to move or interest rates aren't any lower. And finally, if interest rates are lower so that the prepayment option has value, there is no constraint on taking advantage of the lower interest rate.

Exhibit 5 shows a clear pattern of faster speeds among mortgages with lower current LTVs where current market values are estimated by using indexes of home price changes. This pattern helps explain California's reputation for being a fast-prepaying state throughout the 1980s. Housing prices exploded, allowing many homeowners to do equity-takeout refinancings and to trade up to bigger homes. With housing prices having dropped for the last three years in most areas of California, prepayments have slowed dramatically.

The pattern of slower prepayments at higher LTV ranges is maintained for every mortgage origination year, which controls for the coupon rate of the mortgage and the WAM or seasoning/maturity. The differences in the level of cumulative prepayments depend on the relative coupon rates: Mortgages from 1988-1989 have greatest value to their prepayment option, and thus have the fastest prepayments.

Exhibit 5: Payments by Current LTV
For Origination Years 1990 and 1992
March 1994

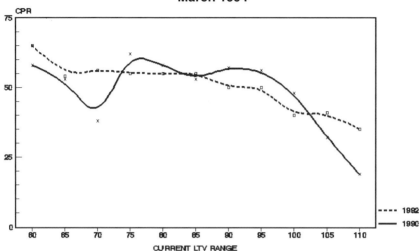

Transaction Type

Mortgages taken out to purchase homes tend to be prepaid more slowly than mortgages taken out to refinance previous higher-rate mortgages. Refinance transactions in which the homeowner takes out cash tend to be more like purchase transactions. Exhibit 6 shows this pattern especially clearly for mortgages originated in the 1992-1993 and the 1986-1987 periods, when rates were low.

Homeowners refinancing an existing mortgage are different from homeowners who just purchased a house in two important ways. First, they have lived in their house for some amount of time. Therefore, they are more likely to have moved to a new stage in their life cycle and to require a different type of house. And second, the fact that they have refinanced their mortgage once already may make them more sensitive to future rate drops because they realize how easy the process can be. Mortgage brokers are more likely to be more aggressive with previous refinancers as well.

Level of Documentation

Non-agency mortgages that are fully documented are loans that would qualify for sale to the agencies, but for the fact that the loan amount is higher than the agencies' limits. (Loans may not qualify for sale to the agencies for other underwriting characteristics such as debt ratios as well, but these reasons are much less common.) Borrowers are required to submit forms verifying income and employment with W-2 forms, pay stubs, tax forms, and lenders verify the sources of the assets to be used for the down payment.

Exhibit 6: Prepayments by Transaction Type
Cumulative Since Issue

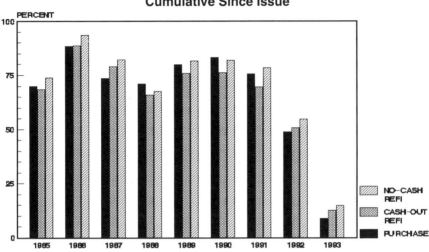

Loans that are deficient in at least one of these areas qualify under "alternative" or "low" documentation programs, usually at a slightly higher interest rate and a lower cap on the permissible LTV. In the extreme, no documentation may have been required as a trade-off for a higher rate and/or an even lower LTV.

Borrowers who qualified for full documentation programs in the last two years have had higher prepayments (see Exhibit 7). First, the spectrum of lenders who will lend to such borrowers is wider; fewer lenders have a low or no-doc program than in the past because of higher default experience (see Chapter 6). Second, borrowers who qualified under a less-than-full-doc program are more likely to have fluctuations in their income — many are self-employed — that may limit their ability to refinance or trade up.

CONCLUSION

Our analysis shows that much more detail is available to incorporate into non-agency prepayment models than agency prepayment models. Using these data to derive an explicit non-agency model will give much more accurate results than simply applying multipliers derived from WAC/WAM comparisons to the results of an agency prepayment model.

Exhibit 7: Prepayments by Documentation Level
Cumulative Since Issue

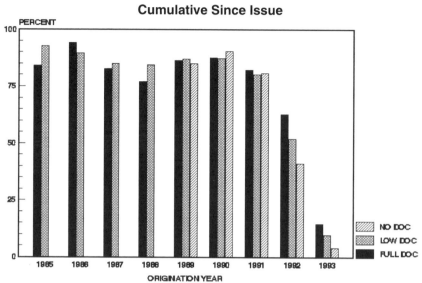

CHAPTER 13

The Volatility of Prepayments on Non-Conforming Mortgages

Sean Becketti
Assistant Vice President / Fixed Income Research
CS First Boston Corporation

Richard Ellson
Director / Mortgage Research
CS First Boston Corporation

Evan Firestone
Director / Mortgage Products Group
CS First Boston Corporation

Karen Auld Wagner, CFA
Vice President / Fixed Income Research
CS First Boston Corporation

The authors would like to thank Teresa Shen of CS First Boston for providing invaluable assistance in the preparation of this chapter.

INTRODUCTION

Our understanding of prepayments on non-conforming jumbo mortgages is significantly poorer than for conforming agency mortgages. This lack of knowledge proved to be costly in 1993, as prepayments in the non-conforming sector soared through the levels of agency prepayments, which themselves caught most market participants off guard. What was particularly disconcerting to investors in the non-conforming private label market is that significant prepayment activity commenced within the first few months of origination. Since many tranches of whole-loan CMOs were issued near par or at a slight premium during this period, the negative convexity of these securities substantially impaired performance.

Unfortunately, the problems did not end in 1993. When interest rates spiked unexpectedly in the first quarter of 1994, it became obvious that the prior year's aggressive pricing speeds and actual prepayments were the product of the near-continuous rally in the market. Prepayments on recently issued whole-loan CMOs slowed markedly, and extension risk rather than call risk became the overriding concern.

For example, pricing speeds on whole-loan CMOs backed by new originations went from around 250 to 275 PSA in February 1993 to over 400 PSA by the end of the year. By the middle of 1994, pricing speeds had declined to approximately 220 PSA. In contrast, pricing speeds for agency CMOs remained in their traditional range of around 175 PSA. The extension problem on whole-loan CMOs caused severe difficulties for the more volatile cash flows such as short companions. This adversely affected the whole-loan CMO market.

Our relative lack of understanding about non-conforming jumbo (whole-loan) prepayments stems from a number of sources. First and foremost is the lack of available data. Although loan-level data are available from private vendors, there are a number of errors and omissions and a general lack of consistency in the raw product. Even when these obstacles are overcome, the available time series are only marginally adequate for modeling purposes.

The majority of the data come from the most recent three years, a period when the market was rallying for the most part. For example, 55% of the total outstanding private label issuance (as of July 1, 1994) occurred in 1993. Therefore, whole-loan prepayment data over an entire interest rate cycle are simply not available. Although loan-level data provide more detailed information than do agency cohorts, the coverage of the agency time series is far superior.

Without adequate data, there cannot be a sound prepayment model for whole loans. As a stopgap measure, some analysts resort to the calculation of whole-loan multipliers: the ratio of whole-loan prepayments (often by issuer) to agency (conventional) prepayments. The best that can be said about these multipliers is that they are naive — the worst that can be said is that they have no value and are actually terribly misleading.

In periods of refinancing, newly issued whole loans prepaid several times faster than comparable agencies. For example, whole loans with eight months of seasoning prepaid at a multiple of four in January 1994 relative to comparable agency cohorts. By May, these mortgages were prepaying at virtually the same rate, with a multiplier of 1.04. This should not be surprising in light of what we know now.

The existing fee structure gives mortgage brokers every incentive to refinance jumbo loans for the thinnest of margins. No-cost refinancings for only 25 basis points were not fiction in 1993, and this behavior will no doubt reoccur in the next rally. Moreover, WAC dispersion in whole-loan pools created refinancing opportunities even though the gross WAC was not in the money.

The reality is that prepayments on whole loans are more bullet-like than prepayments on agencies. Prepayments occur more frequently and on narrower margins. When the mortgages are out of the money, relative prepayments will track the strength of the conforming versus jumbo housing markets adjusted for the greater long-term mobility of wealthier households. Prepayments on newly issued non-refinanceable jumbo mortgages should be quite comparable to prepayments on comparable conforming loans, and they have been. In summary, prepayments on jumbo mortgages now appear to be more predictable than they were before. We should incorporate this information in our investment strategies.

We attempt to answer two questions in this chapter. First, what makes whole loans different, that is, what are the differences between whole loans and agency collateral in the factors that determine prepayments? To answer this question, we analyze a sample of loans in which it turns out that jumbo and conforming mortgages are surprisingly similar, apart from the concentration of whole loans in California. Second, how slow can prepayments on whole-loan CMOs go? We argue that the panic over extension risk was overdone. It is very unlikely that jumbo loans will prepay below 100 PSA for any extended period. We use our analysis of these questions to motivate our investment strategies in whole-loan CMOs. In our judgement, now is a particularly opportune time to invest in this sector.

WHAT MAKES WHOLE LOANS DIFFERENT?

Prepayments are the result of relocation, refinancing, curtailment (partial prepayment), or default. Relocations are the result of changes in family composition, family income, and local and national economic conditions. Refinancings, curtailments, and defaults are influenced by a dauntingly long list of economic factors: swings in the refinancing rate, changes in the borrower's economic circumstances, appreciation (or depreciation) of the home, and changes in lending practices. These factors that influence relocation, refinancing, curtailment, and default are the fundamental determinants of prepayments.

Differences in these determinants account for the differences in the prepayment behavior of whole-loan and agency mortgage securities. Until recently, most analysis of the differences in prepayment behavior relied on anecdotal or indirect evidence on these determinants. For instance, while it is "well-known" that whole loans are concentrated in a few areas, particularly in southern California. It has been hard to quantify some of these well-known differences. A particular problem has been the paucity of data supplied by the agencies on the loan-level collateral backing their MBS. Without detailed loan-level information on both conforming and jumbo mortgages, it is impossible to pinpoint the real reasons for the differences in prepayment behavior.

Fortunately, detailed loan-level data are finally becoming available for both conforming and jumbo mortgages. These data are supplied by loan servicers and whole-loan CMO issuers. The data supplied by servicers record the performance of both securitized and unsecuritized mortgages. These data are beginning to make it possible to develop more sophisticated and more accurate models of prepayments.

Geographic Distribution

The most commonly noted difference between conforming and jumbo mortgages is the high proportion of jumbo mortgages originated in California.[1] Exhibit 1 describes the geographical distribution of a sample of conforming and jumbo mortgages taken from the Loan Performance System (LPS) compiled by Mortgage Information Corporation. This subsample contains fixed-rate, 30-year residential mortgages originated after 1976 on owner-occupied, single-family homes. This subsample was chosen to eliminate extraneous differences between the conforming and jumbo mortgages, and to highlight the differences in prepayment determinants.

Exhibit 1 shows the percentage of jumbo, conforming, and combined mortgages originated in the five states most heavily represented in the sample. The conventional wisdom happens to be correct in this case — California accounts for most of the mortgages in this sample (34%), but it accounts for a disproportionate share of the jumbo mortgages. Fifty-one percent of the jumbos come from California, compared to only 28% of the conforming mortgages.

Once California is accounted for, jumbos are not markedly more concentrated geographically than conforming mortgages. The four states with the next highest numbers of jumbo and conforming mortgages account for 41% of the remaining jumbo mortgages and 39% of the remaining conforming mortgages.

---

[1] We divide mortgages into jumbo and conforming on the basis of the amount borrowed. Our "conforming" mortgages may not meet all the other underwriting requirements imposed by the agencies.

Exhibit 1: Distribution of Mortgages by State

State	Jumbo Mortgages (%)	Conforming Mortgages (%)	All Mortgages (%)
California	51	28	34
New Jersey	8	10	10
New York	6	7	7
Illinois	3	6	5
Pennsylvania	3	5	5
Top Five States	72	56	61

Source: Mortgage Information Corporation and CS First Boston calculations.

Loan Purpose

The loan purpose, the reason for taking out a mortgage, gives important information about the likelihood of future prepayments. Borrowers who have refinanced once are more likely to refinance again. Exhibit 2 displays the distribution of loan purpose in the sample. Twenty-nine percent of jumbo mortgages result from refinancing, compared to 22% of conforming mortgages. And 30% of jumbo mortgage refinancings were initiated in order to cash out equity, compared to 27% of conforming refinancings.

The share of refinancings that represent equity takeouts varies with home prices. When home prices appreciate, borrowers have a strong incentive to cash out. When home prices depreciate, as they have in recent years, borrowers may be inhibited from refinancing at all, even when mortgage rates fall significantly.

Exhibit 3 shows the share of refinancings that represent equity takeouts for mortgages originated from January 1985 through March 1994. The share of equity takeouts increased in the late 1980s, when home prices were increasing. This increase is much larger for jumbo mortgages, though, reaching a peak of 70% of refinancings in 1989 and 1990. As home prices fell in the 1990s, equity takeouts collapsed as well.

Loan-to-Value Ratio

Homeowner equity affects borrowers' incentives to cash out when times are good and to default when times are bad. From the point of view of lenders and whole-loan MBS investors, homeowner equity lowers the probability of default and reduces losses in the event of a default. The loan-to-value ratio (LTV) measures the reverse of homeowner equity; the higher the LTV, the lower the homeowner equity. An LTV of 100 indicates no equity at all.

Exhibit 4 shows the LTV at origination for jumbo and conforming mortgages. The LTVs of jumbo and conforming mortgages are very similar. There are somewhat more jumbo loans with LTVs just over the 80% mark, the threshold for private mortgage insurance.

Exhibit 2: Distribution of Mortgages by Loan Purpose

Purpose	Jumbo Mortgages (%)	Conforming Mortgages (%)	All Mortgages (%)
Purchase	71	78	77
Refinance	20	16	17
Equity Takeout	9	6	6

Source: Mortgage Information Corporation and CS First Boston calculations.

Exhibit 3: Share of Equity Takeouts Among Refinancings

Year	Jumbo Mortgages (%)	Conforming Mortgages (%)	All Mortgages (%)
1985	17	20	19
1986	22	24	22
1987	46	43	44
1988	67	53	56
1989	70	45	53
1990	70	32	42
1991	47	28	33
1992	28	25	26
1993	21	24	23
1994 (Jan-Mar)	25	25	25

Source: Mortgage Information Corporation and CS First Boston calculations.

Exhibit 4: Distribution of Mortgages by Loan-To-Value Ratio

LTV (%)	Jumbo Mortgages (%)	Conforming Mortgages (%)	All Mortgages (%)
0 to 79	65	70	69
80 to 89	26	19	21
90 and above	9	10	10

Source: Mortgage Information Corporation and CS First Boston calculations.

Housing Prices

An increase in the value of the home increases the incentive to initiate an equity takeout refinance. In addition, home price appreciation increases homeowners' wealth, making them likelier to trade up to more expensive homes. Home price depreciation may make it impossible for homeowners to refinance when mortgage rates fall. Home price depreciation also increases the likelihood of defaults. Home price volatility is important as well, since it affects the value of the homeowners' prepayment and default options.

Exhibit 5 shows estimates of both home price appreciation and the volatility of home prices for two California counties. These estimates are derived from the repeat-sales price indexes compiled by Mortgage Risk Assessment Corporation. Repeat-sales indexes estimate price changes by comparing pairs of sales prices on the same properties at different times. The more-familiar median home price series can be misleading when there are shifts in the types and locations of homes that are sold. Because they rely on repeated sales of the same property, repeat-sales indexes do not suffer from this problem and, as a a consequence, provide a more accurate measure of the change in home values.

The pair of charts in the upper half of the exhibit shows the annual rate of change in home prices in the jumbo and conforming mortgage price tiers for Los Angeles County, representing southern California, and Marin County, representing the San Francisco metro area. Over the long term, prices move similarly in both price tiers, although there are significant discrepancies that can persist for several years. For example, prices in the jumbo mortgage tier in Marin county grew much faster than prices in the conforming tier until the 1989 peak, after which they fell off more sharply.

The pair of charts in the lower half of Exhibit 5 shows the annual standard deviation of monthly price changes--a measure of home price volatility. The volatility is very different across counties (note the difference in the scales). Moreover, the volatility at times differs substantially for the jumbo and conforming mortgage price tiers. In Los Angeles County, volatility in the jumbo price tier rose sharply in 1993, at the same time as volatility in the conforming price tier fell, driving volatility in the jumbo price tier significantly above volatility in the conforming sector. In Marin County, volatility in the jumbo sector has been consistently higher than in the conforming sector (and much higher than in Los Angeles) until this year.

Exhibit 5: Home Price Yield Inflation and Volatility

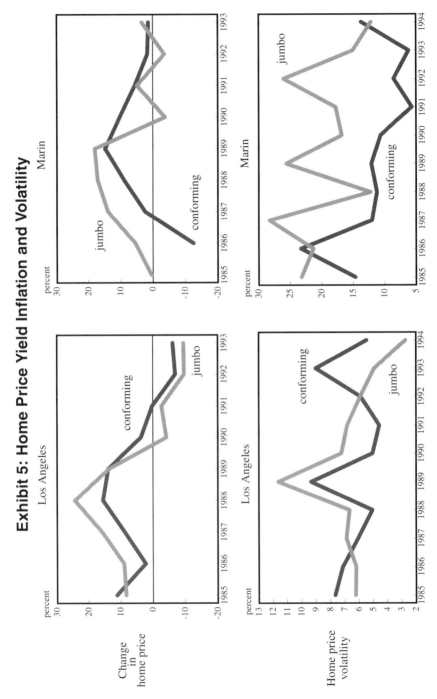

Source: Mortgage Risk Assessment Corporation and CS First Boston calculations.

Exhibit 6: Distribution of Mortgages by Payment Status

Payment Status	Jumbo Mortgages (%)	Conforming Mortgages (%)	All Mortgages (%)
Current	91.7	92.8	92.6
Delinquent	6.6	5.8	5.9
In Foreclosure	1.7	1.4	1.5

Source: Mortgage Information Corporation and CS First Boston calculations.

Delinquency

For agency MBS, delinquency is a precursor to, rather than a determinant of, prepayments. Nonetheless, knowing that a mortgage is delinquent identifies which factors are most likely to trigger prepayment. For whole loans, though, delinquencies mainly increase credit risk.[2] Exhibit 6 reports the payment status of the sample of fixed-rate loans as of March 1994. Jumbo and conforming mortgages displayed essentially identical distributions of payment status in March.

Summary

The most important difference between jumbo and conforming mortgages is the geographic distribution of the loans. Just over half of the jumbo mortgages originate in California, compared to slightly more than a quarter of the conforming mortgages. Aside from the dominance of California collateral among jumbo loans, whole loans and agency collateral are surprisingly similar.

Jumbo loans are somewhat more likely to be refinanced than conforming loans, and jumbo loans respond more sensitively to changes in the incentives to refinance and to cash out equity. This difference may reflect aggressive marketing by mortgage brokers, who find it more profitable to refinance larger mortgages. Jumbo mortgage borrowers are not markedly more levered than conforming mortgage borrowers. Home price inflation and the volatility of home prices are sometimes very different for the jumbo loan price tier than for the conforming tier, but these differences do not follow any simple pattern. Finally, there is no apparent difference in the delinquency experience of jumbo and conforming mortgages.

To oversimplify slightly, the important difference between jumbo and conforming mortgages is that the jumbo mortgage collateral is in California. As a consequence, prepayments on whole-loan CMOs will be

---

[2] Delinquency may increase the prepayment risk of a jumbo loan if the lender is willing to restructure the mortgage, that is, to refinance to avoid a default.

heavily influenced by housing turnover and general economic conditions in California. Refinancing reflects lenders' incentives to market their services as well as borrowers' incentives to reduce their borrowing costs. Lenders have a greater incentive to refinance larger loans, and competition among lenders is particularly fierce in California. These factors tend to magnify the "California effect" on whole-loan prepayments.

WHOLE-LOAN CMO PREPAYMENTS: HOW SLOW CAN THEY GO?

At the height of the 1993 bond market rally, jumbo mortgages (the majority of the underlying collateral in whole-loan CMOs) prepaid significantly faster than agency mortgages. With the collapse of the rally in early 1994, investors' concerns have shifted from prepayment risk to extension risk. Whole-loan MBS investors are faced for the first time with a selection of discounts to evaluate. The gross coupons on many deals reflect historic lows in mortgage rates. These securities are viewed by most investors as less likely to be called than to extend.

How slow can whole-loan prepayments go?[3] The answer depends on how frequently whole-loan borrowers will relocate and how rapidly they will curtail their mortgages. Unfortunately, most of the securitized whole-loan market is only about as old as the bond rally (Exhibit 7). Thus the limited historical data are dominated by refinancing-related prepayments and provide scant evidence on relocations and curtailments. In the absence of hard evidence, some analysts have suggested using prepayment rates as low as 100% PSA as pricing speeds.

We believe extension fears have been overplayed. A PSA of 100 implies that the average homeowner moves no sooner than once every 17.4 years. But mobility data compiled by the Census Bureau indicate that long-term prepayment rates are unlikely to be lower than 150% to 175% PSA for whole-loan products, even for deep discounts.

Is 100% PSA Typical?

Some investors have assumed that 100% PSA represents the rate of prepayments on agency mortgages due to housing turnover alone. This is not the case. The long-term speed of 6% CPR (after 30 months, 100% PSA = 6% CPR) was chosen by the Public Securities Association (PSA) as a reference point only.

---

[3] This section is based in part on Karen A. Wagner, Evan B. Firestone, and Elen Callahan, "Whole-loan CMOs: How Slow Can They Get?" CS First Boston Fixed-Income Research Report, May 26, 1994.

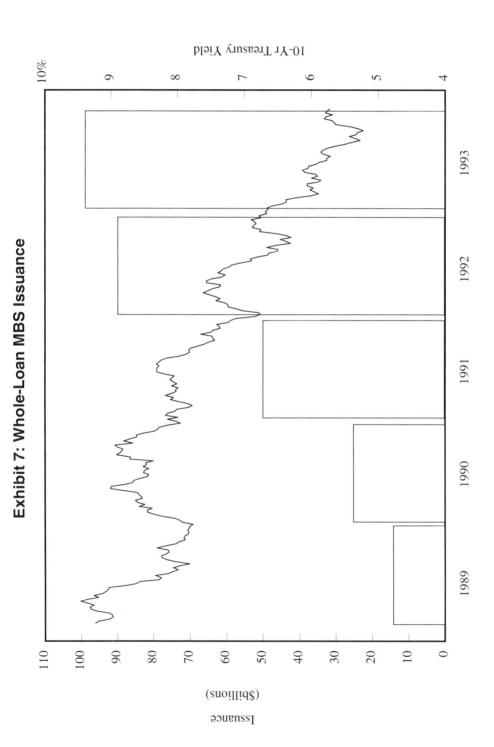

Exhibit 7: Whole-Loan MBS Issuance

Exhibit 8 displays two examples that contradict the notion that 100% PSA represents a typical or baseline prepayment speed. The exhibit charts the actual PSAs from 1988 through 1990 on two discount securities: FNMA 6.5s originated in 1972 and FNMA 8s originated in 1987. Mortgage rates averaged 10.5%, corresponding to a FNMA current coupon of 9.75%, during this period. While prepayments on these securities occasionally dipped below 100% PSA, they were typically much higher, averaging around 120% PSA. The nation was in recession during the 1989-1990 period, which generally suppresses housing turnover. Thus, these data strongly suggest that 100% PSA understates normal housing turnover, even for deep discounts, and even for agency securities.

PSA Speeds and Housing Turnover

There is no historical record comparable to that shown in Exhibit 8 for discount whole-loan CMOs, but we can use information about housing turnover to estimate likely long-run PSAs for these securities. As a first step, we calculate what the PSA standard implies about relocation rates. Exhibit 9 displays the relationship between PSA and the *average time to move*.[4] This measure is not the traditional average life calculation, but rather a weighted average time to recovery of principal assuming no refinancing and ignoring amortization.

As Exhibit 9 shows, 100% PSA implies that borrowers relocate once every 17.4 years, on average. In other words, 100% PSA suggests that people move about as often as *locusts* (which appear every 17 years). Alternatively, if people move, say, every seven years, the correct speed for new collateral is approximately 250% PSA. Over short horizons, of course, prepayment rates may fall below long-term speeds.

Census Data on Mobility

According to the Census Bureau's most recent population report, *Geographical Mobility: March 1991 to March 1992*, an estimated 17.3% of Americans moved in the period studied. This mobility rate implies an average time to move of 5.8 years.[5] Mobility rates vary markedly across subgroups in the population, but, except for rural residents, the Census Bureau does not generally find mobility rates as low as those associated with prepayment speeds of 100% PSA.

---

[4] The average time to move varies slightly with the age of the mortgage because of the seasoning ramp of the PSA. Exhibit 9 displays the implied average time for newly originated mortgages. For additional calculations, see Wagner et al., "Whole Loan CMOs: How Slow Can They Get?"

[5] The mobility rate is the annualized percentage of a given group that changes residence over some period. Thus mobility rates are directly comparable to CPRs, which are annualized percentage rates of mortgage prepayment. If relocation were the only source of prepayments, mobility rates and CPRs would be identical, aside from a small correction for loans that mature. The average time to move is equal to the inverse of the mobility rate.

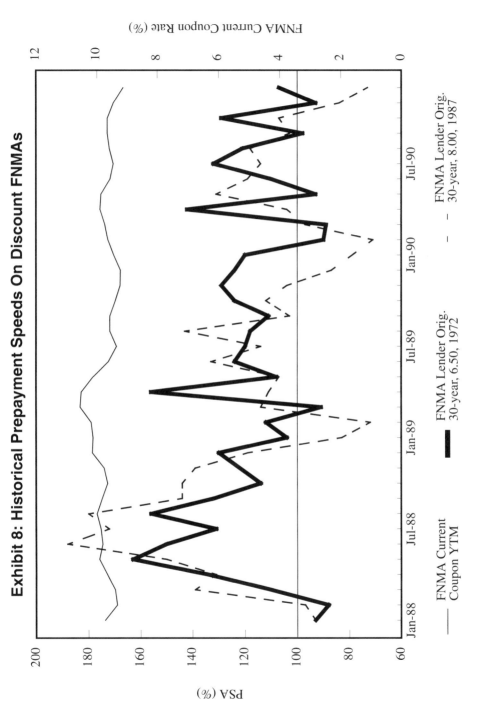

Exhibit 8: Historical Prepayment Speeds On Discount FNMAs

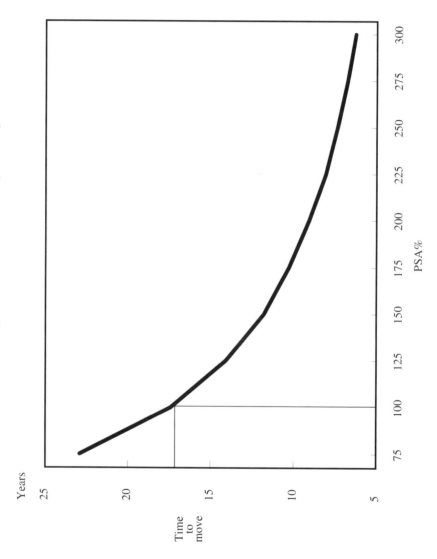

Exhibit 9: Average Time to Move Implied by PSA

Exhibit 10: Long-Term Prepayment Forecast for Discount Whole-Loan CMOs

	Adjustment Factor		Mobility Rate
Total Mobility Rate '91-'92			17.3%
High-income Homeowners: '91-'92 mobility rate			8.5%
Recession Adjustment	20.2%/17.3% =	1.17x	+1.4%
20.2%: Non-Recession Mobility, '84-'85			
Geographic Adjustment	21.4%/17.3% =	1.24x	+2.0%
21.4%: Pacific Region Mobility, Source of Majority of Whole Loans			
MSA[*] Adjustment	21.1%/17.3% =	1.22x	+1.9%
21.1%: Mobility for Those Within MSAs Only (Jumbo borrowers unlikely to be rural)			
Estimated Mobility Rate for Whole-Loan Borrowers =			8.5% - 13.8%
CPR Equivalent =			8.5% - 13.8%
Long-term PSA Equivalent[**]			173% PSA - 300% PSA
Implied Average Time to Move			≈ 10.3 to 6.3 years

[*]MSA: Metropolitan Statistical Area as defined by the Census Bureau.
[**]Assumes new collateral. For collateral seasoned 30 months, the long-term PSA equivalent is 142% PSA-230% PSA.

We can estimate mobility rates on whole-loan collateral by adjusting the Census Bureau estimates for known characteristics of jumbo mortgage borrowers and properties. These adjustments are detailed in Exhibit 10.

The baseline rate for whole-loan borrowers is 8.5%, the rate in 1991-92 for households with incomes high enough to qualify for a jumbo mortgage. The first adjustment is for the recession in 1991-1992. The total mobility rate in 1984-1985 was 20.2%, 1.17 times the 17.3% total mobility rate in 1991-1992. This adjustment adds 1.4% to our estimate. Next we adjust the rate to account for the concentration of jumbo loans in California. The estimated mobility rate in the Pacific region is 21.4%, almost 25% higher than the national average. Finally we increase the mobility rate to reflect the concentration of jumbo loans in urban and suburban areas.

According to these Census Bureau estimates, it appears that housing turnover alone will support long-term PSAs of 150% (9% CPR) or higher for whole-loan CMOs

Note that new mortgages do not necessarily represent new homeowners. In 1993 and early 1994, many whole-loan CMOs contained 65% to 75% refinancings. With mortgage rates at their lowest levels in 20 years, many refinancers had been in their homes for some time. Therefore the average time to move in Exhibit 10 may be overstated for these borrowers.

Curtailments

Curtailments may push whole-loan prepayments even higher than the turnover-based estimates reported above. While borrowers are more apt to curtail premium than discount mortgages, curtailments are likely even on discounts as consumers seek to deleverage their personal finances.

The popularity of 15-year mortgages provides evidence of borrowers' eagerness to deleverage. In late 1993, whole-loan borrowers had the opportunity to borrow 30-year fixed-rate money at 6.5%, tax-deductible. As long as one believed it was possible to earn more than 6.5% over the 30-year horizon, the best strategy would have been to borrow as much as possible (a high LTV) for as long as possible (30 years) and invest the cash available from the lower down payment and lower monthly mortgage payments.

The extent to which people refinanced at 65% LTV using 15-year products indicates that borrowers are interested in a more conservative approach to their finances. For this reason we expect borrowers to continue to use discretionary income to pay down their mortgages regardless of their mortgage rate.

Summary

The rise in interest rates in 1994 has, for the first time, created discount whole-loan CMOs and, as a consequence, investor concern with extension risk. Some investors have voiced fears that prepayment speeds on discount whole-loan securities could fall to 100% PSA. Prepayments may drop this low intermittently, but our analysis of mobility data suggests that housing turnover alone will support long-term PSAs of 150% to 175%. These prepayment speeds imply an average time to move of 10 to 12 years.

INVESTMENT IMPLICATIONS

Investors in whole-loan CMOs earn a spread over agency CMOs. A portion of that spread is attributable to the additional credit risk in a triple-A rated whole-loan CMO. However, the compensation necessary for credit risk is very small; for example, the difference in spread between agency debentures and AAA corporates has ranged from 0 to 15 bps. The bulk of the spread compensates investors for differences in prepayment risk. Therefore, the real focus for most whole-loan CMOs (senior tranches) is on prepayment risk.

Two aspects of whole-loan prepayments should shape investors' strategy. First, jumbo mortgage borrowers are more mobile than conforming mortgage borrowers. Thus, discount dollar-priced CMO bonds backed by discount whole-loans are attractive because the market generally underestimates this mobility difference.

Second, jumbo mortgages refinance more aggressively than con-forming mortgages. CMO bonds that benefit from this greater optionality (whole-loan Z tranches, for example) are also attractive, because the market at the time of this writing does not price in the greater upside potential in whole-loan prepayments.

Discounts Off Discounts: Playing the Mobility Story

Whole loan CMOs backed by collateral 200 bps. or more out-of-the-money are not uncommon today. Most investors regard a 200 bps. rally as unlikely, so the refinancing option is moot. With refinancing unlikely, the primary risk for investors in discounts off discounts is a bad estimate of housing turnover. Note that this type of estimation error is not strongly correlated with interest rate changes. Mobility is affected more by general economic conditions than by interest rates.[6]

As an example, consider Residential Funding's 93-S43, Tranche A5, an AAA-rated vanilla tranche off 7.28% (gross WAC) 30-year collateral. At 175% PSA, the A5 has an 8.26-year average life. It is offered at +185 b.p. to the 7.5-year interpolated Treasury, a dollar price of 84-05. RFC 93-S43 has prepaid at 204% PSA to date. Monthly prepayments have been volatile, which is not uncommon, especially in whole-loan CMOs. Whole-loan pools generally are composed of a smaller number of loans, and monthly prepayment data can be quite noisy. In the nine months since origination, monthly prepayments have ranged from 0.7% to 5.7% CPR.

Exhibit 11 displays the yield of the A5 tranche under various interest rate scenarios. Note that under none of these scenarios are the loans mean-ingfully in-the-money. Even a 200 bp rally would bring the refinancing option less than 30 bp in-the-money. In all the other scenarios, the option is out-of-the-money. Therefore, prepayments are driven mainly by mobility. We have noted the average time to move implied by each PSA.

Under the extreme assumption of a prepayment speed of 100% PSA for life, this investment extends to an average life of 13.5 years and still earns 86 bp over the ten-year benchmark. This performance compares very favor-ably to AAA-rated corporate debt (ten-year bullet), for example, which is cur-rently priced at +40 to +45 bp over the ten-year Treasury.

In the base case (175% PSA) the investor earns a very attractive spread for AAA credit risk and relatively little negative convexity. The upside for the A5 — the likelihood of faster prepayments due to greater mobility than is implicit in the price — is substantial. If prepayments come in at 250% PSA, the investor earns approximately an additional 95 bps (and 299 bp over the benchmark).

---

[6] Wagner et al, "Whole Loan CMOs: How Slow Can They Get?", provide evidence in favor of this contention.

Exhibit 11: Yield Under Different Interest Rates, RFC-93-S43-A5

Rate Scenario	-200	-100	-50	0	+50	+100	+200	+300
PSA (%)	275	250	175	175	175	150	150	100
Implied Time to Move (yrs)	6.4	7.0	9.8	9.8	9.8	11.4	11.4	17.0
Average Life (yrs)	5.17	5.70	8.26	8.26	8.26	9.64	9.64	13.54
Benchmark (yrs)	5.00	5.00	7.50	7.50	7.50	10.00	10.00	10.00
Level (%)	6.70	6.70	6.90	6.90	6.90	7.09	7.09	7.09
Spread (bp)	330	299	185	185	185	136	136	86
Yield (%)	10.00	9.69	8.75	8.75	8.75	8.45	8.45	7.95

MBS investors are paid largely for taking on negative convexity. Yet, in today's market, there are many opportunities where the negative convexity has been largely "wrung out." Bonds priced at conservative speeds, sporting low dollar prices, and with little risk of being refinanced — discounts off of discounts — represent value.

Z Bonds and Whole-Loan CMO Optionality

The greater optionality in whole-loan collateral means that CMOs that benefit from faster prepayments — discount Z tranches, for example — can offer more upside in the whole-loan market than in the agency market.

For example, consider GE 94-09 Tranche A9, a whole-loan support Z tranche. This bond was offered at a spread of 140 bp to the ten-year using a 175% PSA. At the time of the analysis, this corresponded to a 77-26+ dollar price. GE 94-09 A9 is comparable to FNMA 94-31 Tranche ZA, also a Z bond and backed by similar WAC and WAM collateral. The FNMA bond was offered at a spread of 140 bp to the ten-year Treasury at 145% PSA, a dollar price of 79-07+.

Exhibit 12 compares the projected total returns of these two bonds over a one-year horizon and under five different interest rate scenarios (all assumed to be immediate parallel yield curve shifts): unchanged, +/-50 bp, and +/-100 bp. Street median prepayment assumptions are used to analyze the agency Z bond. For the whole-loan Z, we use prepayment speeds that are multiples of the agency speeds. As we note earlier, these multipliers are unstable and provide a poor foundation for portfolio analysis. Multipliers are used here solely to illustrate conventional valuations.

Using these assumptions, the GE 94-09 A9 is projected to outperform the FNMA 94-31 ZA significantly in rallying scenarios and also is likely to outperform in the base case. If rates fall 50 bp, for instance, the total return on the whole-loan bond is projected to be 11 to 15 percentage points higher than the return on the agency bond. The GE 94-09 may underperform in a backup, but only modestly. These results depend heavily on the assumed multiplier, and, as we noted, these multipliers are highly unstable.

Exhibit 12: One-Year Total Return: GE 94-09 A9 and FNR 94-31 ZA

Rate Scenario	-100 bp	-50 bp	Unchanged	+50 bp	+100 bp
Whole-Loan Multiplier	1.8 to 2.0	1.8 to 2.0	1.2 to 1.4	1.2 to 1.4	1.2 to 1.4
GE	33.39 to 33.43%	27.82 to 31.46%	8.53 to 10.61%	1.01 to 4.11%	-6.26 to -3.18%
FNR	21.16%	16.32%	8.53%	2.42%	-3.95%
Difference	12.23 to 12.27%	11.50 to 15.14%	0.00 to 2.08%	-1.41 to 1.69%	-2.31 to 0.77%

CONCLUSIONS

Prepayments on jumbo mortgages were unusually volatile in 1993 and 1994. The extremes of prepayments were experienced within a very short period of time. This prepayment "whipsaw" demonstrates the need for more rigorous analysis in this sector.

Fortunately, better data are becoming available, and more sophisticated models will follow. These data reveal a surprising similarity in the characteristics of conforming and jumbo mortgages, although the geographical distributions of the collateral are quite different. The data confirm that prepayment trends on jumbo loans will be driven largely by conditions in California.

There are two dimensions to this "California effect": economic and institutional. The economic dimension refers to the strength of the California housing market, income growth in the state, migration, and related factors that affect prepayments on discount mortgages. At the time of this writing, the California economy is underperforming relative to national trends. Some may argue that this underperformance is a signal of structural changes in the California economy that will permanently reduce the California turnover "premium." Obviously, no one can resolve this argument at the present time.

There are a number of factors, however, that will support base case prepayments on jumbo loans. These factors include the greater mobility of wealthier households, the ability and the desire to deleverage, the higher probability of living in urban areas, and other factors noted above. Some of these factors are magnified in California. All the evidence suggests that prepayments on discount jumbo loans should exceed 150 PSA. Short-term prepayments may temporarily fall below this level, because of a recession or seasonal factors, for example.

From an institutional perspective, mortgage lending in California is very competitive. Refinancing is in many ways a lender-driven process, and jumbo loans are simply more profitable to refinance. Therefore, refinancing activity in this sector should exceed levels in the agency sector. Furthermore, the refinancing process will commence when loans are only marginally in-the-money. There is no penalty for early refinancing since the process can be repeated easily if mortgage rates continue to decline.

The investment strategies drawn from this analysis are straightforward. Discount whole-loan CMOs currently are priced to very slow life speeds. In our judgment, the market has overestimated extension risk. Hence, cash flow in structured products is likely to be stable under a wide range of interest rates. The incremental spread offered in this sector can be realized.

Given the relative bullet-like profile of the prepayment option, investors should also consider callable securities in this sector such as companion Zs. Compared to the agency sector, the upside in a rally is substantial, and the give-up in a bearish market is minimal.

It is important to recognize that prepayments on jumbo loans have become more predictable, not less. Current market practices (pricing to worst-case PSAs) and the availability of discount product offer new investment opportunities.

Section V

COMMERCIAL MBS

CHAPTER 14

Commercial Mortgage-Backed Securities

David Jacob
Head of Mortgage Research
Nomura Securities International

Kimbell R. Duncan
Mortgage Securities Product Manager
Nomura International PLC

The commercial mortgage-backed securities (CMBS) market today offers investors call protection, strong credits and high yields. With few attractive investment alternatives, investors are beginning to discover the opportunities that various commercial mortgage products offer for superior performance. This chapter describes the CMBS market and highlights opportunities within the market for investors with different investment guidelines.

CMBS are bonds or other debt instruments collateralized by loans that are secured by commercial real estate. Commercial real estate describes income-producing properties that are managed for economic profit. Property types include apartments or other multi-family dwellings, retail centers, hotels, restaurants, hospitals, warehouses, and office buildings.

Our introduction provides investors with a framework for evaluating CMBS. We concentrate on the securitization of *performing* commercial mortgages, as it is our view that growth of the CMBS markets will be stimulated by the refinancing of maturing loans and the financing of new acquisitions rather than the disposition of non-performing loan portfolios.

THE ROLE OF COMMERCIAL MORTGAGES IN A FIXED-INCOME PORTFOLIO[1]

Because of their yield advantage, market size, historical performance, and unique characteristics, commercial mortgages should be a core component of a fixed-income portfolio. Further, the fundamental factors influencing prospective returns for commercial mortgages are currently attractive and suggest tactical allocations in excess of a "normal" long-term allocation. Whether administered by investment staff within a fund or by an advisor, an investment program in commercial mortgages should be executed by investment professionals with real estate experience, because returns will be influenced by performance of the underlying collateral. The choice of an investment vehicle (securitized versus whole loan) should be determined by the investor's total dollars available for investment and liquidity needs.

Historical Performance
Over the past 20 years, commercial mortgages, after credit losses, have provided returns comparable to those of other asset classes, with low volatility (see Exhibit 1).

---

[1] This discussion is adapted from: Patrick Corcoran, Dale Fathe-Aazam, and Alberto Perez-Pietri, "The Role of Commercial Mortgages Within a Fixed-Income Portfolio," *Pension Real Estate Quarterly* (January 1994).

Exhibit 1: Asset Class Returns
1973 - 1993

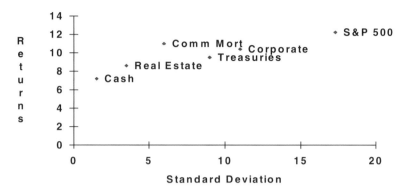

Source: The Prudential Economic & Investment Analysis Group

Analysis of the performance of asset classes by economic subperiods shows that commercial mortgage returns have demonstrated remarkable resiliency in very different economic environments (see Exhibit 2).

Correlation of Returns With Other Fixed-Income Assets

Exhibit 3 shows the correlation of returns of commercial mortgages to other high-grade fixed-income alternatives. Not surprisingly, they show high correlations, as all of the assets' prices move up or down in tandem with Treasury rates.

Treasury-Adjusted Correlations

The raw correlations among fixed-income assets ignore the extent to which a pension fund's liabilities also may have a fixed-income character. A fall in the general level of Treasury interest rates produces appreciation in fixed-income assets and a corresponding increase in the value of the fund's liabilities. If the pension fund roughly "matches" its interest rate exposure for assets and liabilities, its fund surplus will be little affected by changes in interest rates. The high raw correlations within the various fixed-income asset classes are largely irrelevant for such an investor. What matters is the returns net of the common influence of Treasury rates. The impact on the asset correlations if this common Treasury rate movement is removed, is shown in Exhibit 4.

The "Treasury-adjusted" correlations highlight that these assets contribute differently to plan surplus in the absence of interest rate risk. Assets showing the most divergent performance characteristics will yield the highest risk reduction when combined in a portfolio.

Exhibit 2: Performance Analysis by Asset Class and Economic Period (1973 - 1993)

1990 - 1993

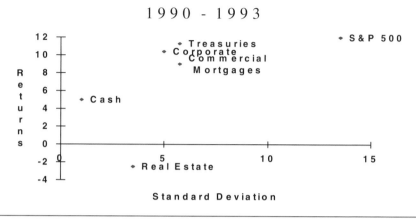

1983 - 1989

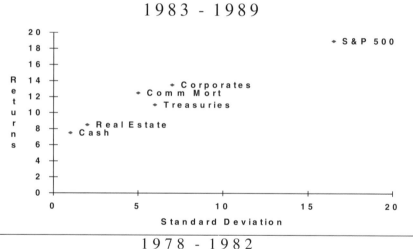

1978 - 1982

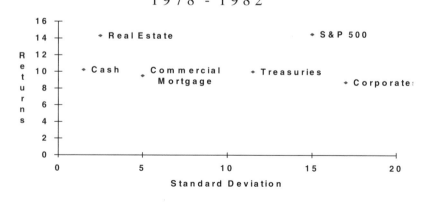

Exhibit 2 (Concluded): Performance Analysis
by Asset Class and Economic Period (1973 - 1993)

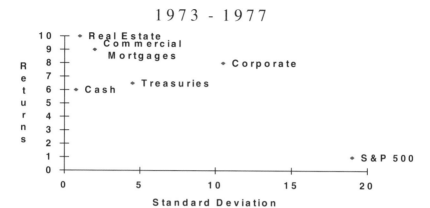

1973 - 1977

Source: The Prudential Economic & Investment Analysis Group

Exhibit 3: Cross-Correlation Matrix (1980 - 1993)

	Treasuries	BBB Corporate	GNMAs	Commercial Mortgages
Treasuries	1.00			
BBB Corporates	0.90	1.00		
GNMAs	0.92	0.92	1.00	
Commercial Mortgages	0.87	0.86	0.87	1.00

Source: The Salomon-Levy Commercial Mortgage Performance Index

Exhibit 4: Cross-Correlation Matrix
Treasury-Adjusted (1980 - 1993)

	BBB Corporate	GNMAs	Commercial Mortgages
BBB Corporates	1.00		
GNMAs	0.59	1.00	
Commercial Mortgages	-0.01	-0.06	1.00

Source: The Salomon-Levy Commercial Mortgage Performance Index

Commercial Mortgages versus Corporate Bonds

The low Treasury-adjusted correlation between corporate bonds and commercial mortgages stems from the different factors driving the two assets.

Corporate bond defaults and spreads over Treasuries are more directly tied to the economy and business cycle risk. The bulges in the corporate spread occurred around the severe recessions in 1974-1975 and 1980-1982. Similarly, in the 1990-1992 expansion episode, corporate bond spreads have narrowed substantially, and commercial mortgage spreads have widened substantially. The economy matters somewhat for corporate mortgages, but there are other factors (such as the demand/supply balance in real estate) that affect mortgage performance.

A unique characteristic of commercial mortgages is that they can play a role as an inflation hedge in a fixed-income portfolio. Rising inflation tends to raise interest rates and hurt fixed-income generally. Yet because real property prices may rise with the general level of prices, decreases in the value of mortgages caused by interest rates are partially offset by gains associated with upward credit migration. In the second half of the 1970s, when inflation rose and bonds suffered capital losses, the credit experience of commercial mortgages was excellent.

Nonetheless, inflation is not the sole agent acting on commercial mortgage credit experience. For example, in the 1988-1992 period, the role of excess real estate supply overwhelmed the modest impact of inflation. [2]

Finally, commercial mortgages are generally originated with fuller call protection than corporate bonds; therefore mortgages have less prepayment risk. In periods of declining interest rates, commercial mortgages experience larger capital gains than corporates.

Commercial Mortgages versus
Residential Mortgage-Backed Securities (GNMAs)

While residential mortgage-backed securities (GNMAs) and commercial mortgages are both collateralized by real estate, their return performance is very different. GNMAs have no credit risk, as they are government guaranteed. They trade at a spread over Treasuries because the underlying single-family residential mortgages, unlike Treasuries, may be prepaid or refinanced at par. This spread increases with interest rate volatility because the probability of prepayment increases. For commercial mortgages, on the other hand, spreads are driven more by the supply/demand balance of the real estate markets. Moreover, commercial mortgages have credit risk but little prepayment risk, because most commercial mortgages are call-protected with yield maintenance prepayment clauses.

---

[2] David Jacob and Randall Zisler, "Real Estate, Inflation, and Interest Rates" (Nomura Securities International, Inc. April, 1994)

IMPORTANT PROPERTY TYPES

An understanding of the various property types and their current market environment is necessary background for our discussions on risk characteristics of commercial mortgage-backed securities backed by loans on such properties.

Multi-family

Mortgages backed by multi-family properties represent one of the largest sectors of the commercial mortgage market. There are over $300 billion of these mortgages currently outstanding. For investors in the residential mortgage market, multi-family mortgages are often their first foray into commercial mortgages. Most are familiar with multi-family properties from everyday experience and are comfortable with the risks of the housing market.

While it is true that multi-family mortgages share many of the underlying characteristics of residential mortgages, the primary buffer against loss is the same as with all commercial properties, namely, a property's ability to generate sufficient income to cover debt service. The presence of an agency market for multi-family MBS also enhances investor confidence in this sector.

Retail

Shopping centers can be categorized into four types: neighborhood, community, regional, and super-regional. Neighborhood properties serve local clientele, offering service and convenience providers such as drug stores, dry cleaners, and banks. They are usually built around a super-market "anchor" and typically total between 65,000 to 100,000 square feet. At the other extreme are the super-regional, which are built around several large department store anchors and range in size from 700,000 square feet to over 1 million square feet. These are typically located near major transportation links and serve large areas in which there are many communities.

Office

The office building sector can be divided into two sectors: central business district and suburban markets. The central business district property is typically a single building centered in a similar environment. It makes up a constellation of large enterprises that contribute to a business-like atmosphere. The suburban property is located outside a metropolitan area and may be isolated from other businesses. This market caters more to the employee by offering amenities such as larger office space, shorter commutes, and available parking.

Hotels

The hotel market can be subdivided into five categories: luxury hotels, upper-market hotels, middle-market hotels, economy motels, and destination resorts. Luxury hotels are marked by extensive personalized services; at the other extreme, economy motels offer limited-service accommodations. Economy and middle-market hotels are today's strongest performers with the increase in cost consciousness of both business and vacation travelers. The weakest performers are big downtown convention-oriented hotels that are in need of renovation and luxury destination resorts burdened by costly overheads.

THE RATING PROCESS

One of the most important financial innovations in the capital markets during the past decade has been the securitization of loans and other receivables. This process involves the transformation of whole loans into securities with attractive investment characteristics such as high credit ratings, enhanced liquidity, and high relative yields. An important element is the process of credit enhancement. Before we discuss methods of credit enhancement and the structuring process, we examine the rating process because the rating agencies exert considerable influence on the rest of the structuring process.

Rating agencies assign ratings on debt and other securitized transactions intended to signal the capacity of an issuer to meet its debt obligations. In the view of the rating agencies, a triple-A rating for a CMBS issue should indicate the same thing as a triple-A rating for a corporate issue about the issuer's ability to make payments on its debt. Consequently, the rating agencies have been careful to establish very conservative criteria for rating commercial mortgage-backed securities. In most cases, these rating criteria are the result of in-depth studies of historical loan performance data. In the course of performing such studies, the rating agencies have sought to identify loan characteristics that influence performance and to establish conservative assumptions regarding defaults and losses resulting from foreclosures.

As noted earlier, one of the barriers to the development of the CMBS market has been a lack of loan performance data. One of the limited sources of commercial loan performance data is the American Council of Life Insurance (ACLI), which collects data from member life insurance companies and reports delinquency and foreclosure results quarterly. Reporting companies hold about 85% of the total mortgages held by U.S. life insurers. This universe of loans currently represents approximately 18% of the commercial mortgage market in terms of principal outstanding.

The ACLI has collected data on an aggregate basis going back to 1965 and by property type since 1988. Delinquencies have ranged from about 0.5% in the late 1960s to a high of 7.53% in the middle of 1992. Cyclical peaks occurred in 1976 and 1992, and cyclical troughs occurred in 1969 and 1981.[3]

The usefulness of this data by itself is limited, as it does not provide information regarding either cumulative defaults or losses resulting from foreclosures on a static universe of loans, which are necessary to develop expectations regarding potential losses on commercial mortgages.

The rating agencies and others have analyzed portfolios of loans to estimate actual cumulative default and loss severity experience. For example, Mark Snyderman of Aldrich, Eastman and Waltch found an average cumulative default rate was 12.1% through 1989 in a study of a universe of 7,205 loans originated by life insurance companies between 1972 and 1984.[4] In another study, Fitch Investors Service analyzed a static universe of 1,524 loans ($15.3 billion) originated by major life insurance companies between 1984 and 1987.[5] Through year-end 1991, the average cumulative default rate was 14%. With many loans restructured rather than foreclosed, however, Fitch estimated the true cumulative default rate was probably closer to 20%. Fitch also estimated that for the remaining life of the loans an additional 10% would default. Thus, they projected total lifetime defaults of about 30% (conservatively). As a comparison, cumulative default rates for corporate securities rated single–B have been in the range of 30% to 40%. The Fitch study of course is limited to a universe of loans originated over a very narrow time span.

The Snyderman study, on the other hand, highlights the importance of the market environment in which loans are originated. For example, loans originated in 1976 and 1977 following a real estate recession during 1974-1975 experienced much lower default rates than loans originated during periods of growth.

Fitch hypothesizes that default rates vary according to the time of loan origination since underwriting standards change during the course of a real estate cycle. Therefore, the current environment of tightening underwriting standards and lower-leveraged financings should result in the superior future performance of loans originated in recent years; these changes should encourage investors to discount past performance data when projecting future performance.

The Snyderman study also analyzes losses on asset sales resulting from foreclosure. It estimates a loss rate of 32% for those loans originated

---

[3] American Council of Life Insurance, "Investment Bulletin No. 1234" (Washington D.C., August 1993).

[4] Mark Snyderman, "Commercial Mortgages; Default Occurrence and Estimated Yield Impact," *Journal of Portfolio Management* (Fall 1991).

[5] Fitch Investors Service, "Commercial Mortgage Stress Test" (New York, June 1992).

between 1972 and 1984. Fitch cites loss severity results from several other studies that give varying pictures of loss experience. For example, from a study of Midwest life insurance companies' portfolios, they report an average loss severity of 21% on foreclosed properties. Fitch qualifies those results by noting that life insurance companies often keep the worst quality properties on their books rather than trying to sell them. Thus, loss severity results on this universe tend to understate reality.

At the other extreme, Fitch quotes a Freddie Mac report claiming that, when the costs of foreclosure are taken into account, losses average 60% on foreclosed multi-family loans. Other data cited show losses from 25% to 57.5%.

When they rate specific transactions, rating agencies adjust their expectations of defaults and loss severities to reflect the differences between the collateral of the transaction being rated and the universe of loans upon which their studies have been performed. S&P uses a default model incorporating loan characteristics such as interest rate, term, and property type which are then used to determine conditional probabilities of default. Incorporating these expectations, they then require sufficient credit enhancement such that the securities experience zero losses in scenarios defined by some assumed probabilities of default and loss severities on the collateral.

For example, Fitch defines an A-level recession scenario as one in which a benchmark universe of loans experiences 30% cumulative defaults. Applying a loss severity factor of 45%, Fitch expects losses of 13.5% over the life of the loans in such a scenario. Expected losses are equal to the probability of default multiplied by loss severity. Consequently, an A-rated security backed by this benchmark universe of loans would require enough credit enhancement so that it experiences no losses in the event that the collateral experiences losses of up to 13.5%.

While adjusted historical loan performance data are instrumental in helping the rating agencies form expectations regarding potential defaults and losses on commercial mortgages, it is the review of transaction-specific characteristics and their impact on expected losses about which investors and issuers alike are most concerned. Although rating agencies differ somewhat in their methodologies, generally each reviews the qualitative and quantitative characteristics of the collateral, the security structure, and legal considerations.

QUALITATIVE REVIEW

Unlike residential mortgages or many asset-backed securities where default behavior can be reasonably modeled to reflect consumer behavior, commercial mortgages are debt instruments that finance businesses.

Hence, in their qualitative reviews, the rating agencies concentrate on the characteristics that most influence real estate performance: property type, location, borrower quality, tenant quality, lease terms, property management, property seasoning, construction quality, insurance coverage, and environmental liability.

Property Type

The risks associated with each property type are obviously very different. Hotels, nursing homes, shopping centers, apartment buildings, office properties, and warehouses are all diverse businesses with different operating margins, cost structures, regulatory constraints, and so on. The fact that these businesses perform differently is borne out by the historical data we have discussed — the ACLI loan performance data and the Russell-NCREIF property performance indexes.[6] Since the timely payment of principal and interest on the debt is dependent upon the availability of sufficient income being generated from underlying properties, the rating agencies review the economics for the property type that collateralizes the loans in the same way that they consider the economics of the borrower's industry when rating a corporate debt transaction.

Multi-family properties, for example, derive most of their income from tenant rents. Since expenses are largely unrelated to levels of occupancy, property managers try to maximize occupancy. Leases usually have terms of one year or less so that projections of revenues are based upon some assumed rate of vacancy in the future. As expected, borrowers and underwriters tend to be more optimistic in their assumptions, while the rating agencies look to the demographics and economic prospects of a region to support occupancy assumptions. Expenses consist of management fees, real estate taxes, insurance premiums, repair and maintenance costs, and other miscellaneous costs (e.g., security, landscaping). Multi-family properties benefit from tenant diversity, which protects against economic downturns. Also, apartment tenants are less inclined to demand the latest technological improvements that in the office market are critical. In general, multi-family properties are considered to be less risky than most other types, according to Standard & Poor's.

When they evaluate securities backed by loans on retail properties, the rating agencies are most concerned with the mix of tenants, the quality of the location, and the economic viability of the tenants' businesses. Unlike apartments, which have many tenants, shopping centers usually have an anchor tenant that serves as the primary draw to the property, and then 10 to 20 specialty stores that serve to diversify the lines of business supporting the

---

[6] National Council of Real Estate Investment Fiduciaries and Frank Russell Company, "The Russell-NCREIF Real Estate Performance Report " (Tacoma, Washington, June 1993).

property. Income is derived from leases of usually three to five years' length. While appearance is very important to shopping center properties, technological obsolescence is not usually a big risk factor. Successful properties generally dominate their local regions and have diverse mixes of tenants and good management teams that focus on cost containment and customer service.

Office properties present a different set of operational parameters. Their leases tend to be very long relative to other property types — extending as long as 20 years. Consequently, it is important that tenants be contractually responsible for operating expenses (including capital expenses). The length of the leases makes the credit quality of the tenants a much more important factor in the debt analysis. In many cases, the ratings of securities backed by loans on office properties may be tied to the credit rating of the dominant tenant. Although leases generally extend beyond the maturity of the loans, the rating agencies consider the risk of retenanting in the case of tenant default. Office properties require technologically updated infrastructures in order to remain competitive and, as a result, the rating agencies may require reserves for future enhancements. Superior office properties are those with quality tenants, state-of-the-art infrastructures, and strong management teams.

Hotels are generally considered to be the most risky type of property. They are clearly different — providing services to short-term guests is a large part of their business operations. Revenues come largely from room rents, but meeting rooms, restaurants, and other "extras" contribute significantly to revenues, particularly at luxury hotels. Small increases in occupancy rates or room prices can go a long way toward improving profitability due to considerable fixed costs. Yet, unlike apartments, offices, or shopping centers, hotel expenses increase as occupancy increases; as a result, maximizing occupancy does not always correspond to maximizing long-term profits. Because the performance of hotels depends largely upon the active management of operations, the rating agencies place particular emphasis on the quality of the property management teams. Well-managed properties with competitive positions in their regions present attractive collateral for commercial mortgages.

Location

The local economies in which properties operate can have considerable influence on their performance. The rating agencies study demographic data including population and household formation trends, the dominant types of industry in an area, and even climate to estimate future demand for a particular property type within a local economy. They analyze the impact of infrastructures such as educational facilities, health care facilities, recreational attractions, and transportation links. The local political climate is also a factor, particularly tax laws, zoning restrictions, and laws governing landlord/tenant rights.

Rating agencies also evaluate existing properties and potential future development that compete with the underlying properties. The review of competing properties helps them ascertain the supply trends in the local economy for the specific property type. Their analysis focuses not only on the relative value between the underlying properties and competing properties, but also on the ability of the local economy to support them (i.e., whether there are potential supply imbalances).

Rating agencies prefer collateral that is diversified geographically to minimize the influence that a local economy has on the performance of commercial real estate. ACLI loan performance data indicate very different results across regional economies for loans backed by similar property types. Obviously, the rating agencies penalize single-property transactions because they are so susceptible to the performance of one local economy. Transactions with properties distributed among many regional economies are rewarded, because this diversity helps insulate the performance of the collateral from a downturn in a particular region. (Large investors of course may be able to take advantage of higher yields offered by single-property transactions and manage their risk through portfolio diversification.)

Borrower Quality

Bad character is virtually insurmountable. In transactions with a small number of borrowers, a review of the borrowers' credit histories is performed to determine the creditworthiness of the borrowers. While CMBS structures are designed to minimize the impact of borrower quality on the credit quality of the securities, borrower quality is still an important consideration when projecting future loan performance. In addition, borrowers who are serious about the real estate business and understand the information needs of fixed-income investors will likely be more forthcoming with ongoing financial information on the properties being financed.

Tenant Quality

Since property income is derived from rents, the ability of tenants to meet their obligations according to their leases is an important consideration in determining the value of most property types. Although tenant "quality" is less applicable to hotels and multi-family properties, the number of rooms/apartments, occupancy rates, and average incomes of occupants or users are important in determining the quality of these properties. On the other hand, the rating agencies review tenant profiles of retail and office properties more closely since the number of tenants is usually much smaller and the length of leases much longer.

Tenant reviews focus on:

• The number of tenants.
• The space occupied by each.
• The credit quality of the dominant tenants.

In some cases, the rating of CMBS backed by loans on properties with one tenant or a dominant tenant may be tied to the rating of that tenant (particularly when the lease payments of the dominant tenant fully cover the debt service on the loans).

Lease Terms

Cash flow is derived from leases, and property value is derived from cash flow. Hence, rating agencies review tenant leases to determine the sustainability of cash flows. Important lease terms are:

• Rental rates.
• Expiration schedules.
• Rent escalation provisions.
• Percentage agreements.
• Expense payment provisions.
• Renewal and cancellation options.
• Tenant improvement rent provisions.

For properties with a small number of tenants, particularly retail and office properties, lease expiration schedules are scrutinized to determine their impact on cash flows. Rating agencies also "mark-to-market" lease terms so that projected cash flows reflect current market rents. As an example, consider the lease expiration schedule in Exhibit 5, where GLA is the gross leasable area for the property, and rents are expressed in units of dollars per square foot per year.

Note that a significant percentage of leases with rents currently above market expire in the first two years. Leases on nearly 51% of the gross leasable area expire in 1995, and the rents on these leases will decline by 40% when renegotiated. In addition, leases whose rents are currently at a discount to market rents will not roll over until 1997. In situations like this, rating agencies would adjust their income projections to reflect the negative impact of the lease expiration schedule.

Rating agencies and lenders prefer leases that extend beyond the maturity of the loans, while borrowers and owners prefer shorter expiration schedules because they anticipate increasing rents.

Exhibit 5: Lease Expiration Schedule

Expiration Year	Number of Leases	% GLA	Cumulative % GLA	Annual Rent	Market Rent
1994	4	16.73	16.73	14	10
1995	7	50.74	67.47	15	9
1996	0	0	67.47	NA	NA
1997	3	18.14	85.61	6	10
Vacant		14.39	100.00	NA	10

In the case of retail properties, emphasis is placed on the mix of tenants and the economic viability of their businesses. Leases are usually three to five years in duration and may include percent agreements tying a portion of rent to sales, thus making cash flows on the properties more sensitive to economic conditions. Rating agencies pay particular attention to the credit quality of a shopping center's anchor and the terms of its lease. Renewal options at fixed rent levels are frequently written into leases and are extended at a cost to the landlord. Hence, leases containing such provisions usually carry higher rental rates.

Tenant quality is most important for office properties, as these leases tend to be much longer than those of other property types. It is also important that tenants be contractually responsible for operating expenses.

Property Management

Management teams can significantly impact the success of a property. Properties that are well-managed exhibit less tenant turnover and lower vacancy rates. The rating agencies review the manager's experience, knowledge of the localized markets, and financial resources. They place particular emphasis on the manager's track record for the particular property type represented in the proposed transaction. They may also require covenants that allow the trustee to replace property management if minimum performance standards are not met or in the case of default.

Property Seasoning

Rating agencies also review the historical performance of the properties — occupancy and cash flow trends. While historical performance data can be very helpful in projecting future performance of properties, older properties may suffer from the negative effects of aging if they become technologically obsolete or have difficulty competing with newer, more attractive, and better technologically endowed structures. Property condition is, however, a better indicator of future performance than age since it reflects a property owner's commitment to long-term viability. In general, some modest seasoning of a property is desirable; the operation of such a building is likely to have stabilized, thereby facilitating analysis of its financial condition.

Construction Quality

Rating agencies require issuers to supply independently compiled engineering reports to indicate a property's construction quality. They review the age, design, operating systems, and physical appearance of each property. The agencies may require issuers to establish reserves against deferred maintenance and/or capital improvements if engineering reports show a need for repairs. Well-maintained buildings are more likely to exhibit stable future cash flows and to remain competitive in future years.

Insurance Coverage

Insurance coverage must be sufficient to protect investors from loss in the case of property damage or interruptions of business resulting from natural disasters, fire, and other types of hazards. The insurers are usually required to maintain a rating of no less than one rating category below the rating of the securities being rated.

Environmental Liability

Rating agencies require environmental reports to be performed on each property. Of particular concern are properties that are, or have been, the site of manufacturing, industrial, or disposal activities. Environmental damage can cause a loss in value and potentially result in substantial cleanup costs. Under the laws of some states, failure to remedy an environmental violation that poses an imminent or substantial endangerment of public health may give rise to a lien on the property that is senior to the lien of an existing mortgage. This, obviously, affects the value of securities backed by such mortgaged properties.

It is unclear now whether bondholders could potentially be liable for costs related to the cleanup of environmental problems on underlying properties according to current U.S. law. Under the Comprehensive Environmental Response, Compensation, and Liability Act of 1980 (CERCLA), a secured lender could be liable as current owner for the cost of environmental clean-up if it had participated in the management of operations. Hence, it is possible that a lender taking title to a contaminated property could incur liability. In certain circumstances, lenders may choose not to foreclose on contaminated properties to avoid incurring liability for remedial actions.

Although the risks appear daunting, the rating agencies require thorough environmental reviews on each property, and take the risk of future liability into account when assigning a rating. In fact, if a property is not free of environmental problems, it is not eligible as collateral for a rated transaction unless reserves have been established within the security structure to cover the costs of cleanup.

QUANTITATIVE REVIEW

Quantitative reviews are concerned with the income being generated by the underlying properties and the leverage characteristics within the capitalization structures. Rating agencies review the debt service coverage and loan-to-value ratios on every loan.

Debt Service

Debt investors are most concerned about the timely payment of principal and interest. The ultimate source for these cash flows is the net operating income (NOI) of the properties collateralizing the loans. NOI, defined as gross annual revenues less operating expenses before federal income taxes, and excluding depreciation, is what is available to meet debt obligations. Properties that cannot generate sufficient cash flow to cover debt payments will default.

The rating agencies review NOI calculations and test the revenue and expense components for reasonableness. Prior year financial statements, with particular attention to whether the past performance is suitable for projecting future potential. They may adjust projected NOI's for special events so that it represents income from stabilized operations. For example, they mark-to-market rents on all leases.

An important measure of the creditworthiness of commercial mortgages is the debt service coverage ratio (DSCR). The DSCR is equal to the NOI from the underlying properties divided by the annual cost of debt service (both principal and interest payments) on the loans. It measures a borrower's ability to meet periodic debt payments; the higher the DSCR, the more creditworthy the loan.

After making adjustments to NOI, the rating agencies require certain minimum DSCRs for various property types in order to achieve specific ratings on securities. Exhibit 6 contains Standard & Poor's indicative minimum DSCRs required for various rating classes on 20-year fixed-rate amortizing securities collateralized by loans on "good"-quality properties. The required DSCRs for various property types differ, reflecting the relative riskiness of the underlying businesses.

Minimum required DSCRs are adjusted upward to reflect the results of the rating agencies' reviews of the qualitative characteristics of the collateral, the security structure, and the legal documentation. It is therefore possible that two structures backed by the same properties will have different required DSCRs because one structure may entail more risk than the other.

Exhibit 6: Indicative Minimum DSCRs for Standard & Poor's

Property Type	Rating	DSCR
Multi-family	AAA	1.75
	AA	1.65
	A	1.50
	BBB	1.40
Office	AAA	2.00
	AA	1.90
	A	1.75
	BBB	1.65
Retail	AA	1.65
	AA	1.55
	A	1.40
	BBB	1.30
Hotels	AAA	2.70
	AA	2.40
	A	2.10
	BBB	1.80

Source: Standard & Poor's

Loan-to-Value

Another measure frequently used to indicate the relative safety of collateralized debt is the loan-to-value (LTV) ratio. The LTV is equal to the loan amount divided by the appraised value of the properties. That is, LTV is equal to total loan amount divided by market value of the property. This is an important measure of the leverage in a transaction and therefore the degree of protection in the event of foreclosure and liquidation. As in residential transactions, it quantifies the amount of equity "buffer".

Compared to residential mortgages, however, commercial mortgages today tend to be much less leveraged — LTVs below 50% are common. The poor performance of Freddie Mac's multi-family loan portfolio, as highlighted by the Fitch analysis of loss severities, illustrates the leverage/loss-severity relationship. The lower the LTV, the more creditworthy a loan.

The rating agencies set maximum LTVs for each property type in order to award various ratings. These different LTV levels are meant to correspond to the default rates and the loss severities that the security is designed to withstand (which vary by rating class). The rate of loss that can be realized on the sale of properties before bondholders experience loss of principal is approximately equal to one minus the LTV.

There are several points to note regarding LTV. First, while the loan amount is known with certainty, estimating the market value of the underlying property is largely subjective. Original cost is obviously not useful. Replacement cost is not used because many properties have come to be valued well below replacement cost in some markets. Recent sale prices of similar properties and actual appraisals are typically used.

The rating agencies determine property values by capitalizing the adjusted net operating income by an assumed market rate of return — called the *capitalization rate* or just the "cap rate." (Here is the link between DSCR and LTV. NOI produces debt service coverage, and NOI determines value.)

The cap rate is analogous to the yield of a property and is higher for property types that are subject to greater uncertainty of business operations. Capitalization rates nationally are between 8% and 12% for most property types at the time of this writing.

Appraisals performed by commercial lenders were once the result of applying cap rates to NOI projections relying on optimistic assumptions about future occupancy rates and rent levels. Today, the rating agencies determine property values by applying cap rates to NOI projections assuming current occupancy rates and market rent levels.

With the capital markets becoming a primary source of financing, capitalization rates are expected to become more volatile as they track returns available on financial assets. This will result in greater volatility in property values.

For a large number of properties, rating agencies may rely on appraisals performed by one or more independent, accredited Members of the Appraisal Institute (M.A.I.). Such appraisals are usually the result of three approaches to valuation: cost of replacement, recent sales of similar properties, and income valuation. Whenever they rely on third-party appraisals, rating agencies review the appraisal methods to test for reasonableness and consistency with their own underwriting procedures. In general, however, rating agencies prefer not to rely on third-party appraisals.

SECURITY STRUCTURE REVIEW

Not all risks associated with commercial mortgages are related to the performance of the underlying properties. The structures of the loans themselves and their interaction with the structure of the securities can introduce the risk that timely payments will not be made to investors. The rating agencies review the payment structures of the loans and the securities, the form of credit enhancement being used, the servicer and trustee of the loans, and the legal considerations for possible introductions of risk.

Payment Structures

Loans on commercial real estate can vary widely with respect to the method of principal repayment and the way in which interest rates are determined. The rating agencies view the risk of various repayment methods differently. They also treat floating-rate loans more conservatively than loans at fixed rates. They require that the security structure address the risks associated with various loan structures.

There are two main repayment mechanisms employed in the commercial mortgage market. Loans can either be fully amortizing to maturity, paying principal and interest each period, or they can pay only interest each period, with principal repaid in one lump sum (balloon) at maturity. Borrowers prefer longer-maturity loans with balloon payments and lenders/investors prefer shorter, amortizing loans.

Balloon loan underlying collateral poses more of a risk to the investor than collateral consisting of amortizing loans. This is because there is a risk that the borrower may not be able to refinance the debt in a timely manner at maturity. Hence, with balloon mortgages, the rating agencies are concerned with "extension risk," or the possibility that the borrower will not make the balloon payment on the due date.

There are several approaches that can provide investors with more assurance that refinancing will take place before the maturity of securities backed by balloon mortgages. For a single-tranche security structure, where the security and the loans mature at the same time, Fitch Investors Service suggests that borrowers be required to prepare items that lenders require (such as new appraisals, engineering reports, and environmental studies) nine months prior to maturity. Moreover, six months prior to maturity, borrowers should be required to have arranged alternative financing or to have obtained signed sales contracts for the underlying properties. If either requirement is not met, Fitch suggests that all cash flows, net of scheduled debt service, be used to amortize the debt and mortgage rates be increased in addition. These features are called "demand notes" and "rate step-ups," respectively. In combination, these requirements provide strong incentive for borrowers to make scheduled balloon payments.

An alternative is to structure the securities so that the final maturity of the securities is beyond the maturity of the loans. In this structure, the targeted maturity of the securities is set prior to the final maturity and corresponding to the maturity of the loans. In the event that the borrower does not make the balloon payment on time, the servicer would be required to make advances to the security holders during this tail period in which foreclosure and liquidation takes place.

The expiration schedule of leases has added importance in the case of balloon mortgages. If a high percentage of leases expire near the maturity of the loan, the refinancing risk of the loan is greater. Hence, the rating agencies prefer to see leases that expire well beyond the maturity of the loans.

Loans with floating or adjustable interest rates are more risky because, as interest rates increase, the cost of debt service increases and therefore the DSCR drops. In order to achieve high credit ratings on securities backed by these loans, the rating agencies require that loans have caps or that issuers purchase interest rate caps from an external counterpart with a credit rating no less than one rating class below the rating on the highest-rated security in a transaction. The rating agencies require that minimum DSCR levels be achieved when the interest rates reach their maximum implied by the caps. If the underlying loans have caps, the securities must have corresponding caps. If the underlying loans are uncapped, and an issuer has purchased caps, the securities may or may not be capped.

The rating agencies further determine if interaction of the loan structures with the security structures introduces risk. For example, the rating agencies penalize transactions where interest rates on the collateral are tied to a different index from the one is used to determine the interest rates carried by the securities.

Form of Credit Enhancement

There are several forms of credit enhancement used in CMBS securitization, and rating agencies review the impact that credit enhancement has on the likelihood of payments being made in a timely manner. If a third party is the provider of credit enhancement, for example, the rating agencies require that its rating be at least as high as the highest-rated security in the transaction. Or, if credit enhancement is achieved internally, rating agencies test to see that payments are made in a timely fashion in the event of delinquencies and may require the establishment of reserves to guarantee the timeliness of payments to security holders.

Servicers

Servicers are responsible for the administration of the mortgage collateral. They perform a variety of important functions:

- Establish collection and distribution accounts.
- Collect and deposit into a collection account:
    Payments of principal and interest by the borrowers.
    Any prepayment penalties due.
    Proceeds from liquidation and insurance.
    Any required advances of principal and interest.
- Transfer funds from collection account to distribution account.

• Make advances from their own funds in the case of delinquencies.
• Make advances for taxes, assessments, insurance premiums.
• Ensure insurance policies are kept current and in force.
• Administer foreclosure proceedings upon default of a loan.
• Employ accounting firms to review their performance.

By assuring timely payment of principal and interest through foreclosure and liquidation and by scrutinizing borrower performance, servicers provide an important level of protection to investors. Therefore, the rating
agencies require that an experienced, well-capitalized servicer is in place. In
many cases, a back-up servicer is also required to be appointed from the
beginning to insure that a smooth transition can be made if the primary servicer is unable to perform its duties.

Because of the importance of the servicer, the rating agencies conduct a thorough review of both the primary and back-up servicers. They look
to see that the historical experience, operations, recovery rates, and financial
conditions are of the highest quality. If the servicers are not of the highest
quality, the rating agencies may require the issuer to hire a "master" servicer
to perform such duties.

Trustee

The trustee holds the mortgage loan documents in trust for the benefit of the
security holders. In the event that a servicer fails to make a required advance,
the trustee is usually required to do so. On each distribution date, the trustee
sends to each investor a statement describing the distribution and the status
of the collateral. The trustee or its designated paying agent makes payments
from the distribution account to security holders according to the payment
rules of the structure. In the event that title to a mortgaged property is
acquired through foreclosure, the deed is issued to the trustee on behalf of
the security investors, and the trustee manages the sale of the properties.
The rating agencies review the experience and financial condition of the
trustee in the same way they review the servicers.

Legal Considerations

The rating agencies review all relevant legal documentation including trust
indentures, pooling and servicing agreements, prospectus supplements or
private placement memoranda, and any other agreements with "outside" entities such as interest rate cap providers. They establish the status of each lien
on the underlying properties. They also review the validity of the proposed
structure and the distribution of cash flows planned by the issuer.

In order to assign a credit rating, the rating agencies require the issuing vehicle to be "bankruptcy remote." A vehicle that meets this requirement
and is most often employed in the securitization of commercial mortgages is

the Special Purpose Corporation (SPC). To qualify as an SPC, an issuer has to meet specific criteria:

- It must not engage in any activity other than owning and managing the pledged collateral.

- It should be restricted from incurring additional debt (except under special circumstances).

- It should be restricted from engaging in a merger, consolidation, or asset transfer with another entity (except under special circumstances).

- It should have at least one independent director.

The rating agencies also require that a transaction be insulated from the insolvency of borrowers, property managers, and others. In general, there may be no liens on the properties senior to the mortgages that collateralize the securities. And, in the case of entities other than the SPC, the rating agencies assume that they go bankrupt to test the ability of the transaction to withstand such events.

RATING IMPLICATIONS

While the criteria outlined are similar to those for rating all commercial mortgage transactions, there are different methods of evaluating transactions backed by pools of loans on many properties and transactions backed by a loan on a single property. On single-property transactions, the rating agencies focus heavily on characteristics such as the economic viability of the property or its management. On transactions backed by pools of loans with many properties, the focus is on the aggregate loan characteristics (if the loans are underwritten using uniform standards and the number of loans is large enough).

If there are a large number of properties in a transaction, for example, the rating agencies are unlikely to perform site inspections on each property or to perform their own appraisals. Rather, they will look at the underwriting criteria of the loan originator and inspect a representative sample of the properties. The more the number of properties in a transaction, the more likely that rating agencies will rely on "statistical inference" in quantifying risks.

The rating process is time consuming. In fact, it can take as long as six months for a transaction to go through the process from beginning to end. When rating agencies are backlogged, they turn down transactions simply because they do not have the resources available to rate them. This can result in many single-rated CMBS issues. Rating agencies are likely to expand their resources dedicated to rating CMBS in response to the increasing use of securitization in financing commercial real estate transactions.

The rating process can be quite subjective, as methodologies employed vary from agency to agency. For example, we noted that the rating agencies make adjustments to required minimum DSCRs according to the results of their qualitative reviews. If the rating agencies make different qualitative assessments, they will likely differ in their required minimum DSCRs.

Yet the purpose of the rating agencies is to perform extensive due diligence on the behalf of investors — the result being the classification of securities according to their relative riskiness. In their efforts to classify CMBS consistently with other types of debt securities, the rating agencies have established very conservative rating criteria. It is our view that this conservativeness means that CMBS face less risk of future downgrade than similarly rated corporate debt.

S&P published a thorough description of its criteria in the *Credit Review* of March 8, 1993. Fitch published its default study results and rating criteria in a special release titled "Commercial Mortgage Stress Test" dated June 8, 1992. Duff & Phelps has recently updated its guidelines in "The Rating of Commercial Real Estate Securities" dated May 1993. Moody's recently published its rating guidelines in "Commercial Mortgage-Backed Securities: A Review of Moody's Rating Approach" published in November 1993.

CREDIT ENHANCEMENT

The rating agencies set minimum DSCRs and maximum LTVs for different rating classifications as a result of their analyses of historical loan performance data, qualitative and quantitative reviews of the collateral, and consideration of the security structure. Usually some form of credit enhancement is necessary in order to achieve these requirements.

For example, if the adjusted NOI from a property backing a loan to be securitized is $10 million per year, and the total debt service (including amortization of principal) is $9 million per year, the DSCR would be 1.11 times. If the rating agencies require a DSCR equal to 1.39 times for the targeted rating, then, in this simplified example, 20% additional credit support would be needed to achieve the desired rating $(1.39 = 1.11 \times 1.20)$.

Exhibit 7: Credit Tranching

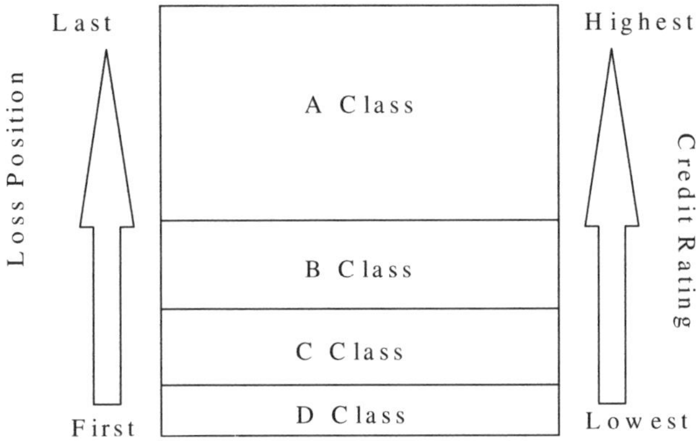

Credit enhancement is the credit support needed in addition to the mortgage collateral to achieve a desired credit rating on the securities. The forms of credit enhancement most often used in the securitization of commercial mortgages are: subordination, overcollateralization, reserve funds, corporate guarantees, and letters of credit. Also, in single-borrower, multiple-property transactions, cross-collateralization and cross-defaulting can further enhance collateral quality.

Subordination

Subordination is the disproportionate sharing of the risk of credit losses by two or more classes of securities. In its simplest form, the senior-subordinate (or "A/B") structure, two classes of securities are collateralized by the pool mortgages, with one class providing the credit enhancement for the other. The subordinated class (B-piece or junior class) is in a first loss position — it absorbs 100% of losses experienced on the collateral until cumulative losses exceed the amount of the subordinated class available to absorb such losses. When delinquencies and defaults occur, cash flows otherwise due to the subordinated class are diverted to the senior class to the extent required to meet its scheduled principal and interest payments. Subordination makes it possible to create highly rated securities from collateral of all levels of quality.

It is possible to transfer credit losses disproportionately across several classes of securities. This is called *credit tranching* and is analogous to the tranching of prepayment risk in CMOs and REMICs backed by residential mortgages. Classes are tranched sequentially with respect to loss position — a class does not experience any losses until the classes with more junior positions have been depleted. This is illustrated in Exhibit 7. In this example, class D, the most junior class, provides credit support for classes A, B, and C. Class C is the second most junior class; it provides credit support for classes A and B, and so on.

There can be any number of credit tranches in a transaction, but the goal of structuring the credit support in this fashion is to minimize the total cost of funds for the issuer. As a result, the issuer's objective is to maximize the size of the higher-rated classes, which carry lower yields and minimize the size of the lower-rated classes, which carry higher yields. The size of each class, however, is dictated by the coverage ratios required for a targeted rating.

From the point of view of the investor, credit tranching provides an opportunity to optimize the risk-return profile. Losses are realized first by the equity in the transaction and then by the most junior class of securities. In this way, the most junior class of securities is really in the "second-loss position." Such classes are popular as more liquid, higher-yielding alternatives to equity investments in commercial real estate. Higher-rated classes span the rating spectrum and allow investors to choose the level of credit risk with which they are comfortable.

Overcollateralization

Minimum DSCRs and maximum LTVs can be achieved simply by issuing less debt or, put another way, by posting more collateral. This is analogous to an issuer buying back the subordinated classes from a senior-sub structure, leaving only the senior classes to be serviced. Only borrowers that do not need to maximize leverage will opt for this form of credit enhancement. Some Real Estate Investment Trusts (REITs), for example, have used overcollateralization when issuing debt designed to introduce modest amounts of leverage to their property portfolios.

Reserve Funds

Although subordination is the predominant form of credit enhancement used, many issuers use reserve funds, either exclusively or in combination with subordination, to provide the required level of credit enhancement. Reserve funds are usually established with an initial cash deposit from the issuer and may be required to grow over time to some specified maintenance level. They are the most liquid form of credit enhancement and are usually in first-loss positions when used in combination with subordination.

Reserve fund balances are usually invested in highly liquid short-term government securities, highly-rated commercial paper, and CDs. Because of the relatively low returns available on short-term securities, reserve funds are expensive credit enhancement alternatives for issuers. Small reserve funds, however, are frequently established in combination with subordination as a source of liquidity within the credit enhancement structure.

Corporate Guarantees

Guarantees may be provided by the issuer or a third party in an amount equal to the required level of credit enhancement. The guarantor will be obligated to cover losses due to delinquencies and foreclosures up to the amount of the guarantee. A guarantor must have a credit rating at least as high as the highest-rated security in the transaction. Corporate guarantees are not used often, but when a highly rated institutional borrower may find it can reduce its costs of issuance by guaranteeing the securities. Usually, commercial mortgages are non-recourse loans; that is, they are secured only by properties and their cash flows. In the case of guaranteed transactions, limited recourse is extended to the guarantor, who is usually affiliated in some way with the borrower.

Letters of Credit

A letter of credit (LOC) obligates the provider to cover losses due to delinquencies and foreclosures up to a specified amount. As with corporate guarantees, the provider must be rated at least as high as the highest rating sought on the securities.

Both corporate guarantees and letters of credit are external sources of credit support. While subordination and reserve funds are set up within the structure of a security and rely solely on the credit quality of the collateral, third-party credit enhancement introduces credit risk not related to the collateral. Subordination is popular with investors since it is not subject to "event risk" or the risk of the downgrading of a third party, but some investors do prefer LOCs or corporate guarantees because of the "name recognition" of the providers/guarantors.

Cross-Collateralization and Cross-Defaulting

For single-issuer, multiple-loan transactions, cross-collateralization and cross-defaulting may be used to enhance the credit quality of the securities further. Cross-collateralization requires the properties that collateralize the individual loans to be pledged against every loan. In the event that the cash flows from a particular property are not sufficient to meet debt service on its loan, cash flows in excess of debt service from one or more of the other properties in the transaction may be used to make up the deficiency. The net operating income (NOI) of the pool of properties therefore is available to meet the collective debt service on all of the loans. Consequently, an individual loan cannot become delinquent or default as long as there is sufficient cash flow from all the properties to cover its shortfall.

Cross-defaulting is an extension of cross-collateralization, in that any loss on the sale or refinancing of one property can be made up on the sale or refinancing of another. In other words, the net proceeds from the refinancing or sale of all properties within a transaction can be applied to the repayment of principal on every loan. An investor will thus not experience loss of principal as long as the net proceeds from the refinancing or sale of the properties are greater than the principal balance of the loans outstanding.

Cross-collateralization and cross-defaulting are powerful credit enhancement mechanisms possible only within single-borrower, multiple-property transactions.

CMBS STRUCTURES

Interactions among the interests of issuers, investors, and the rating agencies determines CMBS structures, and they can be quite diverse as a result. Even so, security structures for CMBS to date have been relatively simple compared to those found in the residential CMO market. Due to significant call protection features of commercial mortgages, the structuring process for CMBS is largely related to the allocation of credit risk; with residential CMOs, the structuring process focuses predominantly on the allocation of prepayment risk.

We have discussed the roles of servicers, trustees, and special-purpose corporations in the context of the rating process. Exhibit 8 demonstrates the interaction of these entities within a CMBS transaction. As we have discussed, servicers and trustees are critical to the debt service process. Servicers interact directly with the borrowers, so it is important that a servicer has experience with the property type backing a transaction. In some cases, an issuer may choose to employ a *special servicer* — one with considerable experience with the specific property type — to oversee the servicing function. The servicer is usually obligated to make advances in the event that income generated from the properties is temporarily insufficient to meet debt service.

The trustee holds the mortgage collateral "in trust" for the security holders and actively manages the distribution of the cash flows collected from the properties. As part of its duties, the trustee monitors the performance of the servicer and may elect to replace the servicer if certain performance standards are not met. The trustee is also responsible for periodic reporting to security holders.

Most CMBS include covenants that protect investors from the activities of the borrowers. One example is include covenants that restrict the ability of the owners to "cherry pick" properties from the collateral (i.e., sell the best properties, leaving the lower-quality properties as collateral). There are several forms that such "adverse selection" prohibitions may take, including:

Exhibit 8: CMBS Transaction Structure

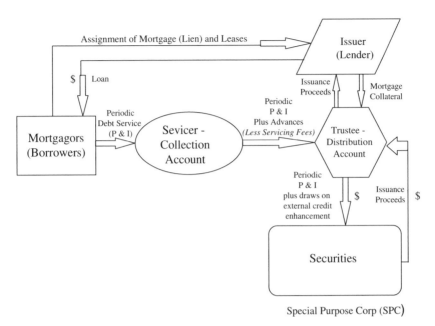

- Owners may be required to retire debt equal to 110% to 125% of the balance of the loan on property being sold.
- Resulting DSCRs have to be no lower than before the sale.
- Collateral substitutions are restricted during non-call periods.

Many CMBS include "locked-box" provisions that give the trustee control over the gross revenues of the properties (see Exhibit 9). Accordingly, the trustee is responsible for prioritizing the distribution of cash flows to debt service, taxes, insurance, and other operating expenses. In many cases, management fees are made subordinate to operating expenses and debt service. Owners have a claim only to cash flows net of expenses (including debt service). The locked-box structure provides strong incentive for owners and managers to operate properties with maximum efficiency, because they have subordinate claims on income.

In order to protect CMBS investors' liens on the properties, borrowers are prohibited from incurring additional debt (or creating additional liens by other means) on properties pledged as collateral to CMBS. This usually includes the issuance of subordinated debt. (It should be noted that, when subordinated classes are created using credit tranching as a means of credit enhancement, no additional debt or liens on the properties are created.) On the other hand, borrowers are not restricted from issuing debt on other properties not already pledged as collateral to mortgages securitized in CMBS.

Exhibit 9: Locked-Box Structure

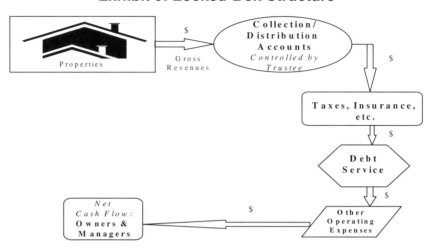

The forms that commercial mortgage-backed securities can take depend, of course, on the payment characteristics of the loans — terms to maturity, call protection and repayment methods, and interest formulas. The securitization of commercial mortgages is still very new, and security structures to date have been fairly simple. As the CMBS market matures, more complex structures will evolve as issuers try to improve the all-in debt execution provided by securitization.

Term to Maturity

Historically, commercial real estate has been financed with long-term, fixed-rate debt. Even as securitization presents new alternatives for borrowers, most still prefer long terms to maturity and fixed interest rates. On the other hand, when the yield curve is steep, many borrowers tend to opt for shorter maturity structures and/or floating-rate structures indexed to short-term interest rates. For example, reducing the term to maturity from ten years to five years may let a borrower save over 50 basis points in annual interest costs.

Call Protection

Everything else being equal, borrowers would like to be able to call their debt at any time without penalty. While such call features are characteristic of residential mortgages, commercial mortgages have historically contained restrictions on prepayments.

Prepayment decisions may be influenced by a variety of economic, geographic, demographic, social, tax, legal, and other factors. In general, if prevailing interest rates fall significantly, debt instruments are more likely to be called. Other factors include the availability of credit for refinancing, changes in tax laws (such as changes to depreciation rules), the borrower's net equity position in the property, "due on sale" clauses, and any prepayment penalties or restrictions.

The risk of prepayment has been acutely felt by investors in the corporate debt and residential mortgage markets as interest rates have plummeted to their lowest levels in 20 years. Callable securities exhibited substantially lower price appreciation than suggested by their initial durations because, as rates dropped, their durations decreased. As a result, many callable corporate bonds and mortgage-backed securities underperformed investors' return expectations.

Most commercial mortgages, on the other hand, have strong call protection features. Typically, loans are non-prepayable ("locked-out") for a substantial period of time prior to maturity. In the event of involuntary prepayments during lockout periods or in the event of voluntary prepayments during designated periods, borrowers may be required to pay prepayment penalties, usually in the form of "yield maintenance premiums."

Many loan structures combine lockouts and yield maintenance. For example, a loan that has a balloon maturity in seven years may call for a lockout of three years, followed by a yield maintenance period of three years and a year without prepayment restrictions. Such call protection features allow commercial mortgages to outperform callable corporate debt and residential mortgages during periods of declining interest rates.

While the calculation of yield maintenance premiums can be quite complicated, they are designed to make investors indifferent to the timing of prepayments. Typically, a yield maintenance premium is equal to the present value of the difference between the interest an investor would earn on the commercial mortgage in the event of no prepayment and what the investor would earn if the prepaid principal were reinvested at some spread to a Treasury security (or LIBOR in the case of floating-rate loans) with a maturity corresponding to the end of the call-protected period.

For example, suppose a voluntary prepayment of $10 million is made during a yield maintenance period that has two years remaining, the loan pays interest monthly at a rate of 8%, and the yield on the two-year Treasury is 5%. The yield maintenance would be the present value of 24 monthly payments of $18,750 (2.25% × $10 million / 12) discounted at an annualized rate of 5.75% incorporating a credit spread to Treasuries of 75 basis points. In this case, the yield maintenance premium would be equal to $424,131.

Repayment Methods and Interest Formulas

Security structures govern the way that loan payments are distributed to investors. One of the most basic security structures is a fixed-rate passthrough with a single senior class and a single subordinated class. Together these represent a 100% ownership interest in the underlying commercial mortgages. Principal and interest less any fees (e.g., due the servicer) would be "passed-through" to the classes according to the percentage each represents of the outstanding balance. The subordination is effected in two ways: first, by the preferential right of the holder of the senior class to receive its distribution before the holders of the subordinate class, and, second, by the allocation of all realized losses to the subordinated class first. Typically, the order of the distribution of cash flows is as follows: interest to the senior class, principal to the senior class, interest to the junior class and, finally, principal to the junior class. Realized losses will decrease the percentage amount of the junior class.

As an example, consider the securitization of a $100 million non-callable seven-year balloon multi-family loan with a 7.65% coupon, an LTV of 71.4%, and a DSCR of 1.40 times. It might be structured as in Exhibit 10.

A slightly more complicated structure would be to strip a portion of the coupon from the senior class (Class A) to create an interest-only class. This would be done to enable senior classes to be priced closer to par (they carry lower yields than the underlying loans due to their enhanced credit quality). For example, in the simple structure set forth in Exhibit 10, the yield of Class A may be 6.65%, thus requiring a coupon strip of 100 basis points to create a par-priced class. The resulting structure would be as in Exhibit 11.

In our view, this coupon strip should trade at a lower yield than the A-1 class for two reasons (assuming the loans are non-callable). First, its duration would be considerably shorter. In this example, the duration of class A-1 would be 5.44 years compared to 3.24 years for class A-2. Second, because it has no principal component, it has less risk arising from the balloon payment because all cash flow (with the exception of the final interest payment) has been received prior to the balloon date. Currently, highly call-protected coupon strips trade at higher yields than similarly rated principal-pay classes due to the perception that they exhibit less liquidity.

The next level of complexity is to credit tranche the loans into several classes spanning the rating spectrum. In this way, issuers can optimize the pricing of risk along the credit curve in the same way that CMO issuers tranche cash flows in time to optimize the pricing of duration along the yield curve. Also, if the loans are amortizing loans or if the loans have long periods of callability, issuers may tranche principal cash flows in time to take advantage of the steep yield curve.

As an example consider a CMBS structure used by Nomura to securitize loans on congregate care retirement residences. The collateral consisted of 33 fixed-rate, monthly pay mortgages with an initial aggregate balance of $167.5 million. The loans pay principal monthly according to a 20-year amortization schedule, with a final balloon payment due at the end of eight years. They contain a prepayment lockout for seven years. Each loan carries an interest rate of 6.85%. The weighted average LTV of all the loans at origination was 79.7%, and the weighted average DSCR was 1.22 times. The securities were structured as in Exhibit 12.

Exhibit 10: CMBS Structure

Class	Size ($)	Rating	Coupon (%)	DSCR	LTV (%)
A	78 million	AA	7.65	1.80	56
B	12 million	BB	7.65	1.55	64
C	10 million	Non-rated	7.65		

Exhibit 11: More Complicated CMBS Structure

Class	Size ($)	Rating	Coupon (%)	DSCR	LTV (%)
A-1	78 million	AA	6.65	1.80[*]	56
A-2	78 million[**]	AA	1.00	N/A	N/A
B	12 million	B	7.65	1.55	64
C	10 million	Non-rated	7.65		

*Classes A-1 and A-2 combined.
**Notional amount.

Exhibit 12: Seven-Class CMBS Structure

Class	Size ($)	Rating	Coupon (%)	DSCR	LTV (%)
A-1	105.5 million	AAA	6.68	1.98	50.2
A-2	8.4 million	AA	6.68	1.83	54.2
A-3	10.1 million	A	6.68	1.68	59.0
B	10.0 million	BBB	6.68	1.56	63.8
C	10.1 million	BB	6.68	1.45	68.6
D	8.3 million	B	6.68	1.37	72.6
E	15.1 million	Non-rated	6.68	1.25	79.7

Principal is allocated sequentially so that class A-2 receives no principal until class A-1 is fully retired, class A-3 receives no principal until class A-2 is fully retired, and so on. The classes are tranched sequentially even though they are protected from prepayments by the long lockout to take advantage of the steepness of the yield curve. In this case, only class A-1 receives scheduled amortization since the balloon payment is due before it fully pays down and its average life at issue was approximately 6.5 years. The average life of each of the other classes is 8.0 years. If the borrower makes partial prepayments between the seventh and eighth years, however, it is possible other classes may receive principal before the balloon date.

Credit losses are allocated first to class E. If losses exceed the coverage provided by class E, losses are then allocated to class D; if losses exceed the protection provided by class D and class E, losses then are allocated to class C; and so on up to class A-1.

The coupons on the securities have been stripped down to 6.68%. The 17-basis point spread between the underlying loans and the securities represents servicing and other fees that are paid on an ongoing basis. Several classes in the transaction were still priced at premiums. We could have stripped a portion of the coupon from each of these to create par-priced classes and interest-only classes. With a long lockout period, however, investors were not concerned about high dollar prices, so the execution was better for premium classes than for combinations of coupon strips and par-priced classes.

Costs

Securitization is not a cheap funding alternative for real estate investors. It entails considerable fees in the issuance of securities that are not incurred with other alternatives. Typical fees in a public offering are: rating agency fees ($100,000 per agency), legal costs ($500,000), registration fees ($75,000), printing costs ($50,000), and underwriting fees (1 to 2 percentage points). This level of fees may make smaller issues prohibitively expensive, forcing borrowers to consider other alternatives. For this reason, conduits that make loans to many borrowers and issue securities backed by pools of loans are likely to play a major role in the future of commercial mortgage securitization.

VALUATION OF CMBS

Because the CMBS market is young, there are no standard structures or benchmark issues. Also, there are no consistent, publicly available sources of historical yield spreads or relative performance data, making it difficult for investors to compare instruments and discern relative value.

Our analysis of the CMBS market suggests that CMBS are attractive compared to other fixed-income instruments. As the market matures, investors will begin to emphasize relative value within the sector. With the development of new tools such as default option-adjusted yield analysis, greater differentiation between CMBS issues will result.

The market will also begin to reflect the different regulatory environments for each sector. For example, the multi-family securities now carry a 50% BIS (Bank for International Settlements) risk weighting for banks and thrifts. In addition, while most CMBS are not SMMEA (Secondary Mortgage Market Enhancement Act)-eligible, those backed by loans on multi-family or congregate care properties are, and therefore can be used as collateral for repurchase agreements. These conditions allow multi-family and congregate care CMBS to trade at tighter spreads.

Relative to Corporate Bonds

Commercial mortgages and CMBS are sometimes seen as substitutes for corporate bonds. Both markets are large and offer a variety of maturities, call protection features, and credit risk. A number of factors, however, make CMBS different from corporate bonds:

- CMBS are "structured financings" in which the collateral is secured by properties and their income. The underlying loans are usually non-recourse to the borrower, so credit analysis focuses on the underlying assets; credit analysis of corporate bonds focuses on the creditworthiness of the borrower.
- The debt service coverage is typically known at the outset of the transaction and is stable, assuming no degradation of the performance of the properties. Corporate bonds, by contrast, are typically general obligations of the borrowers, and debt service coverage is difficult to determine and likely to change in time.
- CMBS typically use structural techniques such as subordination to reduce the risk of underlying businesses to the security holders.
- A CMBS issue is typically insulated from the bankruptcy of each of the parties connected with the transaction. For transactions backed by high-quality properties, it is assumed that downgrade risk is much less than that of corporate bonds.
- The managers of the assets securitizing CMBS must conform to predetermined rules as to how the assets will be managed. Managers of businesses backing corporate bonds are likely to change strategies in response to changes in the markets in which they operate.

Exhibit 13: CMBS Spreads versus Corporate Bonds

Rating	CMBS	Corp
AAA	105	35
AA	135	50
A	180	70
BBB	250	100

7-year average lives, strong call protection. Actual spreads can differ greatly from those shown due to differences in security structures.

Source: Nomura Securities International.

Despite these benefits, it is readily apparent that for comparably rated securities, CMBS trade at much wider yield spreads than corporate bonds (see exhibit 13). There are several reasons cited for the difference in offered yield spreads:

- The presence of a "real estate premium" — the result of fearful memories of the recent bear market in real estate and the subpar performance of poorly structured commercial mortgage transactions from the 1980s.
- The withdrawal from direct lending by some financial institutions because of increased regulatory constraints.
- Investment guidelines of large investor groups that restrict their involvement in new securitized products.
- The relative illiquidity of CMBS compared to corporate bonds.

Although CMBS spreads have tightened significantly more recently, at current spread levels, CMBS continue to represent better value than corporate bonds. Recently, Marriot International Inc. issued $150 million of a ten-year, non-callable note at 105 bps over the ten-year Treasury. The notes were rated Baa1 by Moody's and A- by S&P. According to *The Wall Street Journal*, "investors practically crawled over each other" to buy bonds from this deal. A similarly rated hotel-backed CMBS deal would trade at spreads of between +275 to +300.

Why do CMBS offer much wider yield spreads even though (we believe) the ratings are conservative? Investors are likely being compensated to participate in a young market that is paying a yield premium to attract new sources of capital. This means that there is opportunity for those who can invest in CMBS and are willing to take the time to learn the characteristics of the market.

Because there are divergent opinions on the future performance of various property types, spread levels for similarly rated securities but in different sectors in the CMBS market can differ greatly. Exhibit 14 shows indicative spreads for a few property types at several times during the first half of 1994.

Exhibit 14: Indicative Spreads by Property Type

	January		March		July	
Rating	Fixed	Floating	Fixed	Floating	Fixed	Floating
Multifamily						
AAA	100	L + 65	90	L + 60	85	L + 45
AA	125	L + 80	120	L + 75	110	L + 70
A	160	L + 125	155	L + 115	140	L + 105
BBB	210	L + 170	210	L + 165	190	L + 160
Retail						
AAA	110	L + 70	95	L + 70	90	L + 50
AA	135	L + 90	120	L + 90	115	L + 70
A	165	L +130	155	L + 130	140	L + 105
BBB	210	L + 180	210	L + 180	190	L + 165
Hotels						
AAA	140	L + 100	120	L + 80	110	L + 73
AA	175	L + 140	155	L + 110	130	L + 90
A	220	L + 180	200	L + 142	160	L + 125
BBB	325	L + 250	250	L + 230	225	L + 200
Office						
AAA	130	L + 90	130	L + 90	100	L + 68
AA	165	L + 130	155	L + 120	120	L + 90
A	210	L + 170	185	L + 152	150	L + 120
BBB	315	L + 265	270	L + 240	210	L + 190

Spreads can vary widely from deal to deal, depending on factors including perceived collateral quality, borrower credit history, the number of properties, and call protection.
Source: Nomura Securities International.

In the multi-family and retail sectors, spreads tightened by 25 to 30 basis points over the period. Lower-rated securities tightened the most as investors continued to reach for yield in this low interest rate environment.

However, spreads have tightened much less in the hotel and office sectors. This is partially due to the perception of poor liquidity in these sectors. However, we believe the hotel sector, in particular, is penalized twice for greater uncertainty of business operations of the underlying properties — first, the rating agencies require much higher DSCRs than other property types in order to achieve the same rating and, second, investors require an additional level of protection in terms of higher yield spreads. It is our view that over the second half of 1994 spreads in this sector will begin to tighten relative to the other types of properties as investors become familiar with the characteristics of hotel-backed CMBS.

The office sector suffers from investor fears of continued collateral devaluation. Many transactions backed by prime office buildings, on the other hand, have been received very well due to the name recognition of the property or property owners/managers. Going forward, spreads in this sector will become better defined as more transactions backed by pools of loans on good quality office buildings are brought to market.

How can a portfolio manager track and evaluate opportunities in the CMBS market? First, tracking trends in the commercial property markets is important because these will affect spreads for the various CMBS sectors. In the case of the multifamily sector, for example, this requires being aware of trends in vacancy rates, rent levels, new construction, and so on. We have noted several important factors that affect the performance of different property types.

Second, in order to be able to evaluate relative value in the securities markets, one needs to keep track of evolving structural standards such as call protection features, subordination amounts, or terms to maturity. In addition, one needs to track historical spreads for the various CMBS sectors in order to discern changes in relative value. This can be difficult, as CMBS issues are quite diverse in terms of ratings, structural features, and property types. As the market develops, however, valuation of the various terms will become easier and relative values more discernible.

Default and Loss Scenarios

To evaluate specific CMBS issues, investors should analyze the financials of the properties backing a transaction. Particular emphasis should be placed on the reasonableness of NOI projections, lease rollover schedules, and property valuations. Investors should also evaluate the impact of the security structure on value. For example, investors should determine the servicer's capabilities for the property type being considered and provisions that impact the way cash flows are distributed to various security classes. Once an issue is purchased, investors should monitor updated financial information for the collateral and re-evaluate DSCRs, LTVs, and other measures to see if there is any change in quality that could cause changes in the market's valuation of the issue. For instance, NOI might improve causing a better than expected coverage ratio, which, in turn, would make the bonds a better value. In some cases, ratings may change to reflect changes in quality of the collateral. For example, subordinated classes may be upgraded as senior classes pay down, because their coverages would improve if there is no deterioration of the collateral.

One approach to relative value analysis is to run various default and loss scenarios and observe their effect on realized yields on the securities. For example, consider again the multi-class structure described in Exhibit 12. Exhibit 15 adds some loss statistics.

Exhibit 15: Zero-loss Yields for a CMBS Structure

Class	Face Amount ($)	Rating	Coupon (%)	Zero-loss Yield (%)
A-1	105.5 million	AAA	6.68	6.66
A-2	8.4 million	AA	6.68	7.06
A-3	10.1 million	A	6.68	7.46
B	10.0 million	BBB	6.68	8.01
C	10.1 million	BB	6.68	10.61
D	8.3 million	B	6.68	11.50
E	15.1 million	Non-rated	6.68	22.33

Suppose we evaluate the impact of each of the following seven scenarios on realized yields for each class:

1. A total of three properties default, one each at the end of each of years three, four, and five.
2. 10% of current balance defaults at the beginning of the second year.
3. 10% of current balance defaults at the beginning of the fifth year.
4. 20% of current balance defaults at the beginning of the second year.
5. 20% of current balance defaults at the beginning of the fourth year.
6. 20% of current balance defaults at the beginning of the sixth year.
7. 30% of current balance defaults at the beginning of the sixth year.

In each default scenario we assume a 50% recovery rate at the end of 12 months. During this year no advances are made to the security holders by the servicer. Exhibit 16 summarizes the resulting yields for each scenario by class.

Note that the timing of and the amount of defaults have different impacts on the various classes. Classes A-1 through A-3 experience no reduction yield for all scenarios, and class B, which carries a BBB rating, experiences a reduction only in scenario 7. The realized yields for class C are not severely impacted in any scenario, and only classes D and E, the most junior classes, experience negative yields for these scenarios.

It is worth mentioning that these scenarios are quite onerous since we assume 50% recovery rates after 12 months with no advances being made. (Recall that Fitch finds average recovery rates to be better than 60%.)

Exhibit 16: Resulting Yields for Each Scenario by Class

Class	Zero Loss Yield	Scenario						
		1	2	3	4	5	6	7
A-1	6.66%	6.66	6.66	6.66	6.66	6.66	6.66	6.66
A-2	7.06%	7.06	7.06	7.06	7.06	7.06	7.06	7.06
A-3	7.46%	7.46	7.46	7.46	7.46	7.46	7.46	7.46
B	8.01%	8.01	8.01	8.01	8.01	8.01	8.01	7.16
C	10.61%	10.61	10.61	10.61	9.39	9.79	10.12	9.70
D	11.50%	11.50	11.28	11.50	7.62	9.75	10.58	-5.71
E	22.33%	11.03	7.66	12.45	-156.7	-42.30	-4.38	-10.62

Rate of Return Analysis

Another approach to assessing relative value is total rate of return analysis. Expected total returns can be calculated in order to compare the amount of spread widening that may be experienced for breakeven total returns. The most difficult aspect of such analysis is estimating the horizon price of the security in question. One way to do this is to estimate the change in NOI that would lead to a downgrading (or upgrading) that would cause the securities to trade at spreads commensurate with the lower (higher) rating category.

Suppose you want to analyze a double-A class from a hotel issue that is trading at 180 basis points over the seven-year Treasury. After reviewing the future prospects of the properties, you project there is a 25% chance that the NOI will drop from the original estimate, causing the DSCR to drop from 2.70 to 2.40. At a capitalization rate of 9%, the LTV will increase from 58% to 66%. If, due to this deterioration, the rating agencies were to downgrade the security to an A rating, the appropriate spread would go from 180 basis points to 235 basis points. Assuming no change in interest rate levels, this spread widening would lead to an approximate 2.5% change in price. Offsetting this price depreciation would be the 180 basis points earned over Treasuries plus any price appreciation from down the curve. Investors can apply expectations of various scenarios to come up with expected total rates of return.

Option Pricing Method

Investors can use option pricing theory to price the credit or default option that the lender has extended to the borrower. The security holder can be viewed as having purchased a bond with no credit risk and having sold a default option to the borrower. Assuming that the value of the properties follows some process, you can build a tree of property and loan values with corresponding probabilities. By making the assumption that the borrower will default when the LTV is greater than some threshold (usually 100%), one can solve for the fair value of the default option.

Exhibit 17: Asset Category Contributions to the RBC Factor

Asset Category	Rating Range	Security Types	RBC Factor (%)
U.S. Government	NA	Treasuries, GNMAs	0
NAIC1	AAA - A	Agency Debentures, Corporate Bonds, MBS, ABS, CMBS	0.3
NAIC2	BBB	Agency Debentures, Corporate Bonds, MBS, ABS, CMBS	1
NAIC3	BB	Agency Debentures, Corporate Bonds, MBS, ABS, CMBS	4
NAIC4	B	Agency Debentures, Corporate Bonds, MBS, ABS, CMBS	9
NAIC5	CCC	Agency Debentures, Corporate Bonds, MBS, ABS, CMBS	20
NAIC6	Default	Agency Debentures, Corporate Bonds, MBS, ABS, CMBS	30
*Whole Loans**			
		Single- and Multi-family Residential Mortgages	2
		Other Mortgages (including commercial)	3
Real Estate			30

* Capital requirements for whole loans may be adjusted further to reflect an individual company's default and loss experience relative to the experience of the industry as a whole.

In this framework, the default option will be more valuable, the higher the initial LTV, the longer the term to maturity, and the more volatile the NOI. The greater the value of the default option, the higher the yield should be for the securities. A comparison between the default option-adjusted yields and the market yields can be used as a rich-cheap indicator.

NAIC Capital Guidelines

Under the new risk-based capital guidelines, insurance regulators will mandate minimum levels of capital for insurers as a function of their assets and liabilities. The variable that the regulators will focus on is the ratio of an insurer's actual capital to its risk-based capital. Exhibit 17 is a summary of the risk-based capital (RBC) factors for each asset category.

CONCLUSION

The CMBS market represents an opportunity for investors who are able to evaluate the risks of this market. While there appear to be many specific risks in individual securities (especially single-property transactions), we think a diversified portfolio of CMBS can significantly outperform a similarly rated corporate bond portfolio. As investors become more comfortable with this market, and as standardization takes hold, liquidity will improve and spreads will tighten. Portfolio managers willing to do the work now will benefit from improved liquidity.

CHAPTER 15

Commercial Mortgage-Backed Securities Portfolio Management

Mark Warner
Vice President
BlackRock Financial Management

Exhibit 1: Indicative Yield Spreads as of 12/31/93

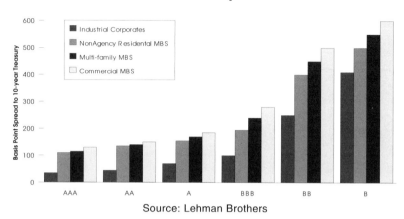

Source: Lehman Brothers

The opportunity for investment in commercial mortgage-backed securities (CMBS) has grown as the result of greatly diminished participation by traditional real estate lenders. The 1980s boom in real estate construction was financed largely by thrifts, banks, and insurance companies. What followed was a glut of new space that increased vacancy rates and depressed rental rates. Regional economic recessions combined with this overbuilding led to large devaluations resulting in enormous portfolio losses.

Poor portfolio performance and increasingly stringent capital requirements that have reduced returns caused many of the traditional lenders to retreat from this sector. At the same time, largely because of RTC-sponsored securitization efforts, the capital markets have emerged as a viable funding vehicle.

The displacement of traditional lenders and the need to attract new capital have created an attractive opportunity for investors. In each rating category, CMBS offer a positive yield advantage to similarly rated corporate debt. Yield spreads between CMBS and domestic corporate debt range from 80 basis points for investment grade securities to 250 basis points for below-investment-grade-rated debt.

As with other emerging sectors in the debt markets, spreads initially are wider than their long-run level in order to attract new capital to the sector. Markets for securitized jumbo residential loans and asset-backed securities are familiar examples of this pricing phenomenon. Considerable spread tightening occurs as investors become more knowledgeable about a sector's risks and characteristics. Investors in CMBS are likely to benefit by a similar tightening of spreads as performance characteristics, rating agency methodology, and other factors become better understood. Exhibit 1 shows comparative yield spreads among similarly rated ten-year average life bonds as of the end of December 1993.

Exhibit 2: Commercial Securitization over Time
RTC versus Non-RTC

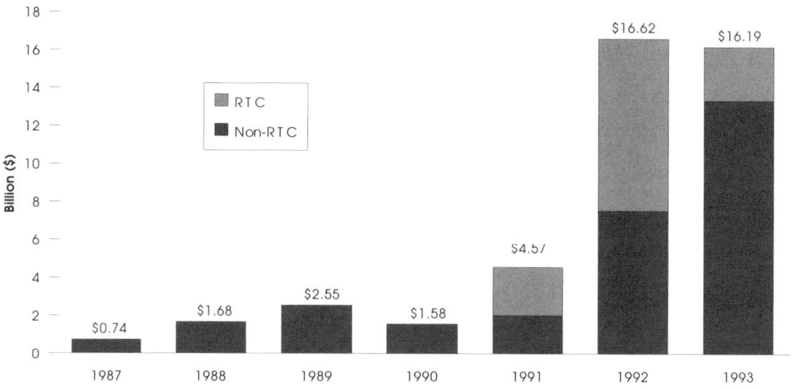

Source: Lehman Brothers

Securitization of commercial mortgages into CMBS is the primary way the RTC has been able to dispose of its inventory of performing and non-performing commercial mortgage loans. During the mid to late 1980s, CMBS issuance never exceeded $3.0 billion annually. Beginning in 1991, CMBS issuance grew to $4.6 billion, jumping to $16.6 billion in 1992. Through October of 1993, CMBS issuance totaled $14.6 billion, of which 84% was non-RTC. Total issuance in 1993 is projected to be approximately $17 billion. The RTC has nearly completed its disposal of commercial real estate mortgages and will not re-emerge as the dominant issuer of CMBS. (See Exhibit 2.)

Projections for 1994 issuance of CMBS range from $20 billion to $30 billion. The growth of non-RTC CMBS will be fueled by an estimated $150 to $200 billion of commercial mortgages maturing in each of the next three years. As these loans are mature on the books of traditional lenders, the combination of reduced asset allocation to commercial real estate and higher risk-based capital requirements will force borrowers to look to the capital markets for financing.

WHAT ARE COMMERCIAL
MORTGAGE-BACKED SECURITIES?

The underlying security for CMBS is the first-lien mortgage loan. These loans have recourse to the real estate ownership itself. The fundamental value of each property is determined by the rents paid by tenants. Ultimately, each mortgagee looks to the tenants' leases as the security for debt service payments.

Exhibit 3: CMBS by Sector

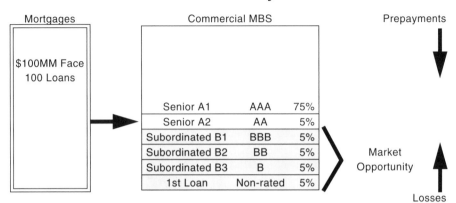

Securitization of mortgages has occurred most frequently with loans on the following property types:

1. Apartment buildings (multi-family housing)
2. Shopping centers (neighborhood, community, regional, or super-regional)
3. Office buildings
4. Warehouses
5. Hotels
6. Nursing homes
7. Mobile home parks

CMBS are backed by mortgage loans ranging from a single property to hundreds of properties. When pools of mortgages are used to secure CMBS, the collective principal and interest payments from the borrowers are used to pay each class of bondholders. Pools of mortgages thereby reduce investment risk through the diversity of properties and the regional economies in which they are located. (See Exhibit 3.)

Typical mortgage terms available today are 7- to 10-year final maturities with amortization schedules of between 25 and 30 years. These loans require balloon payments of principal at maturity.

The refinancing of maturing balloon mortgage loans has been the focus of participants in the commercial real estate markets from 1991 to 1993, principally because of the large number of such mortgages originated in the late 1980s at the peak of real estate valuations. Current mortgage origination standards mandate far lower financial leverage and higher cash flow coverage of debt service payments. This combination has stopped speculative development of new space and has given investors renewed confidence that commercial mortgage financing will remain a viable sector of the capital markets.

INVESTMENT CHARACTERISTICS

The yield advantage of CMBS does not come at the expense of added call risk. The underwriting standard for commercial loans typically includes lockout provisions prohibiting prepayments of principal or yield maintenance penalties that require a borrower to pay the present value of future mortgage cash flows discounted at the applicable Treasury yield. These prohibitions or penalties eliminate or severely diminish the borrower's incentive to refinance. Consequently, the call risk of CMBS more closely resembles that of call-protected corporate bonds than of residential mortgage-backed securities.

Credit risk is the most important risk for holders of CMBS because the underlying mortgages are neither guaranteed by federal agencies nor protected by private mortgage insurance. Instead, property losses are first absorbed by equity owners and then holders of first-loss securities. Holders of junior debt are cushioned from losses by requirements that equity and first-loss securities must be wiped out before more senior debt realizes a loss.

While the period from 1991 to 1993 has seen negative returns to ownership of real estate equity, the hiatus in new construction and more recent renewed economic growth have combined to stabilize rental rates and reduce vacancies. These trends are confirmed by declining market vacancy rates and fewer delinquent mortgages held by domestic life insurance companies.

Another risk is the possibility of extension of maturing balloon mortgage loans. Although a loan is performing, dislocations in the capital markets can make financing sources temporarily unavailable. The structure of CMBS typically provides for this possibility by allowing the servicer of the mortgage loans to extend the maturity of a loan for up to two 12-month periods. This provision is designed to get borrowers past temporary periods of dislocation without forcing foreclosure actions. Today's underwriting standards, which require lower leverage and more conservative debt service coverage assumptions, mitigate the risk of future mortgage extension.

These combined structural enhancements make CMBS an attractive risk-adjusted value for fixed-income portfolios. Yield spreads of 100 basis points to investment-grade-rated corporate bonds and superior call features compared to residential MBS justify an investment allocation to CMBS. At current levels, CMBS offer attractive yields and the possibility of further spread tightening. Although spreads have narrowed since the emergence of CMBS in 1992, investors still are well-compensated for the risks.

INVESTMENT PROCESS

A manager must undertake an active due diligence process before the purchase of any CMBS. Four elements of the security must be reviewed: property risk, credit support, servicing, and legal documentation. This review is done even before the purchase of AAA-rated bonds.

The mortgage pool underlying any potential CMBS purchase is analyzed for several risks:

1. Large loan concentrations
2. Market concentrations
3. Major tenant exposures

Among the largest loans, anchor tenant lease terms are analyzed for expirations during the term of the mortgage and rent levels above current market. Any possibility of cash flow interruption must be met with increased levels of credit support appropriate for a security's rating. Rents and vacancy rates for markets with mortgage concentrations are compared to assumptions used in appraisals done by the underwriter. Assumptions must be checked for their accurate reflection of current market conditions, and where necessary, adjustments should be made.

Extensive discussions should be held with the rating agencies to determine appropriate levels of credit support for each class of bondholders. The ability of the pool to absorb credit losses without affecting the investment-grade-rated classes is a central part of the analysis. The rating agencies take a very conservative view of credit risk and require subordination well in excess of anticipated loss levels.

Credit protection is determined by stress analysis that incorporates "worst case" scenarios for tenant lease rollover and rental rates. The securities are designed to maintain payments to bondholders even under conditions of declining occupancy and debt service coverage.

Requirements for the servicer are twofold: (1) to advance delinquent payments of principal and interest and (2) to work out or foreclose upon mortgages that become delinquent. The requirement for principal and interest advances by the servicer through the liquidation of REO property is not universal across securities. Each prospectus must specify the exact terms of the advancing requirement.

Further, the reporting standards for CMBS must be clear. The servicer should collect and compile annual property operating statements. An appraisal and loss estimate should accompany a servicer's report to the Trustee prior to the start of foreclosure action. The primary benefit of better information flow will be improved liquidity for the bonds.

Building an efficient portfolio of CMBS requires active diversification. Proper diversification requires tracking exposure by property type (multi-family, retail) and geographic as well as industry concentration. Even in the same market, property types follow different cycles because their tenants differ among service sector firms, manufacturers, exporters, and so on.

Diversification by manufacturing and service sector firms minimizes the risk that geographically separated regional economies are driven by the same underlying industries (oil, military spending, for example). This decreases the chance of false diversification such as occurred in portfolios diversified geographically by states (Texas and Colorado, say) but that which turned out to be highly correlated with changes in oil prices.

The due diligence process works to reduce the risk of cash flow interruption to non-agency mortgage securities. All aspects of the securitization process must be scrutinized: credit risk, servicing, and legal documentation.

INDEX

Information . . .
your blueprint for success.

The Mortgage Data Report

The Investor Resource Book

The Mortgage Securities Source Book

Customized Investor Reports

We are committed to providing in-depth information and direct access to a variety of mortgage products, including mortgage-backed securities issued by RFMSI, Inc., an affiliate of Residential Funding Corporation.

For more information contact Warren Loken at 612-832-7498.

Leadership in Housing America ˢᵐ

"All-Pro"

Why punt when you can score a touchdown?

GAT Precision™ gives your team the power and ability to get the ball into the end zone. With over 3400 agency and whole loan CMO structures, fixed-rate and ARM passthroughs, and Treasury securities, you can't be beat!

With Precision on your team, structuring isn't a desperate Hail Mary. The newly-enhanced CMO model accurately captures the senior-mezzanine-subordinate structures of whole loan-backed deals. The shifting of interest feature in these deals is fully captured down to the loan level. It's all part of Precision's game plan.

We maintain an enormous database for you and update it daily. We reverse-engineer new deals as they come to market. We update factors, coupon resets, prepayment histories, and geographics on the deals so you'll never be sacked by blitzing prepayments and interest rate hikes.

And if you'd like to create a new deal or reverse an old one, go for it. Apply Precision's powerful analytics to stress-test the deal. Run prepayment vectors. Generate price/yield tables. Determine the PAC collars.

You're the quarterback. Generate three-dimensional graphs, mark-to-market a portfolio, analyze the average life volatility of a CMO portfolio, and generate option-adjusted durations and convexities. Apply Precision's powerful analytics to MBSs.

As a Precision user, you'll make decisions with more confidence. Our contacts in the industry help us gather timely and accurate data. Our mortgage experts reverse-engineer even the toughest CMO structures. Our client support staff is responsive and dependable. Count on Precision. We're on your team.

"I'm Open!"

GAT Precision™ lets you complete a fast break. Through its open architecture, you can rack up assists by interfacing with Princeton Financial Systems' PAM™ or CAMRA™ PORTIA™ Bankmaster™ Sendero, TAS™ and Knight-Ridder's Money Center for Windows™ No clumsy interfaces. Nothing but net.

Precision combines a Windows interface with a database of over 3400 CMO structures, complete with historic and geographic data, powerful analytics, and portfolio capabilities. Precision brings all-star experience to your team.

It's a no-look pass to import and export files. Generate portfolio analytics, reverse-engineer newly issued CMO and whole loan structures, create synthetic blends, and calculate OAS. Play above the rim and get fast results without giving up accuracy.

As a Precision user, you can generate three-dimensional graphs, mark-to-market a portfolio, analyze the average life volatility of a CMO portfolio, generate option-adjusted durations and convexities, and run regulatory reports such as FFIEC, Regulation 126, FASB 91...and that's just for starters. We'll even customize reports for you.

And because many investors need to analyze their MBS holdings, GAT has recently added specific pool data to Precision. Now you can apply Precision's powerful analytics to MBSs.

With Precision on your side, you'll make decisions with more confidence. Our contacts in the industry help us gather timely and accurate data. Our mortgage experts reverse-engineer even the toughest CMO structures. Our client support staff is responsive and dependable. Count on Precision. We're on your team.

GLOBAL ADVANCED TECHNOLOGY

G A T
Analytics • Consulting • Research

Fixed-Income Analytics
- **Integrative Bond System™ (IBS)**
- **GAT Precision™**
- **CMO Subroutine Library**
- **Simulations Interface Platform (SIP)**
- **Custom Software Integration**

Financial Strategies Consulting
Annual GAT Fixed-Income Conference
Research and Publications

40 WALL STREET   NEW YORK, NY

GLOBAL ADVANCED TECHNOLOGY

WIN THE GAME
Precision
A CMO Analytical System

**Get GAT on your team!
Call Rhoda Woo
212·785·9630**

Credit Rating

Investors need to understand credit considerations affecting residential housing and mortgage markets in order to make informed investment decisions. Duff & Phelps Credit Rating Co. provides in-depth research on significant developments in the credit analysis of mortgage-backed transactions.

The following topical reports and publications are available to you free of charge. Please call for more information.

- Rating Policy for Residential Mortgage-Backed Securities

- Innovative Deals Rated Under New Residential Policy

- Securitization of B & C Quality Loans

- Los Angeles Area Housing Prices

- The Impact of U.S. Military Base Closings on Private-Label Residential Mortgage-Backed Securities

- Rating of Prepayment Sensitive Cash Flow Securities

- Credit Enhancement for Mortgagor Bankruptcy Risk in Residential Mortgage-Backed Securities

- Credit Enhancement for Special Hazard Risk in Residential Mortgage-Backed Securities

The Rating Guide alphabetically lists all companies and transactions with their ratings. This monthly handbook is supplemented by a weekly newsletter, *Credit Decisions*, updating readers to any interim rating activity.

Structured Finance Review provides a bi-monthly review of newly rated structured securities and includes timely articles on industry trends.

Press releases on recently rated transactions are mailed weekly to investors and are also available through real time electronic delivery.

InformationManagementNetwork

Leading-Edge
Financial Conferences
and Seminars

A Sampling Of Our Comprehensive Annual Events Includes:

Asset Allocation
Asset Securitization
Asset/Liability Management
Collateralized Mortgage Obligations
Commercial Mortgage Securitization
Derivatives in Investment Management
Equity Style Management
Fixed Income Accounting
Fixed Income Analytics
Fixed Income Portfolio Management
Fixed Income Pricing & Valuation
Foreign Currency Risk Management
Health Care Finance
Hedge Fund Investment Management
International Securities Lending
Mortgage-Backed Securities
Private Placements
Real Estate Investment Trusts
Repurchase Agreements
Whole Loan CMOs

To be added to the IMN mailing list
or to discuss customized programs,
please call us at **(212) 398-0050.**

STRUCTURED FINANCE

RATINGS AND ANALYSIS FOR EVERY STRUCTURED TRANSACTION RATED BY STANDARD & POOR'S

S&P's Structured Finance delivers ratings and analysis for more than 3,600 issues in the United States and major overseas markets, as well as relevant rating criteria and legal commentary.

Mortgage pass-throughs, whole loan-backed CMOs, asset-backed securities, preferred stock, and more.

Each quarterly edition of Structured Finance brings you updated ratings information for a wide variety of transactions, including securities backed by residential, multi-family, and commercial mortgages; consumer assets; trade receivables, and other forms of collateral. Included in each issue are:

Credit Analyses, all newly published analyses of structured transactions with detailed explanations of the ratings assigned. Included in each analysis is a transaction summary that allows you to gain a fundamental understanding of the transaction before reading the whole analysis.

Credit Ratings which let you see at a glance the current and "at origi-

nation" collateral pool information, plus a wealth of other key data.

Credit Comments that will keep you up-to-date on the latest developments in the structured market, and the **Historical Index** that will help you locate relevant articles in other S&P publications.

And for an additional fee, Structured Finance subscribers can also be notified by fax of new S&P rating announcements.

Call 212 208-8830 for subscription information.

European Sales Office, contact Steven Flaws 071-826-3510.

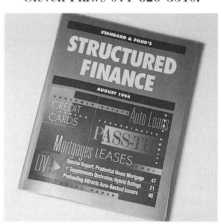

The Distinction Between Seeing and Vision.

As the market for securitized assets becomes more complex, issuers and investors are looking for analysis that can bring it into focus.

At S&P, our analytical teams have seen it all. They have the experience and the expertise to evaluate today's securitized marketplace with its complex and constantly evolving range of new assets and structures.

So if you want to know more about our criteria and the transactions rated by S&P, call Michael Crane at 212 208-1399 for information that can open your eyes.

Standard & Poor's
A Division of McGraw-Hill, Inc.

FRANK J. FABOZZI

858 Tower View Circle, New Hope, PA 18938
Phone: (215) 598-8930 Fax: (215) 598-8932

BOOK ORDER FORM

Name:

Company:

Address:

City: _____ State: _____ Zip: _____

Phone: (_____) FAX: (_____)

Book	Price	Quantity	Sub-Total
☐ Collateralized Mortgage Obligations: Structures & Analysis (Second Edition) Fabozzi, Ramsey, and Ramirez, (Fabozzi Associates, 1994).	$42.95		
☐ CMO Portfolio Management Fabozzi (ed.), (Fabozzi Associates, 1994)	$41.95		
☐ Valuation of Fixed Income Securities Fabozzi, (Fabozzi Associates, 1994)	$39.95		
☐ Whole-Loan CMOs Fabozzi, Ramsey, and Ramirez (eds.), (Fabozzi Associates, 1995)	$54.95		
☐ Fixed Income Mathematics Fabozzi, (Probus, 1993)	$45.00		
☐ Advanced Fixed Income Portfolio Management Fabozzi and Fong, (Probus, 1994)	$65.00		
☐ The Handbook of Fixed Income Securities (Fourth Edition) Fabozzi and Fabozzi (eds.), (Irwin, 1994)	$90.00		
☐ Municipal Bond Portfolio Management Fabozzi, Fabozzi, and Feldstein, (Irwin, 1994)	$80.00		
Shipping($3.00 for first book; $1.00 for each additional book):			
TOTAL:			

MAKE CHECK PAYABLE TO FRANK J. FABOZZI.
NO CREDIT CARDS SALES.

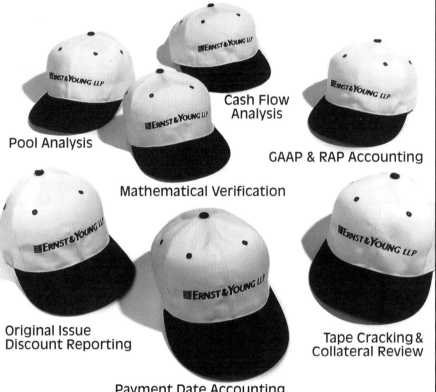

Does the Mortgage-Backed Securities Market Leave You Confused?

Let Us Be Your Guide,,,

Lewis S. Ranieri	Kenneth C. Weiss	Louis C. Lucido	Clifford E. Lai
Chairman	*President*	*Chief Operating Officer*	*Chief Investment Officer*

For More Information, Contact Christopher J. Hannon
or Robert G. Absey at 212-980-8400

HYPERION CAPITAL MANAGEMENT, INC.

Specialists in Mortgage-Backed Securities

520 MADISON AVENUE, NEW YORK, NEW YORK 10022

HYPERION CAPITAL MANAGEMENT, INC.

Hyperion Capital Management, Inc. is a fixed income investment manager with a special expertise in the management of mortgage-backed securities. With presently $4 billion in assets under management our institutional clients include pension funds, endowments, foundations, and insurance companies. The firm additionally advises on over $9 billion in assets for such entities as the Resolution Trust Corporation (RTC). Through our joint venture with AIG Investment Corporation, Hyperion also offers domestic fixed income capabilities to institutional investors globally.

Hyperion Capital was founded in 1989 by Lewis S. Ranieri, formerly the vice chairman of Salomon Brothers and widely recognized as the "father" of the mortgage-backed securities market. Mr. Ranieri's experience is complimented by that of the investment team in which each member averages over 10 years experience in the fixed income and mortgage-backed securities markets.

Hyperion Capital's approach to the mortgage-backed securities market focuses on the identification of relative value. Our investment process incorporates the insight and experience of our investment team with our proprietary and specialized mortgage-backed analytics. Additionally we look to our extensive network of affiliate companies which are engaged in the areas of mortgage finance, loan origination and real estate advisory to provide us with additional insight into the mortgage market.

Products and services we provide to the institutional investment community include:

- Mortgage-Backed Securities Specialized Portfolios
- U. S. Fixed Income Short and Intermediate Duration Portfolios
- Credit-Sensitive Mortgage-Backed Securities Portfolios
- Insurance Investment Management Services
- U. S. Fixed Income Arbitrage Portfolio

Our ultimate goal, for all of our clients, is to provide incremental returns through the understanding and management of risk. Let us be your guide in this increasingly complex market. Call us at 212-980-8400.

520 MADISON AVENUE, NEW YORK, NEW YORK 10022 212-980-8400

The Chase Manhattan
Rent-A-Shelf
Program

With years of securitization experience, we are pleased to offer the mortgage industry The Chase "Rent-A-Shelf" Program:

- Deal Securitization Services
- REMIC Administration
- Trustee/Custodial Services
- REMIC Taxation & SEC Reporting
- Access to Chase "CORIS" Bulletin Board Information System
- Master Servicing

For more information contact Sam Katzman at (201) 307-6534

 CHASE

Rising To Meet Your Every Need.

EQUAL HOUSING
LENDER

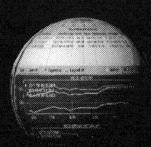

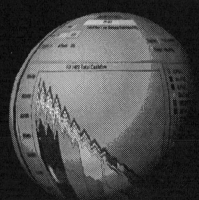